Small Business Solutions

Microsoft®
Windows® 2000
Professional

Don Gilbert

PUBLISHED BY
Microsoft Press
A Division of Microsoft Corporation
One Microsoft Way
Redmond, Washington 98052-6399

Library of Congress Cataloging-in-Publication Data
Gilbert, Don, 1948-
    Small Business Solutions for Microsoft Windows 2000 Professional / Don Gilbert.
      p. cm.
    Includes index.
    ISBN 0-7356-0856-3
    1. Small business--Management.   2. Microsoft Windows (Computer file)   I. Title.

  HD62.7.G537   2000
  658.02'2'0285544769--dc21   99-089909

Printed and bound in the United States of America.

1 2 3 4 5 6 7 8 9   WCWC   5 4 3 2 1 0

Distributed in Canada by Penguin Books Canada Limited.

A CIP catalogue record for this book is available from the British Library.

Microsoft Press books are available through booksellers and distributors worldwide. For further information about international editions, contact your local Microsoft Corporation office or contact Microsoft Press International directly at fax (425) 936-7329. Visit our Web site at mspress.microsoft.com.

Acquisitions Editor: Christey Bahn
Project Editor: Kim Fryer
Technical Editor: Steve Sagman

For Sandra

Contents

Contents

Contents

Part 4

Connecting a Computer Online

11 Step One: Connect to Your Internet Service Provider 203

Part 6
Networks and Windows 2000 Professional

Acknowledgments

This book owes a great deal to the efforts of Steve Sagman (technical editor) and Gail Taylor (copy editor) at Studioserv. Steve provided not only a firm hand on the technical tiller but also the kind of invaluable perspective that comes from being an experienced editor, small business owner, and established author.

Thanks also to Christey Bahn (acquisitions editor), Barb Ellsworth (content manager), and Kim Fryer (project editor) at Microsoft Press for their parts in helping to conceive, manage, and produce this book.

I want especially to thank my wife, Sandra, for taking the time to read and provide insights on each chapter and for her many talents and contributions, all of which have made it easier for me to write the book.

Introduction

By now, it's likely you've already heard a lot about Microsoft Windows 2000 Professional, the latest industrial-strength operating system from Microsoft. If you're involved in a small business or home office, you might suspect you need the power and features of Windows 2000 Professional while wondering how hard it is to set up and maintain without costly support calls. Whether you're looking for immediate help with your new Windows 2000 Professional platform or still testing the waters to see if it'll work in your business, you've come to the right place. Welcome to the world of Windows 2000 Professional and step this way (no hard hats, safety goggles, or pocket protectors required).

This book is about solutions for issues that small businesses face with computers and operating systems. First, it points out how Windows 2000 Professional can address many of the shortcomings of consumer operating systems such as Microsoft Windows 95 or Microsoft Windows 98 in the business environment, mostly by ensuring reliability and the safeguarding of your data. And second, it provides detailed steps for setting up and using Windows 2000 Professional. While Microsoft has done an excellent job of making Windows 2000 Professional user friendly and easy to install and configure, someone still has to do the work. If you're that person, and you're also operating a small business, time (or lack of it) is probably one of your biggest areas of concern. This book answers that concern by getting right to the steps you need without a lot of conceptual overhead. It also concentrates most on the features of Windows 2000 Professional that are really useful for small businesses. As the saying goes, the typical small business owner wears many hats. Keeping a small business healthy and viable often means doing lots of things yourself rather than hiring or contracting someone else to do the work. The same goes for your computers. You'd rather not pay a consultant for the basic tasks you should be able to do. In most cases, with the solutions in this book and the initiative you have for getting things done, you can successfully install and manage Windows 2000 Professional yourself.

Who Should Read This Book?

If you're involved in setting up and maintaining computers and have purchased or are considering Windows 2000 Professional, you'll find this book helpful. And if you're not totally comfortable in that role, you'll find this book tailor-made for you. The procedures in this book are common and useful tasks like installing printers, adding programs, performing backups, faxing documents, and so on.

On the other hand, this book makes the assumption that you've been using some fairly recent version of Windows, such as Microsoft Windows 95, Microsoft Windows 98, or Microsoft Windows NT 4.0. Because it assumes you have basic skills, such as using a mouse, opening and closing programs, and navigating folders in Windows Explorer, it devotes space to the more important issues facing readers coming to Windows 2000 Professional for the first time.

What You Need to Know and Where To Find It

What you need to know about Windows 2000 Professional really depends on how you use the computers in your office and how your office is set up (for example, whether you use a network or are connected to the Internet). You can think of the set of maintenance and administrative tasks you might need to perform as a kind of graduated list, starting with administering a single-user system, continuing on to administering a multiple-user system, graduating to administering a networking system, and finally finishing with performing advanced administrative tasks. You can read just the parts of this book that apply to your particular use of the computer running Windows 2000 Professional.

The Parts in This Book

This book is divided into seven parts, each of which identifies an individual aspect of using or administering Windows 2000 Professional.

The chapters in Part 1, "Windows 2000 Professional and Your Business," provide an overview of Windows 2000 Professional features including their relevance to small businesses, and they also explain what setup decisions you should make before installing Windows 2000 Professional.

The chapters in Part 2, "Five Steps to Setting Up Windows 2000 Professional," cover the basic setup procedures for installing Windows 2000 Professional, printers, hardware, and software. Part 2 also contains a chapter that provides a quick look at the new visual features of Windows 2000 Professional and shows you how to configure your desktop environment.

Part 3, "Creating Accounts and Keeping Your Data Safe," contains chapters that show you how to increase the security of your system and plan for the possibility of a catastrophe when your data might be lost. The most important step you can take to make your data secure from deliberate or inadvertent damage is to create user accounts for all users of your system and require users to log on. Chapter 9, "Creating and Managing Accounts," devotes a good deal of space to this effort. If the computer you're setting up will be used by more than one person, be sure to read this chapter. The other part of keeping your data safe is making sure your data is backed up, so this part covers using Windows Backup in detail also.

The chapters in Part 4, "Connecting Your Computer Online," describe using the built-in tools and services of Windows 2000 Professional to connect an individual computer to the Internet, hook up e-mail in Outlook Express, and work with the fax services that come with Windows 2000 Professional.

The two chapters in Part 5, "Windows 2000 Professional Knobs, Dials, and Switches," cover the changes to the user interface in Windows 2000 Professional, mostly focusing on coming to this operating system from Windows 95 or Windows 98. A great many of these changes occur in the Control Panel, due to differences in functionality between operating systems, so most areas of the Control Panel not described in other chapters in the book are visited and described here.

Part 6, "Networks and Windows 2000 Professional," describes almost every way you can connect computers together, from connecting to an existing network, to creating your own network, to connecting two computers together using a direct connection or dial-up networking. This part also contains a chapter on connecting your portable computer, which describes the Offline Files feature, and a chapter on using the new Internet Connection Sharing feature, which allows you to share a modem.

There's a good chance you will seldom, if ever, need to use advanced administration tasks—this is definitely the deep end of the pool. But, it's also where you see how deep Windows 2000 Professional actually goes in the area of configurability, security, and variety of services that become more important the larger your business grows. Part 7, "Advanced Administration Tasks," concentrates on one multipurpose tool called the Computer Management Console—it contains most of the advanced administration functionality typically used in Windows 2000 Professional. While Part 7 touches on all of the parts of this tool, it describes only a few in detail. You can read this part if you're just curious or if you need to learn about the power of Windows 2000 Professional that's beyond what's offered in other Windows operating systems.

I think you'll find Windows 2000 Professional a pleasure to use and you'll likely discover that the "professional" part of the name isn't marketing hype. If your small business can profit from using professional-quality tools and services—and what business can't?—you're going to like Windows 2000 Professional.

Windows 2000 Professional and Your Business

Chapter 1

Is Windows 2000 Professional Right for Your Business?

If you haven't already purchased a copy of Microsoft Windows 2000 Professional or a new computer with this operating system installed, you're probably now in the process of deciding whether (or perhaps when) to move to Windows 2000 Professional. This chapter should help you make that decision. If you already own Windows 2000 Professional or have decided to buy it, this chapter will serve as an overview of the features that make the most sense for small businesses and a conceptual preview to the rest of the book.

Historically, small businesses have been slow to embrace Microsoft Windows NT, the predecessor to Windows 2000. They have had several reasons for this, but probably the biggest one has been the overhead required to configure and manage computers running Windows NT. Small business owners have perceived that they'd need a computer science degree and an arsenal of computer and network administration tricks to run Windows NT. Because small business owners are focused on their businesses and not on their computer systems, this often equates to hiring someone for the job, either as a full-time employee or on a contract basis. And the decision to upgrade comes down to cost. "What am I getting for all this extra expense and hassle?" is the question that they usually ask. The answer, more often than not, has been "not enough to make me switch from something that's working (well, most of the time anyway)."

The fact remains that small businesses have computing needs much closer to those of large scale businesses than to the needs of consumers. Few businesses can tolerate down time or lost data, least of all businesses that have few resources to spare. Yet because the step to Windows NT has often seemed too great for busy small business owners, most have had to be satisfied with using consumer operating systems like Microsoft Windows 95 and Windows 98. Fortunately, Microsoft has been well aware of this problem and has designed Windows 2000 Professional with small business owners in mind.

Have the developers at Microsoft done enough to make you want to switch to Windows 2000 Professional? In this chapter, you'll take a look at the compelling features of Windows 2000 Professional for small businesses and at just how much you really need to know to install, configure, and maintain it.

Because most small business owners use either Windows 95 or Windows 98 on their current computers, as opposed to Windows NT, the focus of this chapter is on highlighting the advantages of Windows 2000 Professional over those consumer operating systems. Windows 2000 Professional has many improvements over Windows NT 4.0 as well, mostly in the areas of ease of use, installation, and hardware support.

Windows 2000 Features Designed for Business

The features of Windows 2000 Professional that appeal most to small business owners are largely those that increase the productivity of their businesses. While things like total cost of ownership (TCO), the measure of what your computer really costs to run, are important, small business owners will appreciate the more tangible features like fewer reboots, more protection against data loss, easier learning curves for employees, and so forth. The remainder of this section covers these key Windows 2000 Professional features:

- Reliability—the basic ruggedness and robustness of the system
- Ease of use—not only user interface improvements but also the ease with which you can install and configure the operating system and hardware components
- Security—the safety of your data from data loss, corruption, and the possibility of theft
- Networking capability—the ability of Windows 2000 Professional computers to work in a network of other computers
- Mobile computing—better experiences when using your portable computer, both in and out of the office

Reliability

The reason given by most small business owners who have decided to move to Windows NT in the past, and to Windows 2000 Professional recently, is the need for reliability. Small businesses typically don't have the deep pockets of corporations and need to be extremely cost conscious and sensitive to waste issues, especially when it involves time. A typical small business owner can't afford to have employees sit around while a computer is down or while an employee (or the owner) tries to recover lost work from a hung program that requires a reboot. And small businesses that rely on their computers for customer contact or sales can hardly afford to lose a customer's business because of a computer malfunction.

Microsoft developed Windows NT for this very reason: to provide an operating system that is robust and industrial strength. Windows 2000 Professional is superior to the consumer versions of Windows in several areas and, in many cases, it improves on Windows NT in reliability. These include:

- Decreasing the number of times you have to reboot

- Increasing protection against viruses in drivers you install

- Increasing the stability of programs
  Each of these is discussed in further detail next.

Decreased Rebooting

A standing joke among system administrators is that operating systems would work infinitely better if you didn't have to run programs on them. Unfortunately, no operating system does much for you without programs, but given enough rope, some programs will inevitably hang themselves. To achieve high reliability, Windows NT and Windows 2000 Professional shorten the rope given to programs, in part by blocking direct access to the hardware devices on the computer.

Simply put, crashes in Windows 95, Windows 98, and MS-DOS are often caused when a program makes direct calls to some hardware device on the computer and runs into a problem. Usually, you can't exit the program at this point and even shutting down the program from the Task Manager can leave the hardware locked and unusable. Windows NT prevents programs from directly accessing the hardware and puts a layer of the operating system, called the hardware abstraction layer (HAL), between programs and hardware. Windows 2000 Professional, because it is an extension of the Windows NT platform, has the same HAL architecture.

Applications that run in Windows NT and Windows 2000 are also run in a true *preemptive multitasking* environment, unlike those running in Windows 95 or Windows 98. This means that a badly behaved program can't hog the computer's processing power—this was a performance problem to be sure, but also a potential reason for rebooting.

Windows 2000 Professional has also drastically reduced the number of reboots required when you reconfigure the computer. The number of configuration changes requiring a reboot has dropped from 50 in Windows NT 4.0 to only 7 in Windows 2000 Professional. And when a reboot is required, Windows 2000 Professional boots much faster than either Windows NT 4.0 or Windows 98.

Driver Verification

Another cause of computer instability can sometimes be traced to device drivers. A driver is the software that connects the operating system with the hardware inside or attached to your computer. Microsoft has incorporated in Windows 2000 device drivers the same VeriSign code-signing technology it uses for Internet downloads. Driver verification is really a security feature, but keeping unknown code off your computer helps to keep your computer reliable.

On the Internet, it's important that you not download viruses. When you're about to download a file, a digital signature in a file causes a dialog box to show the name of the company that created the file. This dialog box asks your permission to continue and lets you know it's safe to put the software on your computer because the company has registered its name with VeriSign. The same verification is now attached to device drivers, and all drivers shipped with Windows 2000 Professional have a Microsoft digital signature, as do all driver updates Microsoft supports. Non-verified device drivers can't be installed in Windows 2000 without your knowing about it and accepting it. Because so many people use the Internet to obtain driver updates, using digitally signed drivers and having an operating system that recognizes signed drivers are important steps in keeping your computer robust and virus resistant.

Program Installation

An area with definite room for improvement in Windows was program installation and removal. How many times have you loaded some software that started copying files to your computer only to be stopped and asked if you wanted to overwrite an existing file of the same name? If you clicked No, you were left wondering if the new software would be installed correctly. If you clicked Yes, what program might you have just broken by overwriting its files? Program installation errors can affect the stability of Windows; when a program expects certain versions of files to work with, the program can hang or crash if those files are missing or changed. Windows 2000 Professional addresses this problem with the Windows Installer Service, a feature you won't see but that nonetheless makes installing programs considerably easier and less error-prone than before.

The Windows Installer Service provides a standard for installing and removing applications and for repairing and updating application components. Application installation programs are written to conform to this standard and the end result is a more stable experience for users. Even applications that don't conform, such as older applications, aren't allowed to install in ways that will make the system unstable.

You might experience the features in this service in two ways—either using a stand-alone Windows 2000 Professional computer or using a Windows 2000 Professional computer connected to a network administered with Windows 2000. Here are the advantages you'll see from the stand-alone perspective, all of which apply to networked computers as well:

- DLL (dynamic-link library) files are installed into separate folders instead of into a common area. One of the original Windows concepts was to create libraries of program calls that could be placed in a common area and shared among different applications. Unfortunately, this concept runs into problems when different versions of a common file are installed by different programs. The Windows Installer Service now forces installed DLLs to be kept separate—you won't be asked to decide whether or not to overwrite files you've never heard of when you install a new program; existing DLLs will never be overwritten except by an update of the application.

- If an installation fails partway through, the service restores the computer to the state it was in before the installation began.

- Applications must list their critical files so that Windows 2000 can monitor those files and replace them if they are removed or become damaged.

- Removing applications is more robust because all components are tracked throughout the system and in the registry. Because DLLs are kept in separate folders, removing them doesn't cause questions about whether to remove a shared component. Also, tracking the components makes updating the software more reliable.

- Configuring programs is easier because independent software vendors (ISVs) are encouraged to segment their software into small components so you can install only what you need.

When an application for Windows 2000 Professional is installed on computers connected to a Windows 2000 Server network, network administrators can perform the installation from the server without visiting each computer on the network. This is known as just-in-time installation. Administrators can place (or *publish*) an application in the new Windows 2000 Server Active Directory to enable installation by users on client computers. Users can install the application across the network when they double-click a file that requires the application. Alternatively, administrators can place a shortcut on the user's Start menu that causes the application to be installed over the network when the user chooses that application on the Start menu.

Ease of Use

One of the biggest obstacles to overcome in gaining acceptance by small businesses was ease of use. Microsoft's challenge was to take an operating system with the capabilities and flexibility of Windows NT, originally designed for computer professionals and corporate users with IT support, and make it as easy to use as a consumer version of Windows. When Windows NT adopted the Windows 95 look and feel, it took a big leap in that direction, but Windows NT still had plenty of management tasks that seemed better suited to an NT administrator than to a small business owner.

Microsoft has managed to meet that challenge in significant ways. Windows 2000 Professional has achieved a good balance between usability and power by simplifying the user interface and placing most administrative tools out of the way in a configurable toolbox called the Microsoft Management Console (something most users will never need to deal with). It has also raised the bar on ease of use in quite a few areas, making this version of Windows even easier to use than Windows 95.

In addition to improved user interface features, Windows 2000 Professional has made significant improvements in the area of setup and hardware installation. Plug and play is now implemented (for the first time in a Windows NT-based product) and it is better than Windows 98 in some respects. Also, Windows 2000 Professional setup has been streamlined and simplified considerably compared to Windows NT 4.0. For details about installing printers, hardware, and software, see Chapters 5, 6, and 7.

Here are a few of the advances in ease of use that you'll find in Windows 2000 Professional. (You'll find a complete description of all of these improvements in Chapters 14 and 15.)

How Easy to Use Is Windows 2000 Professional?

If you're wondering whether you can install, configure, and maintain Windows 2000 Professional without the need of a Windows NT administrator, the answer is a resounding yes! This book will take the guesswork out of the process, of course, but running Windows 2000 Professional isn't a far stretch from what you're used to in Windows 95. Microsoft expects ordinary mortals to use Windows 2000 Professional, not just computer professionals.

Under the hood, Windows 2000 Professional is far more configurable than either Windows 95 or Windows 98. This means you have plenty of opportunities to take advantage of advanced features if you want, or ignore them if you'd prefer. As with almost everything else in the world, the advanced features in Windows 2000 Professional are seldom in the easy-to-use category, although you might find that many aren't all that complicated, either. You can learn to employ these advanced features yourself if you're so inclined, hire a consultant, or have an employee learn these skills. On the other hand, you might decide that the basic services of Windows 2000 Professional—the ones described in this book—are enough for the needs of your small business. If you use Windows 2000 Professional only for its built-in reliability, you are still making a good business decision.

The bottom line is that if you've managed to set up and maintain a Windows 95 or Windows 98 computer, you should have no problem with the same tasks in Windows 2000 Professional. Nor should you have a problem adjusting to some of the new tasks you'll encounter.

Start Menu Improvements

The Start menu in Windows 2000 Professional is less cluttered and more configurable than in any previous version of Windows. The Start menu can also monitor which Start menu programs you actually use and hide those that you don't use (these are made available with one mouse button click). You can also browse and open documents and folders in the My Documents folder right from the Start menu (see Figure 1-1).

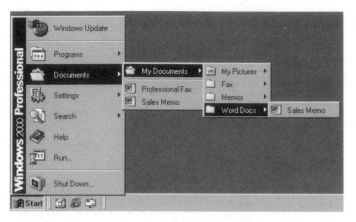

Figure 1-1

You can open documents from the Start menu.

Open, Save As, and Browse Dialog Box Improvements

These dialog boxes, common to most applications in Windows, now have a column of buttons on the left side so you can quickly navigate to familiar places, like the Desktop or My Documents folder. Even better, a History button provides you with a list of recent file names and locations you've accessed, as shown in Figure 1-2. What's more, these dialog boxes are now resizable, so you can view more files, and they also incorporate recently used file lists and an AutoComplete feature for fast and accurate access to files you've used before (see the accompanying sidebar).

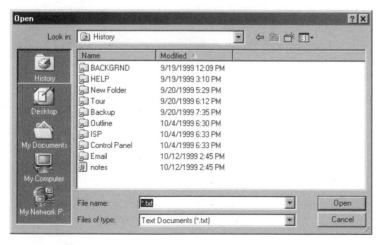

Figure 1-2

Click the History button to see recently opened folders.

11

Recently Used File Lists and AutoComplete

All dialog boxes in Windows 2000 Professional that require you to enter a filename remember the files you've used in the past and present them in a drop-down list box, filtered by the file type (for example, if you're saving a file in Notepad, and the Save As Type box shows Text Documents (*.txt), all recently saved .TXT files are shown). AutoComplete is a technology borrowed from Internet Explorer and Microsoft Office that remembers filenames you've entered before in specific areas like Open, Save As, and Run dialog boxes. As you type, the AutoComplete feature displays possible completions for the filename based on what you've typed there before.

Windows Explorer Improvements

Windows Explorer has improved the access to its Explorer Bar (the area on the left in Windows Explorer). Just as in Internet Explorer, you can click the Search, Folders, and History buttons on the Standard toolbar to change the Explorer bar. History now shows not only Web components, like URLs, HTML files, and Web graphics but also all files of any type that you've opened on your computer, as shown in Figure 1-3. So recalling a document you worked with last week is considerably easier now. Also, in any Explorer window, you can just click the Search button to open the Search Explorer Bar. Or you can use the Start menu's Search options to open the same Search Explorer Bar, which allows you to look for files and folders, computers on a network, people in an address book or on the Internet, or just about anything on the Internet (assuming you have an Internet connection of course).

My Documents and My Pictures Folder Improvements

The My Documents folder is the same as in previous versions of Windows but it's more accessible now. The common dialog boxes provided by Windows 2000 Professional for opening and saving files make the My Documents folder accessible with the click of a button. The My Pictures folder is also much improved with the addition of a built-in picture viewer (see Figure 1-4) that enables you to zoom in or out, print, or view the picture full screen.

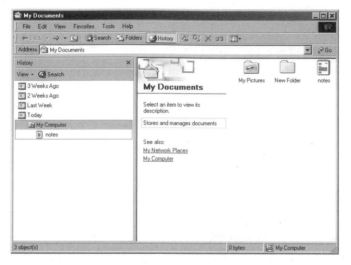

Figure 1-3

The History Explorer bar in Windows Explorer shows Web sites and all files you've recently opened.

The picture viewer is actually part of a Folder Customization feature that enables you to personalize the look of any folder. If you've tried customizing folders in Windows 95 or Windows 98, you'll be pleasantly surprised that this feature is much improved and easier to use in Windows 2000 Professional.

Figure 1-4

The My Pictures folder offers a built-in picture viewer.

Faster File Searching

When enabled, the Indexing Service feature in Windows 2000 Professional runs in the background and builds an index of all of the files on your computer and on a network, so searching your entire hard drive is extremely fast. The Indexing Service can automatically index text files, HTML files, Microsoft Office documents, and e-mail files. Microsoft has published a standard so that ISVs can provide filters that enable unique documents used by their applications to be indexed as well.

Better Placement of Some Windows Components

A few things have been renamed and shuffled around in the user interface for easier access. For example, Dial-Up Networking is now called Network And Dial-Up Connections and it's now located directly under Settings in the Start menu instead of being buried under Start/Programs/Accessories/ Communications.

Security

Windows NT has always provided strong security features for its workstations and networking solutions and Windows 2000 builds on those strengths. The concept of security encompasses the set of services that helps protect you from the possibility of losing data and helps keep your data private. Windows 2000 Professional guards against the following types of damage to data:

- Unauthorized damage—data being intentionally deleted by someone who shouldn't be accessing the computer containing the data

- Inadvertent damage—data being inadvertently deleted or changed by an authorized user of the computer

- Virus damage—data being maliciously destroyed by a virus that attacks the computer

- Hardware failure damage—data being destroyed by your hardware, including things like a hard drive crash or archive tape degradation

The remainder of this section explains how Windows 2000 Professional provides safeguards against each of these potential damages and helps you to minimize the risks of losing your crucial business data. Be sure to read the chapters in Part 3 to learn how to enable security and backup features on your computer.

Preventing Unauthorized Damage

The strongest defense against unauthorized damage is to password protect your computer. Windows NT password security, implemented in Windows 2000 Professional, isn't easily defeated, unlike the password security offered in Windows 98, which is mostly designed for network access and doesn't do anything to keep someone away from the data on your hard drive. Windows 2000 Professional allows you to bypass password protection during installation if you know that you will be the only person using the computer. However, it's a good idea to enable password protection even if you think nobody else will be using your computer.

Preventing Inadvertent Damage

Small businesses often need to pool resources, and computers are resources that often get shared. When more than one person uses a computer, it's easy for data to get deleted or changed by mistake. Windows has the Recycle Bin to help protect against deletions, but users can delete data directly without using the Recycle Bin (just hold down the Shift key when you delete) and, of course, after the Recycle Bin is emptied, your data is gone. Windows 2000 Professional has the option of using the New Technology File System (NTFS) to protect against possible data loss. NTFS enables you to restrict access to files and folders to a specified user or group of users, so you can put private, sensitive, or important data in a locked folder. All of this is done easily from the Properties dialog box for the file or folder, as shown in Figure 1-5 on the next page.

Other inadvertent damage can occur when users add or remove resources such as printers or hardware devices without informing the appropriate person (like you). While this might not cause data loss, it's often a source of irritation and loss of time when you have to reconfigure the computer after someone has changed it. By using accounts and passwords, you can limit the access of users to keep them from reconfiguring the computer.

Preventing Virus Damage

The first defense against viruses isn't built into any version of Windows yet: a good virus checker. However, digital signing of device drivers, described earlier, is a security step that has been added to Windows 2000 Professional.

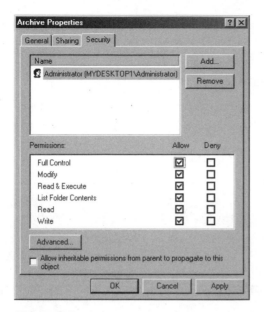

Figure 1-5

In the Properties dialog box for a folder or file, you can set permissions.

Also, because Windows 2000 Professional, like Windows NT, logs all events that occur on your computer, it's much easier for someone to track the damage that was done by a virus or attempted on your computer. While this might not be detective work you want to do yourself, it's a record that someone with advanced knowledge of Windows 2000 Professional can use to help track down the source of the problem.

Hardware Failure Damage

No operating system can prevent hardware damage, but it can make dealing with the recovery from hardware damage easier. The best defense against data loss due to hardware failure is to diligently back up your computer data. Windows 2000 Professional's Backup Service is an excellent tool (see Figure 1-6), which makes backing up and recovering data a snap.

Because Windows 2000 Professional supports more hardware than any version of Windows NT, you can archive important data to media other than tape, which is known to degrade over time. For example, CD-R and CD-RW media are currently becoming attractive archive solutions. Tape is still a good medium for daily backups, especially when it comes to backing up large hard drives.

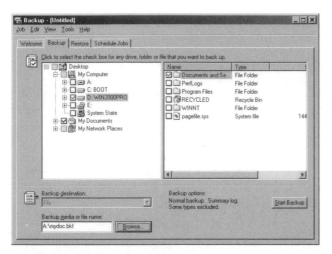

Figure 1-6

The Backup utility in Windows 2000 makes backing up and recovering data easy.

Networking Capability

Computer networks have been used in large-scale businesses for decades. Lately, more and more small businesses are seeing the benefits of creating small office networks, especially as the price of the networking components comes down.

How does Windows 2000 Professional improve the networking scenario for small businesses? This depends on whether you're interested in a domain network or a workgroup network. Domain networks provide the best solution when you have many computers to connect together. A Windows 2000 domain network—one that combines a Windows 2000 Server with Windows 2000 Professional workstations—has many benefits, not the least of which is the new Active Directory service. The subject of Windows 2000 Server networking is beyond the scope of this book; however, you'll find a summary description of Windows 2000 Server features in Chapter 16, which describes how to connect your Windows 2000 Professional computer to a client/server network.

If you've decided your business isn't large enough to invest in a domain network with its inherent expense and complexity, you can still reap the benefits of networking computers together with a workgroup (or peer-to-peer) network. Workgroup networking has been part of Windows since Windows 3.11 (also known as Microsoft Windows for Workgroups),

What Is a Network?

A network is a connection between any number of computers that allows one computer on the network to use the resources, such as files and printers, of another computer. The computer sharing the resources is said to be a *server* of those resources; the computer using those resources through the network is called the *client*.

Networks come in two flavors: *domain* networks and *workgroup* networks. A domain network, also called a *client/server* network, has at least one computer acting as a server (most often as a file server) and other computers acting strictly as clients of the resources on the server. The server is typically a computer running Windows NT Server or Windows 2000 Server. Client computers can be any variety of PCs that have network interface hardware running the appropriate communication protocol for the network.

Workgroup networks, also called *peer-to-peer* networks, don't have a dedicated server. Instead, each computer on the network acts as a server for its own resources, such as files and printers, which can be shared or not. Any computer that uses a resource shared by another computer on the network acts as a client; but it's also potentially a server of its own resources to all other computers on the network.

which added to the operating system the Microsoft LAN Manager services that ran on top of Windows 3.1. Windows 95 and Windows 98 provide built-in support for networking and file and printer sharing, as does Windows 2000 Professional. Windows 2000 Professional adds a feature to workgroup networking: the ability to share a connection to the Internet. The benefits of implementing a peer-to-peer network in your office are as follows:

- The ability to share files. You can share whole hard drives or individual folders and define who has access to the files in them. This can be a great improvement over using removable media (floppy disks or Iomega Zip disks, for example) to transport files between computers. You can also back up data from shared folders over a network, so computers that don't have backup hardware attached can back up to those that do. You can even share removable media, so if you have a removable hard drive or Zip drive on just one computer on the network, you can use it from any of the computers.

- The ability to share printers. With the cost of printers coming down every day, it's not uncommon for every computer in an office to have a printer. But is this really the best way to handle printing? By sharing printers, you can have access to the best printer for the job. So if you have a laser printer, for instance, anyone in the office can use it for fast black-and-white output; likewise, your color printers can be freed up to do more time-intensive color print jobs. It's also easier to maintain fewer printers used by more people, supplying them with toner and ink supplies, than to have many different printer brands, each with its own supply list.

- The ability to share Internet access, also called Internet Connection Sharing (ICS). ICS enables one computer on the network to act as a gateway to an Internet service provider (ISP), which then provides Internet and e-mail access to every computer on the peer-to-peer network. What's even better is that you don't need to install any separate *proxy* software to share the connection or create a *firewall* to protect your business from hackers on the Internet. The technology for Internet Connection Sharing is as bullet proof as a proxy and built into the operating system.

Mobile Computer Advantages

Several improvements in Windows 2000 Professional make it an excellent choice for portable computer users. These improvements include the following:

- Power management based on the OnNow design initiative
- Easier dial-up connections to the office network when you're on the road, and easier direct connections to another computer in your office
- Offline files and folders—a significant improvement over Briefcase

Chapter 19 provides detailed information on using Windows 2000 Professional features on your portable computer, but here is an overview of the major advantages.

Power Management Features

Power management is a feature built into portable computers so that they can conserve battery power. Typically, the computer's basic low-level operating system (called the BIOS) provides the support for this feature and the Windows operating system takes over control when Windows is loaded. Many portable computer manufacturers use different power management implementations; some include everything in the BIOS, some use drivers for one service or another.

Until recently, most portable computers used the APM (Advanced Power Management) standard for conserving power. A new standard called ACPI (Advanced Configuration and Power Interface) is now available in portables and Windows 2000 Professional fully supports this as its default. If your portable doesn't use ACPI, you can enable support for APM for basic services like suspend and resume and for battery level indication.

If you're installing Windows 2000 Professional on a current computer with an APM BIOS, you won't see any improvement over the power management in Windows 98. However, you will see advantages if you're buying a new portable that has an ACPI BIOS and Windows 2000 Professional. ACPI takes over support for PC card hot swapping (inserting and removing PC cards without rebooting) and hot docking (connecting a portable to a docking station without rebooting). ACPI includes support for managing device, processor, and system low-power states, managing multiple batteries, and providing the ability to hot swap IDE and floppy disk devices. ACPI also supports the latest battery subsystem interfaces, including Smart Battery and Control Method Battery (CMBatt).

Of course, if you've been using Windows NT 4.0 on your portable computer, the power management in Windows 2000 Professional is a long-awaited and welcome addition to the Windows NT story.

Making Connections

Small businesses buy portable computers so that their users can be productive when away from the office on business trips or at home. The ability to access files on your office computer or network while away from the office is convenient and often crucial. Windows 2000 Professional supports two types of dial-up connections to your office:

- Remote access server (RAS) connections. RAS provides a telephone-line connection directly from your remote computer's modem, through the phone lines, to the modem on your office computer.

- Virtual private network (VPN) connections. VPN connections use Internet connections accessed by both your remote computer and your office computer. The VPN connection "tunnels" through the Internet to provide a secure connection to your office's network.

You use the Network Connection Wizard, accessed from the Network And Dial-Up Connections folder, to establish both of these connections. Of the two, RAS connections are probably the easiest to implement for small business users.

When you're in the office, you need a means of connecting your portable to other computers in your office. If you have the computers in your office on a network, then a network interface on a PC card is the best connection because it provides your portable with access to all the computers on the network. If not, Windows 2000 Professional supports direct connection to a single computer through a serial or parallel cable or through an infrared link. You use the Network Connection Wizard to establish this type of connection, too.

Working Offline

Taking work home away from the office requires putting the files and folders you need on your portable before disconnecting and then copying them back to your office computer or network when you reconnect. In Windows 95/98 and Windows NT Workstation 4.0, you use Briefcase to do this, which requires dragging files and folders into and out of the Briefcase component. Windows 2000 Professional provides an alternative to the Briefcase utility called Offline Files.

Tip

Chapter 19 covers the detailed steps of using offline files and folders.

Let's say your portable is connected either to a network or directly to another computer and you are working on some files stored on the other computer that you find in a shared folder in My Network Places. When you leave the office, you want to be able to work on those same files. When you connect again the next day, you want the files on your portable to be copied back to the computer on which they're stored. Offline Files is exactly what you need.

To use offline files, you do everything from your portable. You simply right-click a shared file or folder on the network in Windows Explorer and select Make Available Offline. This first time you do this, a wizard helps you set everything up. All files and folders selected as offline are copied to a cache on your portable's hard drive. There are a number of ways you can synchronize files between the network location and your portable's cache:

- Click Tools and choose Synchronize in Windows Explorer, and then click Synchronize.

- Right-click on the specific file or folder in Windows Explorer and click Synchronize.

- Set up Offline Files to synchronize whenever you log off and log on, after the computer has been idle for a period of time, or at scheduled times. You set all of this up from the Synchronize selection on the Tools menu in Windows Explorer.

You can use the Folder Options dialog box in the Control Panel to set Offline Files options (see Figure 1-7).

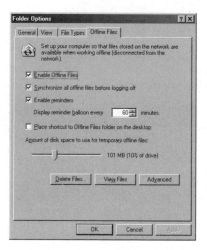

Figure 1-7

Configure Offline Files in the Folder Options dialog box.

When you do go offline, you work on the files as if you are connected to the network—they maintain the same location, names, and hierarchy. You can set up Windows 2000 Professional to remind you with an information balloon that you're working offline every 60 minutes (also configurable). When you reconnect your portable and synchronize, changes you made in your offline files are copied back to the network location, any new files are added, and any deleted files are removed from it. Windows 2000 Professional watches for version changes, so if a file is changed both online and offline between synchronization, it notifies you and you can set it up to create two files with different names so you can resolve differences.

Briefcase isn't gone, however; you can still find it in Windows 2000 Professional. If you don't want to create a connection from your portable to your office computer or network, you can use Briefcase to synchronize files to a floppy disk drive.

Windows 2000 Professional and Your Applications

Most small businesses rely on a few critical applications on a daily basis. These applications might be current, state-of-the-art Windows 32-bit software, slightly older 16-bit Windows software, or maybe even much older MS-DOS–based programs. In small business offices, different computers often run different operating systems. While your business might not have any MS-DOS computers still around (although some small businesses still do), it's likely you have one or more computers running Windows 95 or Windows 98.

Whatever your collection of computers, operating systems, and applications, the question remains: where does Windows 2000 Professional fit in the picture when it comes to running the software you now own or might want to own in the future? Let's take a quick look at what might make a program compatible or not compatible and then see what kind of applications are designed to work best with Windows 2000 Professional.

How to Determine if Your Current Software Is Compatible

Microsoft has a database that lists what programs are tested to run on Windows 2000 at this address: *www.microsoft.com/windows/professional/ deploy/compatible*. If your application is recent, you might find it on the supported list. If it's an older application, it might still work, depending on how it was written. Be sure to check with the company that created the application to see if a Windows 2000 Professional upgrade is available for it. Most software companies have Web sites that will provide updates and information, so they're a good place to start.

Windows 2000 Professional should run most well-written Windows applications. Microsoft has done more testing of applications on this platform than on any Windows NT platform. But testing only determines if it doesn't work—the software vendor must make the fix. Fixes are available in the form of upgrade packs, which you can use during Windows 2000 Professional setup to help the system upgrade your software. Again, you should be able to obtain those from the software vendor's Web site.

You can begin checking compatibility of your current applications before you even install Windows 2000 Professional by running the winnt32.exe program in the Windows 2000 Professional CD's /i386 directory. At the MS-DOS command line, run winnt32.exe with the /checkupgradeonly option (type *winnt32 /checkupgradeonly*). This runs the setup program without installing anything and generates an upgrade report (see Figure 1-8), which includes application incompatibilities as well as hardware incompatibilities. You can ignore the hardware incompatibilities if you're not planning to upgrade the particular computer on which you run the check, but the software report is worthwhile if you plan to migrate these applications to a computer running Windows 2000 Professional.

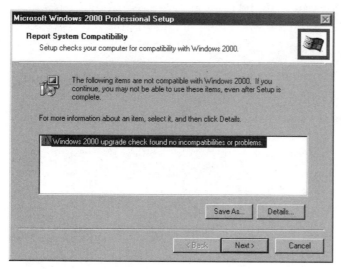

Figure 1-8

The upgrade check can find incompatible hardware and software before you install Windows 2000 Professional.

Chapter 7 addresses installing and testing programs in Windows 2000 Professional, and you'll find the specific procedures in that chapter.

Understanding Windows Compatibility

Applications on Intel-based computers have followed an evolution that has matched the evolution of the Microsoft operating systems (leaving aside other operating systems like OS/2, for the sake of brevity). Understanding this history sheds some light on the compatibility of legacy applications, those programs written prior to the release of Windows 2000 Professional, and it might give you some perspective when testing your older applications in this new operating system.

The earliest Microsoft operating system was MS-DOS, which ran 16-bit applications. The phrase *16-bit* defines the width of the CPU instructions and addresses—like freeways, wider means more traffic at greater speeds. It was common for MS-DOS programs to make *interrupt calls* directly to hardware devices such as video cards or disk drives. Device manufacturers invited this kind of activity by publishing ways to talk directly to the hardware since it was often the fastest way (and sometimes the only way) to do some things like display graphics.

The first Windows operating systems used 16-bit applications also, but these applications used different program calls—calls to the operating system software, the Windows application programming interface (API)—in order to work with the graphical Windows user interface. Since Windows ran on top of MS-DOS, you could easily run 16-bit MS-DOS applications from Windows, although the MS-DOS programs didn't use the Windows API. However, MS-DOS programs could still circumvent Windows and access the hardware directly; if something went wrong with the program or the hardware, you'd have to reboot Windows to recover. If any other programs were running at the time, it was very likely you lost work.

When Windows NT arrived, so did *32-bit* applications. In fact all components in this operating system are 32-bit. In Windows NT, 16-bit applications (both Windows and MS-DOS) run on a Virtual DOS Machine (VDM), which behaves just like an independent 16-bit Windows environment on the inside but is actually a 32-bit component to Windows NT. You can even run several of these at once. However, there are a few things that 16-bit programs can't do in this environment—most importantly, calling the hardware directly. Windows NT makes all hardware calls, regardless of how many bits its program has, through a hardware abstraction layer (HAL), which isolates hardware from programs that are running.

> ### *Understanding Windows Compatibility* (*continued*)
>
> Windows 2000 is based on Windows NT technology and, while the names are slightly different, it still works basically the same way. Windows 16-bit programs run in what is now called a Win16 NT VDM, MS-DOS programs run in an MS-DOS NT VDM, and both of these virtual, 16-bit subsystems get translated to a Win32 subsystem that then calls the core operating system.

Should You Keep Your Older PC for Legacy Applications?

Although Windows 2000 Professional runs most "well-written" programs, plenty of applications in the market aren't going to run in Windows 2000 Professional, at least not without an upgrade. These might be well-written programs from the standpoint of what they do for you, but they don't pass the reliability standards of Windows 2000 Professional. You might be using one or more of these programs, especially if you have older software.

If you do have applications that don't run in Windows 2000 Professional, that's not necessarily a reason to abandon these applications just yet. It's also not a good reason to abandon the benefits of Windows 2000 Professional. With the price/performance ratio of computers these days, it's probable that the computer hardware on which you're running your older applications has depreciated to very little (especially compared to its worth if you still rely on applications that run on it!). So it costs you little in terms of investment to stay with what you have until you find a replacement.

Does that mean you should wait to buy a new computer with Windows 2000 Professional until you upgrade your software? Nobody can really say but you—it's sort of a chicken and egg problem; which comes first? However, in general terms, it's a good idea to keep up with major shifts in computer technology so your company doesn't fall behind. While this may not mean buying every operating system upgrade that appears, there are times when you can hear the gears shift. Moving from MS-DOS to Windows was one shift; moving from 16-bit Windows to 32-bit Windows was another; and moving from consumer-based Windows to NT-based Windows is the most recent change you'll want to make, now that Windows 2000 Professional has made Windows NT easier to use.

Shouldn't I Wait for the Point 1 Version?

It's a popular belief that Microsoft always releases the best version of its product after the first release, when it has time to fix bugs. While it's true that bug fixes always follow after any product releases, the Internet has changed the way that updates are propagated. Microsoft has built the Windows Update functionality into all recent versions of Windows, including Windows 2000 Professional, which enables you to get bug fixes and enhancements right from the Start menu. By doing this, Microsoft has stabilized its process of releasing new versions of operating systems.

Use Programs Certified with the Windows Logo

When looking for new applications to run on Windows 2000 Professional, you should look for the Windows 2000 logo on the box and make sure that the program is certified to run on Windows 2000 Professional. Microsoft has enhanced the Windows logo program for Windows 2000 applications to take advantage of the more stringent requirements of this operating system. Any application that passes the certification for Windows 2000 Professional will also work on any previous 32-bit version of Windows (Windows NT, Windows 95, or Windows 98).

The list of specifications for a Windows 2000 Professional application is quite extensive and it has been available for a couple of years. To name just a few of the newer requirements: Windows 2000 Professional applications must install correctly, without trying to overwrite system files, they must comply with the security requirements of the operating system, and they must comply with the OnNow/ACPI power management capabilities for mobile users. The Windows 2000 Application Specification that spells out all of this is more than 40 pages long, so I won't go into any more details here.

In summary, almost all Microsoft Windows applications will work as is, or with an ISV-provided update pack, in Windows 2000 Professional. Many small businesses have used the excellent integration of Microsoft products and operating systems to their advantage by using Microsoft software such as Microsoft Office 2000 for Small Businesses. But you can be sure that the competitive software industry is busy making excellent Windows 2000 Professional applications as well. The Windows 2000 logo just helps sort out what works best on Windows 2000 Professional.

Now that you've read the overview of Windows 2000 Professional features, you're probably eager to get to the details of setting up and using this operating system. Before you run Setup, however, there's one more chapter you should be sure to read so that you'll understand the decisions you'll be making when you install Windows 2000 Professional. Chapter 2, "Decisions to Consider Up Front," provides a summary of issues to consider regarding Windows 2000 Professional and your business computers, including hardware requirements, upgrade paths, security options, networking possibilities, and more. After covering these basic decisions, this book concentrates on helping you to dig in and learn to use the cool new features of Windows 2000 Professional.

Chapter 2

Decisions to Consider Up Front

If you've made the decision to use Microsoft Windows 2000 Professional in your small business, you'll need to make a few decisions, if you haven't already done so. Because you always want to give important decisions some advance consideration, you'll read about them here so you can sort them out before you set up your computer.

The first decision you should consider is what computer hardware you'll use; you'll make this one, obviously, before you run Setup. Setup will present many other choices, and you'll want to look at them in advance to get an idea of the other decisions you need to make. This chapter will serve as an introduction to all of those decisions, while later chapters will provide further information about each one. You can always reconfigure things after you install Windows 2000 Professional; however, it's usually easier to set things up right the first time, especially when you know beforehand what you want to do.

This chapter will help you look at possible solutions to the following questions:

- Should you upgrade your current computers to Windows 2000 Professional or buy new computers with this operating system preinstalled?

- Do you want to enable multiple users on your system using password-protected accounts?

- Should you format your hard drive with Windows 2000 Professional's preferred file system, NTFS?

- Is now a good time to implement a network in your office and, if so, what type of network should you consider?

Should You Upgrade Your Current Computers to Windows 2000 Professional?

The first things to determine are what computer hardware you'll need to run Windows 2000 Professional and whether to upgrade your current computer or purchase a new computer with Windows 2000 Professional preinstalled.

For the majority of small business cases, Microsoft suggests upgrading to Windows 2000 Professional as a preinstalled operating system on your next new computer purchases rather than upgrading over the operating systems on current computers. This is because almost 80 percent of small businesses today use consumer Windows operating systems, and the upgrade path from consumer operating systems to Windows 2000 Professional might not always be the easiest solution. It can involve issues that take more time and effort to resolve than most small businesses owners want or need to spend. Microsoft has been vigorously promoting Microsoft Windows NT 4.0 as the platform for those who eventually want to upgrade to Windows 2000 Professional. This message seems to have been well received, based on the significant growth in sales of Windows NT 4.0 to small businesses prior to the release of Windows 2000 Professional. Microsoft wants users to have as good an experience installing Windows 2000 Professional as they have using it after it's installed.

Many small business owners, however, will want to try upgrading their current Microsoft Windows 95 or Windows 98 computers anyway.

This section will help you decide whether you want to upgrade from a consumer operating system by showing you the issues you are likely to encounter in this process.

Is Your Current Hardware Compatible?

Before you do anything else, take a look at the minimum hardware requirements for Windows 2000 Professional, listed in the following table, to get an idea of how much horsepower and disk space you'll need. Note that the values in this table state the minimum requirements; however, you'll really want as much memory and as much hard drive space as your budget will allow.

Table 2-1 Minimum Hardware Requirements

Component	Minimum Requirement
CPU	Pentium 166 MHz or higher, or Digital Alpha-based CPU
Hard drive	At least one hard drive with 800 megabytes (MB) on the partition containing the operating system files, with at least 2 gigabytes (GB) total disk space recommended
Memory	32 MB (64 MB or more is recommended); 4 GB is the maximum supported memory
Display	Video display adapter and monitor with Video Graphics Adapter (VGA) resolution or better
CD-ROM drive	12X or faster, required if not installing over a network
Accessories	Keyboard and mouse or other pointing device

To help you determine what peripheral hardware works with Windows 2000 Professional, you can use the hardware compatibility list (HCL.TXT), which is located in the Support folder on the Windows 2000 Professional CD. You can also look up the latest hardware compatibility list for all of Microsoft's supported operating systems on the Web at *www.microsoft.com/hwtest/hcl*.

Also, as mentioned in the previous chapter, you can test a computer you currently own for software and hardware compatibility by running the Windows 2000 Professional setup program on the setup CD with a special option. This runs only the compatibility-checking part of the setup and doesn't install anything. On a Windows 95 or Windows 98 computer, insert the Windows 2000 Professional CD-ROM, click Start, and then click Run.

Type the command *[Drive Letter]:winnt32.exe /checkupgradeonly* and press Enter. Figure 2-1 shows the command to use if your CD-ROM is designated as drive letter D.

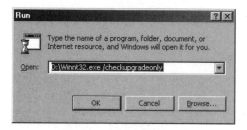

Figure 2-1

You can run the setup program to check your hardware for compatibility.

The resulting dialog box shows a listing of the incompatible hardware that Setup finds. You can save this information to a text file from the dialog box. While this is a good place to start, you shouldn't use this as the final list—the hardware compatibility list (HCL) is the ultimate source. Even if a device is listed in the HCL, however, you might want to use the driver from the manufacturer, for example if the manufacturer's driver contains updates not included in the driver provided by Microsoft.

Should You Upgrade Windows 3.1 or MS-DOS to Windows 2000 Professional?

If you're considering upgrading an older computer running a Microsoft operating system prior to Windows 95, save yourself the headache. First, it's unlikely that the hardware is current enough to be compatible with Windows 2000 Professional, and upgrading older computers to the required specifications can be a complicated process. To begin with, you'll need to replace almost everything, including the motherboard and BIOS. You'll probably need a much bigger hard drive, since Windows 2000 Professional alone takes up more disk space than computer owners even dreamed of having when Microsoft Windows 3.1 was popular. (The word "gigabyte" wasn't in most people's vocabulary then!)

Additionally, upgrading any operating system prior to Windows 95 isn't supported by Windows 2000 Professional Setup. This means you'll need to copy your data to another disk or set of diskettes, reformat the hard drive, and then do a clean installation. Alternatively, you can repartition the hard drive, or install a second hard drive, and dual boot between operating systems (*see "Dual Booting Windows 2000" on page 36*). So upgrading an old computer is more like building a new computer from scratch. In short, it's easier and probably just as cost-effective to buy a new computer with Windows 2000 Professional already installed. You might want to visit Microsoft's Windows 2000 Professional site (*www.microsoft. com/windows/professional*) and check out the Windows 2000-Ready PC program for brand-name computers that are certified to work with Windows 2000 Professional. The more compatibility headaches you can eliminate up front, the happier you'll be.

Should You Upgrade Windows 95 or Windows 98 Computers?

Now comes the most often-asked question: should you upgrade your current Windows 95 or Windows 98 computers to Windows 2000 Professional? Microsoft supports this option in Setup; however, you should consider the issues before you decide what's right for you. As always, there are both hardware and operating system issues involved. If, after weighing all the options, you decide to use your existing computer, you'll need to choose how to install it using one of three options:

- Update your current operating system (keeping current applications and settings).

- Remove your old operating system and data (by formatting) and install a clean version of Windows 2000 Professional.

- Dual boot your current operating system along with Windows 2000 Professional.

Finally, you'll need to decide what file system to use—you can stick with your current file system, upgrade, or use a combination. Here's a look at each of these decisions in more detail.

Hardware

While you might not need to make drastic hardware upgrades if your computer is of fairly recent vintage, you'll probably need to replace at least some hardware components in your current system. Of these, memory and hard drive size will probably be the biggest concerns, especially for older Windows 95 computers. And you'll need to check the BIOS version to make sure it will support the larger hard drive you plan to install. Check with your computer manufacturer for BIOS information and upgrades. If the hardware upgrades you'll need to make look at all intimidating, it's probably not worth upgrading.

Operating System

On the operating system side of things, upgrading from Windows 95 or Windows 98 seems like the logical choice because you keep your settings and don't have to reinstall software. However, this route can sometimes run into problems, often due to registry differences. The registry is the database that contains configuration information for everything in your computer. Because registries differ between NT-based and consumer-based Windows operating systems, transferring registry settings from Windows 95 or Windows 98 can sometimes be troublesome. For example, your current Windows 98 registry might have been corrupted by some program in the past (often without your knowing it), causing problems when Setup tries to preserve your configuration in Windows 2000 Professional.

More important, it's probable that some of your current applications won't work when you upgrade. Since Setup doesn't enable you to uninstall Windows 2000 Professional and recover your old operating system, you could be stuck without access to those programs if they aren't installed on another computer in your office. If those programs are critical to your small business, you could be in trouble. It is safer to install Windows 2000 Professional on one computer first, and then test your applications on it before jumping in and upgrading all your computers. Or consider the third option, dual booting, which lets you return to Windows 98 when necessary, as described later in this chapter.

File System

The final issue to consider is what file system to use. If you're currently using Windows 95, your hard drive is likely formatted with the FAT file system. If you're using Windows 98, you might be using FAT or FAT32. Windows 2000 Professional is compatible with both of these but has its own preferred file system called New Technology File System (NTFS), which enables features like compression, encryption, file permissions, and hard drives larger than those allowed by FAT or FAT32. If your business data is on the same partition as your current operating system (for example, you only have a C: drive on your computer and it contains your business data), you'll need to determine if you want to convert that partition to NTFS during setup. *See "Using NTFS Plus Accounts" on page 40 for more information on making this decision.*

Caution

While FAT and FAT32 partitions can be converted to NTFS during setup, there is no backward conversion utility. Be sure to back up your data before doing any file system conversion.

Regardless of whether you have Windows 95 or Windows 98 installed, if you decide to use an existing computer for Windows 2000 Professional, it's often best to do a clean installation to avoid possible registry and application incompatibility, described earlier. You can do this either by reformatting the hard drive containing your current operating system when installing Windows 2000 Professional, or by installing Windows 2000 Professional in a dual-boot configuration. In both cases, you choose the Clean Installation option—if Setup finds an existing operating system, it creates a dual-boot configuration; otherwise, it always boots to Windows 2000 Professional.

Performing a clean installation requires reinstalling applications and business data and setting up your preferences in Windows 2000 Professional, but it's the one way to make sure you start with a solid foundation.

Caution

Before upgrading your current computer to Windows 2000 Professional, be sure to back up your entire computer in case you want to revert to the original operating system. Also, you should back up data files separately (in addition to the full backup) by copying them to a removable disk so you can copy back the data files when you reinstall the application in Windows 2000 Professional.

Should You Upgrade Windows NT Computers?

If you're one of the many small business owners currently using Windows NT, you'll definitely want to upgrade to Windows 2000 Professional. Upgrading works best if your current operating system is Windows NT 4.0 (Service Pack 4 or later), which supports NTFS 5.0. Windows 2000 Professional was originally called Windows NT 5.0, so it's really the next upgrade to Windows NT. Chapter 3 describes the upgrade process to Windows 2000 Professional.

Dual Booting Windows 2000

If your current computer's hardware is up to the task of running Windows 2000 Professional, you might want to consider installing Windows 2000 Professional as a second operating system in addition to your current operating system. This is called *dual booting* and is configured in Windows 2000 Professional Setup when you choose the Clean Install option on a system that already has an operating system. In a dual-boot configuration, each operating system is totally independent from the other; when the computer boots, you are given the option to choose an operating system. If you don't make a choice within a specified time period, one of them boots by default. You might want to use dual booting if any of the following conditions apply:

- You have programs you need to use occasionally that run in your current operating system but don't run in Windows 2000 Professional.

- You want to evaluate Windows 2000 Professional before you actually install it as your main operating system.

- You want to transition slowly from your current operating system to Windows 2000 Professional.

- You have peripherals or devices that run in Windows 98 but not in Windows 2000 Professional.

Setting up a dual-boot configuration for Windows 2000 Professional has one caveat: you need to install Windows 2000 Professional on a different partition or on a different hard drive from the one where your primary operating system is installed. If you have a second hard drive installed, or if you're comfortable with creating and configuring partitions in MS-DOS or using third-party partitioning software, this is pretty straightforward.

Caution

While reconfiguring partitions isn't brain surgery, you can potentially do permanent damage to data on your hard drive if you aren't careful. Be sure you know what you are doing before attempting this.

If you decide to dual boot to Windows 2000 Professional, you'll need to decide whether you want to format the Windows 2000 Professional partition as NTFS or leave it as FAT or FAT32. Unless your current operating system is Windows NT 4.0 (SP4 or later), your current operating system won't be able to access any files on the partition you format as NTFS for Windows 2000 Professional. If you have doubts, the safest way to go when dual booting is to format the Windows 2000 Professional partition as FAT32. NTFS has many benefits, as described elsewhere in this book, and you can always upgrade to NTFS later; but if you intend to work on the same files in both Windows 2000 Professional and another operating system, both operating systems will need to be able to access the files, and FAT32 is the best common denominator.

See Chapter 3 for some guidelines on dual booting Windows 2000 Professional with another operating system.

What Level of Security Do You Need?

Another set of decisions involves which security features, if any, you'll want to enable and manage on your Windows 2000 Professional computer. Here's a brief overview of the security issues you'll be dealing with so you can think about what's right for you.

Are You Concerned About Security?

When asked if computer security was a concern to them, a majority of small business owners, in surveys conducted by Microsoft, answered that they were, indeed, concerned about losing data. For them, security means safety. Fewer of those surveyed actually linked the concept of security with privacy. Privacy is a concern that many small businesses take to heart, especially those working on confidential projects or with customer information. Privacy is also important when it comes to keeping your data safe because by protecting the privacy of data you're also protecting it from being altered or deleted.

Safety and Privacy Issues

The most obvious safeguard against losing data and the easiest way to make sure a hardware failure, such as a hard drive crash, doesn't bring your business to a halt is to keep your data backed up. Windows 2000 Professional has an excellent, easy-to-use backup utility for doing just that.

Note

Small businesses that have implemented servers with SCSI hard drives should also consider using RAID technology, which guarantees redundancy of data on these hard drives. RAID, which stands for redundant array of independent disks, is a storage system consisting of two or more equal-sized disks that appear to the operating system as a single disk. Data is "mirrored" on all disks so that if one disk fails, it is still available on other disks without interruption to users. Installing and configuring a RAID storage system is best left to computer professionals and isn't covered here.

Besides backing up, you can take other steps to help limit the risks of losing data due to innocent mistakes or malicious vandalism (say, from a disgruntled ex-employee). Establishing user accounts, using password protection, and enabling file and folder permissions and encryption are the tools provided by Windows 2000 Professional for protecting privacy.

There are other reasons why privacy should be a concern for small business owners. Any business with customer data on its computers needs to maintain the confidentiality of that data. For example, a customer who has entrusted a credit card number to you when ordering something definitely doesn't want that number stolen from your office. Also, business records you keep on your computer contain a wealth of information that might make your business vulnerable to a number of attacks—including theft of intellectual property, check or credit card fraud, computer hacking, and so on.

If you use a portable computer in your small business, you're probably already aware of the ever-increasing incidents of portable computer theft. Laptops are easy to steal, and if you have unsecured business data on your portable, you might be putting your business or customers at risk.

Security Decisions to Make

The main decisions you'll need to make in the area of security are these:

- Whether you'll want to enable multiple users on your system using password-protected accounts
- Whether you need the privacy capabilities provided by Windows 2000 Professional's preferred file system, NTFS

Windows 2000 Professional Setup gives you the option of making decisions up front on both of these issues.

Tip

Chapter 4, "Getting Comfortable," provides some of the basics on accounts and password protection so that you can be secure shortly after running Setup on your computer. Chapters 8, 9, and 10 in Part 3, "Creating Accounts and Keeping Your Data Safe," cover security issues in detail and provide the specific steps for managing accounts, setting passwords, and backing up your data.

How Much Control Do You Want over Access to Your Computer?

The amount of control you want to exercise over access to your computer is mostly a factor of how much time and effort you want to devote to this job. In general terms, the levels of this control are as follows:

- Using no security—you can use no security features and still have a fully functional installation.

- Establishing accounts—you can establish accounts for all users and add password protection.

- Using NTFS plus accounts—you can set permissions on folders and files, or add encryption to fully safeguard access to their contents.

- Taking full control—you can perform all of the user account management tasks usually performed by a system administrator.

Using No Security

If you don't have more than one person accessing your computer, you probably don't need to enable user accounts. Setup gives you the option of automatically logging on to Windows 2000 Professional without using a password, whenever you reboot. In this mode, you'll be logged on as the user name you entered during setup. However, even if you decide not to set up user accounts, it's a good idea to require a password even for yourself and to log off when you're not at your computer. This is especially true if you have data on a portable that you take out of your office, but it also safeguards against unauthorized access when you're in the office. The steps to setting up password protection are at the end of Chapter 4.

Establishing Accounts

If you do have multiple users on the Windows 2000 Professional computer, you should at least set up accounts for each user, as enabled in Setup and described in Chapters 3 and 9. This accomplishes several things:

- It enables you to define the authority of users on the computer, restricting some users from installing or removing programs, for example, and giving others full access to everything.

- It prevents unauthorized access to the computer by anyone without a password.

- It keeps normal users (anybody with standard or restricted access rights) from viewing any files on the system other than their own.

- It allows all users to have their own profiles on the computer, including their own backgrounds, desktop themes, programs on the Start menu, My Documents folders, and so on.

Using NTFS Plus Accounts

You can't consider security without taking into account the privacy features of NTFS. The ability of NTFS to selectively enable or block access at the file or folder level is an appealing feature for many small businesses. Using NTFS, you can determine who has access to specific folders and files and you can define exactly what those people can do on the system. For example, among other options, you can assign permissions as follows:

- Have full access to the file (read, write, and execute).

- Read the file but not make changes (write) to it.

- Execute a file but not make changes to it.

Where would NTFS permissions be useful? You might want to enable them, for example, on a portable computer that contains sensitive information. If you keep files or folders on a hard drive formatted as FAT, anyone can access the hard drive and open the files without running Windows 2000 Professional (using an MS-DOS boot diskette). However, files set with permissions on NTFS are accessible only to users who log on with the permission to open the file.

Taking Full Control

Because Windows 2000 Professional is an extension of Windows NT, you have at your disposal many more options for fine-tuning the access privileges of users on your system to files and to programs, beyond simply setting up user accounts and passwords. For example, users can be allowed or denied specific capabilities such as changing the system time or shutting down the system. Typically, you won't need to go beyond setting up accounts and passwords; if you work closely with everyone who uses the computer you can probably do without this extra administrative overhead. Also, administration isn't all or nothing—you can do a little or a lot. You'll have to decide if the needs of your small business warrant the time to pursue advanced administration—but it's good to know that the capabilities are there if you do need them. Part 7, "Advanced Administration Tasks," describes how to accomplish many of the things small business owners will want to do in this area.

Is a Network in Your Future?

If you haven't yet linked your computers together in a local area network, you're not alone. Historically, the fear of networks among small businesses has been akin to the fear of Windows NT, often bringing to mind complex and expensive solutions that might have seemed out of reach.

Windows 2000 Professional provides a solution that makes it easy to establish a network, even if you've never done it before. You'll find setting up a simple network of a few Windows 2000 Professional computers straightforward. Once it's set up, you'll be able to share files, folders, hard drives, printers, and even Internet access among the computers in your office.

If you've been putting off linking your office in a network, now might be a good time to consider creating a network. For one thing, network interface cards (NICs)—the hardware you need to connect to a local area network (LAN)—have become relatively inexpensive. They're also available as PC cards for portables and they even come as USB devices. Also, because Windows 2000 Professional has plug and play support, many of these network interface devices just install automatically—no need to deal with interrupts, memory resources, and all those other gory details. Plus, Windows 2000 Professional incorporates a new feature called Internet Connection Sharing that enables you to share the modem on one of your Windows 2000 Professional computers so that all computers on the network can access the Internet and use e-mail over a single Internet service provider (ISP) connection in your office.

What Type of Network Fits Your Business?

Although this book doesn't focus on networks—I'll happily leave that subject to others (a good recommendation is *Small Business Solutions for Networking,* from Microsoft Press)—here are a few questions you can consider to help make the decision about whether or not to link your office in a network.

- Do you have a need to share printers or files between computers? If you answer yes, you'll probably want to establish a network at some point.

- Are you planning on linking fewer than ten Windows 2000 Professional computers? If the answer is yes, you'll likely want to create a peer-to-peer network soon. Windows 2000 Professional computers are designed to work together easily on a peer-to-peer network. See Chapter 17 for the steps to do this.

- Do you have fewer than ten Windows computers, only some of which are running Windows 2000 Professional? You can create a peer-to-peer network with other computers running Windows 3.1, Windows 95, Windows 98, or Windows NT. You might need to hire someone to help you set this up because linking different operating systems in a network can be more complicated.

- Do you have more than ten computers of any type that you want to link? If so, you'll want to implement a client/server network, using either Windows 2000 Server or Windows 2000 Small Business Server. While both of these provide excellent network solutions, they are well outside the scope of this book. You'll probably need to hire a consultant to do this work unless you, or someone in your business, is trained in this area.

Although this book doesn't address setting up your own domain network, the chapters in Part 6, "Networks and Windows 2000 Professional," do provide quite a bit of network information. You'll find chapters that help you connect to an existing domain network, set up your own workgroup network with Windows 2000 Professional computers, share files and folders, and set up Internet Connection Sharing.

Chapter 3

Step One: Run Windows 2000 Setup

When designing Windows 2000 Professional, the developers at Microsoft recognized that one of the reasons Microsoft Windows NT was less popular with small business and home users than with corporate users was its reputation for being too difficult to install. To address this concern, Windows 2000 setup is considerably easier, partially because of the plug and play capabilities now built into Windows 2000, and also because of the increased focus on usability that permeates the whole operating system. The end result is that you'll find setting up Windows 2000 Professional on your computer to be no harder than setting up a computer with Microsoft Windows 95 or Microsoft Windows 98, and in many ways it's easier.

This chapter helps you figure out where to start for your particular installation scenario and then describes the steps you'll go through. Each scenario is broken down into the major stages that Windows 2000 Setup goes through, with each stage delineated by a reboot of the computer. All of this is automatic, so you really only need to follow the steps provided by Windows 2000 Professional Setup once you get going. However, the steps are provided here so you can find answers to any questions that you might have.

Before you run Windows 2000 Setup, be sure to read Chapter 2, "Decisions to Consider Up Front," which provides information about the minimum hardware requirements for running Windows 2000 Professional and the decisions you'll need to make, including:

- Whether to upgrade an existing operating system or perform a clean installation.

- Whether to dual boot with an existing operating system.

- What network information you'll need if you're connecting to a network.

- Whether you'll want to set up Windows 2000 Professional for multiple users.

- Whether to use NTFS disk formatting.

Scenarios for Installing Windows 2000 Professional

How you install Windows 2000 Professional depends on your unique situation, which probably falls into one of these categories:

- You're setting up a new system on a blank, formatted disk drive or you want to reformat the drive in an older computer that has an existing operating system and install Windows 2000 Professional in a clean install, as the only operating system. You'll find a description of this process in "Setting Up a New System," on page 48.

- The computer is already running an operating system and you want to upgrade it to Windows 2000 Professional to keep your programs and settings. Read "Upgrading to Windows 2000 Professional," on page 51, for an overview of the setup process.

- The computer is already running an operating system and you want to keep that operating system and install a new copy of Windows 2000 Professional, dual booting between operating systems. In this case read "Installing Windows 2000 Professional to Dual Boot," on page 54, for an overview of the setup process.

Preparing to Run Setup

To prepare for setup, you need to verify that your computer has compatible hardware, and you should know whether you want to clean install, upgrade, or dual boot. You should also decide whether you'll be upgrading to NTFS during setup and whether you'll want to set up your computer for multiple users or just one person. Here's a checklist of what you'll need before you run setup:

- Windows 2000 Professional CD, or Setup startup disks if you're installing to a blank hard drive—Even if you've made startup disks (as described on page 48) you'll need the CD and the CD case, which contains the product key.

- Network names and information—If you're connecting to a domain (client/server) network, you'll need to know the name of the domain, and you might also need to know about special network services or protocols required. You can get this information from your network administrator or IT contractor. If you're connecting to a workgroup (peer-to-peer) network in your office, you'll need the workgroup name. Note that you can connect to a network after running setup. Chapter 16 in this book describes the process of connecting to a network and building a simple workgroup network.

- Pen or pencil and paper—It's a good idea to have something to jot notes on during setup. Also, you'll be asked to create a password so you'll need to write it down and remember it.

Additionally, if you're upgrading an existing operating system to Windows 2000 Professional, you can provide Windows Setup with upgrade packs for programs or updated driver files for hardware that you have on your current system. The setup process for upgrading generates an upgrade report that point outs software or hardware that's not currently supported. (*You can also run this upgrade report from the command line before running Setup, as described in Chapter 2, on page 32.*) To see if there are upgrade packs or drivers available for the software or hardware you're running with Windows 2000 Professional, contact your software or hardware manufacturer or visit their Web sites.

Setting Up a New System

If you've bought a new computer with Windows 2000 Professional as the operating system, you'll want to follow the computer manufacturer's instructions for setting up your computer. Look through your computer's documentation for a setup guide, which will tell you how to connect your computer hardware and run Windows 2000 Setup. Each manufacturer has its own set of hardware and configuration issues and often installs its own programs and utilities.

On the other hand, you might have a computer with a blank hard drive, no manufacturer's setup instructions for Windows 2000, and a copy of Windows 2000 Professional to install. This would be the case, for example, if you've removed an existing operating system in preparation for installing a new copy of Windows 2000 Professional that you've purchased. If you want to overwrite a current operating system, you don't really need to format the drive first—you can do this as part of the setup process.

To run Windows 2000 Setup on a computer with a blank hard drive, you'll need either a bootable CD-ROM drive (available in some recent model computers) or you'll need the Setup startup disks. If you don't have these, you can create them by following these steps.

To create Setup startup disks:

1. Obtain four blank floppy disks and label them "Windows 2000 Professional Setup Boot Disk," "Windows 2000 Professional Setup Disk #2," "Windows 2000 Professional Setup Disk #3," and "Windows 2000 Professional Setup Disk #4."

2. Insert the Windows 2000 Professional CD in the CD-ROM drive and exit the Windows 2000 Professional CD application if it appears.

3. Insert "Windows 2000 Professional Setup Boot Disk" in the floppy disk drive.

4. Click Start and then click Run.

5. In the Open box, type *D:\BOOTDISK\MAKEBOOT A:* (assuming D: is your CD-ROM drive letter and A: is your floppy disk drive letter).

6. Follow the instructions on the screen, which prompt you to insert each of the blank disks in order.

With the Setup startup disks in hand, you can install Windows 2000 Professional on any computer, including one that already has an operating system, as described in three stages: starting Setup from the startup disks, rebooting to Windows 2000 Setup, and rebooting for the final time.

Starting Setup From the Startup Disks

To begin the installation, follow these steps:

1. Insert the disk labeled "Windows 2000 Professional Setup Boot Disk" in the floppy disk drive and power up the computer.

2. Insert the remaining Setup startup disks when requested.

3. When the Setup Notification screen appears, press Enter to continue.

4. In the Welcome To Setup screen, press Enter.

5. Insert the Windows 2000 Professional CD in your CD-ROM drive when asked, and press Enter.

6. Read the Windows 2000 Licensing Agreement and press F8 if you agree to its provisions.

7. Select a partition in which to install Windows 2000 Professional and press Enter. If you want to replace the current operating system, press D to delete the system partition. You will be warned about deleting a system partition containing files. After deleting the partition, press C to create a new, unformatted partition, providing the size of the partition when asked (it should be at least 800 MB, preferably larger). Then select the new partition and press Enter.

Caution

Delete a partition only if you're sure you don't need anything on it. All data on the partition will be lost.

8. If the partition you selected is unformatted, you can choose to Format the partition as FAT or NTFS. Select one and press Enter. If the partition you selected is already formatted, you're given the opportunity to format it as FAT, format it as NTFS, or convert it to NTFS.

9. Remove the last Setup disk. Setup now copies files to the Windows 2000 installation folders, initializes the files, and then reboots.

Rebooting to Windows 2000 Setup

When Windows 2000 boots, Windows 2000 Professional Setup runs and installs devices. This is a good time to go find something else to do for a while.

After devices are installed, continue with these settings:

1. If necessary, change the system or user local settings and the keyboard layout on the Regional Settings page, which appears after Setup installs devices. These settings can be adjusted from the Control Panel after you run Setup, so you don't need to worry about this now.

2. Enter your name and organization name in the Personalize Your Software page.

3. In the Your Product Key page, type the product key, which you'll find on the CD package.

4. In the Computer Name And Administration Password page, you can replace the default computer name if you want. Also, type an Administrator password. Be sure to write this down and keep it in a safe place.

5. In the Date And Time Settings page, set the date and time zone. Setup now copies network software to the hard drive.

6. In the Network Settings page, which appears when the copying is finished, choose whether to use Typical or Custom settings for networking. If you don't know, choose Typical—you can always add networking components later.

7. In the Workgroup Or Computer Domain page, select whether to use a client/server (domain) network or a peer-to-peer network (workgroup). If you aren't adding the computer to a network, choose None, in which case you still choose Workgroup. Enter the workgroup name if you already have a workgroup network.

   Finally, Setup installs Windows components and performs the tasks of installing start menu items, registering components, saving components, and removing temporary files.

8. After Setup finishes these tasks, click Finish.

Rebooting for the Final Time

The computer reboots one more time to start Windows 2000 Professional and the Network Identification Wizard runs to collect information.

To respond to the wizard and complete your installation:

1. Click Next at the Network Identification Wizard's welcome page.

2. In the Users Of This Computer page, you're asked if you want users to enter a name and password to use the computer or whether you want Windows to assume one person has logged on (and doesn't require a password screen). If you choose the latter, you can choose yourself as the person who logs on by default (using the name you entered earlier in Setup) and then type a password for yourself, or choose to log on as the Administrator. Click Next when you're done.

3. Click Finish to exit the wizard.

Upgrading to Windows 2000 Professional

While upgrading is almost always the best approach when you're currently running Windows NT 4.0, and upgrading is listed as the preferred option in the Setup program, you need to have considered the issues described in Chapter 2 when upgrading from Windows 95 or Windows 98. You can upgrade in a single stage.

To upgrade to Windows 2000 Professional, follow these steps:

1. Insert the Windows 2000 Professional CD. A dialog box tells you that the CD-ROM contains a newer version of Windows than the one you're presently using and asks if you would you like to upgrade to Windows 2000 (see Figure 3-1). Click Yes.

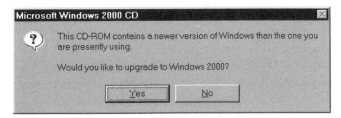

Figure 3-1
Inserting the Windows 2000 CD automatically starts the setup process.

2. The welcome page of Windows 2000 Setup provides the options of upgrading to Windows 2000 or installing a new copy of Windows 2000 (see Figure 3-2). The default choice is to upgrade. so you can just click Next.

Figure 3-2

The Windows 2000 Setup Wizard asks if you want to upgrade or install a new copy of Windows 2000.

3. Read the license agreement, accept it if you agree, and click Next.

4. Enter the 25-character product key, which you can find on your Windows 2000 CD case, and click Next.

    The Preparing To Upgrade To Windows 2000 page appears now (see Figure 3-3). If you have an Internet connection, you can click Click Here to visit the Microsoft Web site (*www.microsoft.com/windows/professional*) for the latest information and to download any upgrade files for setup that might be posted there.

5. A Corporate Connection Status page might appear now to determine what network environment you are connected to (this doesn't appear in all upgrades). Choose one of the options that describes whether you're connected to a LAN, either directly or through a dial-up connection. If the page doesn't appear, Setup has probably automatically determined your LAN connection status.

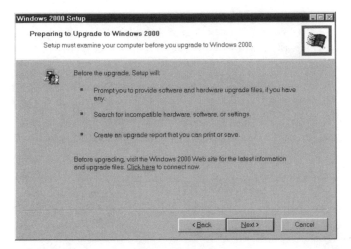

Figure 3-3

The Preparing To Upgrade wizard page tells you what the wizard will do.

6. You're now given the opportunity to provide upgrade packs for your current applications that you might have received from the manufacturer. You can add them by selecting Yes, I Have Upgrade Packs, clicking Next, and then browsing to the files. If you don't have any upgrade packs, you can just click Next.

7. In the Updating To Windows NTFS page, choose whether to upgrade your file system to NTFS. After making your decision, just click Next, and Setup loads the setup information file.

8. The Creating An Upgrade Report page now appears and Setup visits all programs and system files on your computer, searching for incompatible software or hardware. You can get this report before running Setup, as described on page 32 in Chapter 2, so this report might come as no surprise, in which case you will have already had a chance to look for solutions to any incompatibilies.

9. When Setup finishes scanning your programs, the Provide Update Plug And Play Files page appears, identifying hardware whose drivers don't work in Windows 2000. At this point you can click Provide Files and provide any upgraded drivers that you might have gathered in advance. (You can add this hardware later, so don't worry if you don't have the files now.)

10. Setup now generates a report (see Figure 3-4) informing you of incompatibilities encountered. At this point, you can visit the

Web sites of software or hardware manufacturers to see if they have Windows 2000 updates available that you can download.

Tip

It's a good idea to save the report by clicking the Save button, or print it by clicking Print, so you have a record of the incompatibilities found.

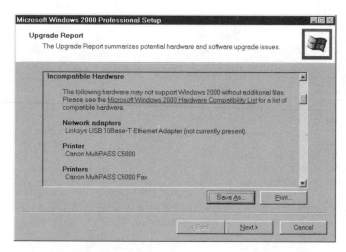

Figure 3-4
Read the upgrade report to check for incompatible hardware or software.

11. Finally the Ready To Install Windows page appears. When you click Next, the rest of the installation process is automatic, so you can go do something else for the time it takes to finish upgrading your computer.

Installing Windows 2000 Professional to Dual Boot

If you instruct Setup to install a new copy of Windows 2000 Professional and it finds an existing operating system on your computer, Setup leaves the current operating system in place, by default, and installs Windows 2000 Professional in a dual-boot configuration.

What's a Dual-Boot Configuration?

When you start the computer in a dual-boot configuration, you will see a menu with options to run Windows 2000 Professional or your old operating system. If you don't choose either option within 25 seconds, Windows 2000 Professional will start by default.

Windows 2000 Setup alters the boot sector on the hard drive, which the computer uses to determine where to find the operating system. In Windows 95 and Windows 98, this boot sector just runs Windows. In Windows NT and when Windows 2000 is installed in a dual-boot configuration, the boot sector loads a file that displays a menu so you can choose which operating system to run. A hidden configuration system file called BOOT.INI contains the information displayed in this menu, sets the timeout, and sets the partition to jump to for the chosen operating system.

You should install Windows 2000 Professional in a different partition from the one in which your current operating system is installed. This is primarily because you'll need to install programs independently in Windows 2000 Professional and your current operating system and this can cause problems when the two operating systems are both in the same partition. Another reason for installing operating systems in different partitions is that your current operating system might not work with NTFS. If you want to use NTFS with Windows 2000 Professional, you'll need to use a separate partition for the NTFS volumes and you might as well put Windows 2000 Professional there also.

The installation is described in four stages: starting Setup from the current operating system, rebooting and performing disk activities, rebooting to Windows 2000 Setup, and rebooting for the final time.

Starting Setup From Your Operating System

To install Windows 2000 Professional in a dual-boot configuration, begin with these steps:

1. Insert the CD-ROM and when a message tells you that the operating system is newer than yours and asks if you want to upgrade, click No.

2. In the Microsoft Windows 2000 CD window (see Figure 3-5), click Install Windows 2000.

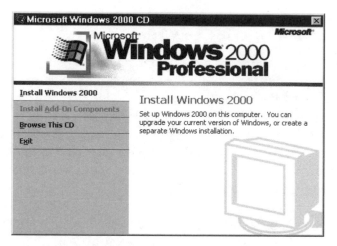

Figure 3-5

Start Setup by clicking Install Windows 2000 in the Microsoft Windows 2000 CD window.

3. When the Windows 2000 Setup Welcome page appears, select Install a New Copy of Windows 2000 (Clean Install).

4. Read the license agreement and, if you agree, accept it.

5. Type the 25-character product key, which you can find on your Windows 2000 CD case.

6. In the Select Special Options page (see Figure 3-6) click Language Options if you want to select the language to run and also install character sets for many languages. You can click Advanced Options if you want to copy the Setup CD files to a location on your hard drive, change the default folder for the system files (instead of \WINNT), or specify that you want to choose the installation partition during Setup. You can click Accessibility Options to select the Microsoft Accessibility tools you want to use during Setup. You can select either the Magnifier or the Narrator.

   Next Setup loads the setup information file, evaluates the disk space, copies installation files to the hard disk drive, and then restarts your computer.

Rebooting and Performing Disk Activities

After the computer reboots, you'll see Windows 2000 Professional Setup on the operating system selection menu. The Setup option is quickly chosen

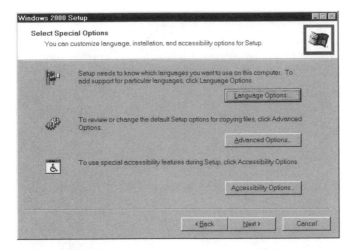

Figure 3-6

The Select Special Options page of the setup wizard gives you installation choices.

by default in five seconds, and the computer copies hardware files and then starts Windows 2000 Setup in a DOS-based mode. You can press Enter to continue. At this point you can continue, repair an installation (if you have an emergency repair disk), or exit.

To continue with the installation:

1. When you select Continue, you're given a choice of partitions in which to install the new copy of Windows 2000 Professional. After you select the partition, Setup examines its disk space. If the disk has enough space, the installation proceeds.

   If you don't have enough disk space, press F3 to exit Setup. When you reboot, select your original operating system (do this quickly—Windows 2000 Professional Setup is programmed to start within seconds of the appearance of this selection menu). Free up disk space and restart your computer, which then runs Setup at the point where you left off.

2. If you're installing in a partition different from the one containing the current operating system (as recommended), you're given the opportunity to format the partition using NTFS, format the partition using FAT, convert the partition to NTFS, or leave it as it's currently formatted. Formatting will destroy data on that partition—converting will not. However, you can't convert back to FAT formatting once you've converted to NTFS, so make this decision carefully.

Rebooting to Windows 2000 Setup

After the computer reboots again, Windows 2000 Professional opens in Windows graphical mode. Setup automatically configures hardware devices on your computer, which can take quite a while to complete.

After devices are installed, continue with settings:

1. The Regional Settings page now appears, enabling you to change the system or user locale settings and the keyboard layout. These can be adjusted from the Control Panel after running Setup, so don't worry about changing them now if you'd rather not.

2. In the Personalize Your Software page, enter your name and organization name.

3. In the Computer Name And Administration Password page, a 15-character name is fabricated for you from your organization name, but try to think of something more descriptive—this name will appear on any network you're connected to now or in the future. Enter a password for the administrator and be sure to write down the administrator password and keep it somewhere safe. If you lose this password, you'll have to reinstall Windows 2000 Professional to enter another administrator password.

4. If Setup detected and installed a modem, you'll be asked to provide some modem information.

5. In the Date And Time Settings page, set the date and time zone. Setup now copies network software to the hard drive.

6. In the Network Settings page, which appears when the copying is finished, choose whether to use Typical or Custom settings for networking. If you don't know, choose Typical—you can always add networking components later.

7. In the Workgroup Or Computer Domain page, select whether you're using a client/server (domain) network, a peer-to-peer network (workgroup), or none, in which case you still choose workgroup. Type the workgroup name if you do have a workgroup network.

Tip

All of this network configuration can be changed later and is described in Chapter 16, so don't worry if you don't have the answers at this point.

Finally, Setup installs Windows components and performs the tasks of installing Start menu items, registering components, saving components, and removing temporary files.

8.   After Setup finishes these tasks, click Finish.

Rebooting for the Final Time

The computer reboots one more time. This time, the Microsoft Windows 2000 Professional operating system comes up as the default in the operating system selection menu. Let Windows 2000 start automatically by waiting or pressing Enter to select it. When it starts, the Network Identification Wizard runs immediately to collect information.

To respond to the wizard and complete your installation:

1.   Click Next at the Network Identification Wizard's welcome page.

2.   In the Users Of This Computer page, you're asked if you want users to enter a name and password to use the computer or whether you just want Windows to assume one person has logged on (and doesn't require a password screen). If you choose the latter, you can select the name you entered earlier or the Administrator and then type a password for that user. Click Next when you're done, and click Finish to exit the wizard.

Uninstalling a Dual-Boot Configuration

You might be wondering what to do if you've installed Window 2000 Professional in a dual-boot configuration but later decide to remove it. You might have decided to test Windows 2000 in a dual-boot configuration by putting it on a second partition on a computer running Windows 98. If that doesn't work out for some reason and you you'd rather install Windows 2000 Professional on another computer, you'll want to remove it from the first computer and revert to booting directly to your old operating system.

Windows 2000 Professional doesn't include an uninstall program, but you can remove the files by hand and then fix the boot sector on the hard drive so the computer doesn't bring up the operating system selection menu when you boot. To remove the files, boot to your old operating system and remove all the files and folders under the WINNT and Documents And Settings folders. (Make sure you really delete them by pressing Shift+Del, otherwise you'll end up with a very large Recycle Bin!) In order to revert the partition table to its original state before you installed Windows 2000 Professional, you'll need to create a system disk.

To create a system disk in your old operating system:

1. Insert a blank disk in your A: drive.

2. At an MS-DOS command prompt, type *FORMAT A: /S*. This will format the disk and copy system files to it.

3. Copy the SYS.COM file from the WINDOWS\COMMAND directory to the disk (for example, type *COPY C:\WINDOWS\ COMMAND\SYS.COM A:*).

Now you can reboot your computer with the disk in the A: drive. After it boots, at the command prompt type *SYS C:* (assuming your operating system is on the C: drive). After the system files are transferred, remove the disk and reboot, and the computer will boot to your original operating system.

Installing Windows 2000 Professional Unattended

You can run Setup using an answer file to provide the input you would normally provide by answering prompts on the screen. Network administrators in large corporate environments often use unattended installation to save time when installing Windows 2000 Professional on many computers. Because this book is targeted to business owners or managers in a small office environment who aren't network administrators, this scenario isn't covered here.

If you're interested in an unattended installation, the I386 folder on the Windows 2000 Professional CD contains a file named Unattended.txt, which you can use as a template. Also, the Windows 2000 Professional Resource Kit, available from Microsoft Press, offers lots of information.

A plug and play printer or any other plug and play hardware that's connected to your computer before you run Windows 2000 Setup should be installed automatically as part of the setup process. However, if you haven't yet hooked up a printer or other hardware, or if the device isn't plug and play, you'll find steps for installing your printer in Chapter 5 and for installing hardware in Chapter 6. The next chapter will give you a chance to get comfortable with Windows 2000 Professional and see what's familiar and what's new with the look and feel of the latest Windows.

Chapter 4

Step Two: Make Yourself Comfortable

Now that you've run Setup, it's a good time to sit back, adjust the mirrors, and check out the Microsoft Windows 2000 Professional scenery. While the chapters in Part 5 will take you through a closer look at the Windows 2000 Professional user interface, this chapter helps you make a few adjustments to get settled in before continuing the installation and setup. Besides, you are probably curious about how Windows 2000 Professional looks, so now's a good time to check it out. The best part about this topic is that it'll be familiar territory if you're coming from Microsoft Windows 95 or Windows 98.

This chapter starts with the Getting Started application, the first thing you see when you run Windows 2000. It helps you set up display options and explains some Start menu changes you'll see. It also provides a survival kit for the basic security features of Windows 2000 Professional so you'll understand enough to get by until you get to account management in Chapter 9.

> ### Note
>
> This book compares Windows 95 and Windows 98 user interface features with Windows 2000 Professional to help you with the transition. In most cases, it uses only Windows 95 for the comparison unless there was a change to the feature in Windows 98.

What to Do with Getting Started

After you run Setup, and whenever you boot or log on, Windows 2000 Professional opens with a musical fanfare and presents the Getting Started application (see Figure 4-1). After you actually do get started, you'll want to disable this application from automatically appearing, but first, you'll probably want to take a look at what it offers.

The right pane of Getting Started displays some graphical tips on basic Windows features like the Start menu, the Control Panel, and the Microsoft Internet tools. (These graphics rotate every few seconds like a Web page advertisement—click in the right pane to flip through them faster if you want.) The left pane gives you some menu choices, which you'll learn about in a moment, but first here's how to deal with Getting Started if it's getting in your way.

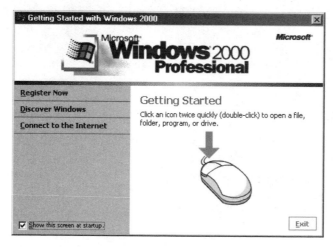

Figure 4-1

The Getting Started application in Windows 2000.

Exiting and Restarting Getting Started

The first thing to know about Getting Started is that you can open it from the Start menu at any time. So feel free to exit it now and come back later if you want.

- To exit Getting Started, click the Exit button in the lower right or the Close button in the upper right.

- To open Getting Started, click Start, point to Accessories, point to System Tools, and then click Getting Started.

When you exit Getting Started the first time, you'll see another new feature of Windows 2000 Professional: the informational balloon, in this case pointing to the Start button and telling you what it's for (see Figure 4-2). Click the Start button or the balloon to get rid of it. The balloon pointing to the Start menu appears only once, after you exit Getting Started the first time (this occurs once for every user on your system with an account). You'll see similar informational balloons occasionally in Windows 2000 Professional when the system notifies you of some change that it either causes or detects.

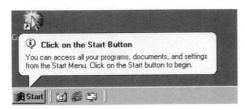

Figure 4-2
Informational balloons provide tips on using Windows 2000 features.

Until you disable it, Getting Started comes up every time you log on. You may want to wait to disable it until after you've registered Windows 2000 Professional, just to keep a reminder that you should register. To prevent Getting Started from appearing whenever Windows starts, clear the Show This Screen At Startup check box, located in the lower left corner of the Getting Started window.

Getting Started Options

Getting Started gives you three choices (actually four, if you consider that exiting is an option—one that many people take first). This section covers these options.

Register Now or Register Later?

Register Now opens the Microsoft Windows 2000 Registration Wizard, which has you fill in some information and then connects to Microsoft and registers your copy of Windows 2000 Professional. When you choose this option, you'll also discover whether your modem connection is working. Part 4, "Connecting Online," covers everything about making connections, from configuring your modem to connecting to an ISP and e-mail service. You might want to postpone registering until you've read Chapter 11, where you'll find modem troubleshooting tips.

If you prefer to take the plunge now, however, go ahead and click Register Now—if you run into any modem or connection problems, you can cancel the Registration Wizard and try again later.

Discover Windows

Discover Windows is an informative multimedia tour of the new Windows 2000 Professional user interface features. If you have the time to explore the menus in this tutorial, you'll find some helpful information about what's new in Windows 2000. One nice aspect of Discover Windows is that it provides animations showing new user interface features and how to use them. All of the features shown in Discover Windows are also covered in this book, but in a less animated fashion.

Note

Clicking Discover Windows actually runs a program that resides on the Windows 2000 Professional CD. It isn't copied to your hard drive by Windows 2000 Setup, so unless your computer manufacturer has installed it on your hard drive, you'll need to have the Windows 2000 Professional CD in the CD-ROM drive.

Connect To The Internet

Choosing Connect To The Internet runs the Internet Connection Wizard, which creates a dial-up or network connection to an Internet service provider (ISP). As with registering, you may want to wait to run this wizard until you've read Part 4, which covers connecting to the Internet and troubleshooting modem problems.

Note

If you do click Connect To The Internet and then want to cancel, the Internet Connection Wizard opens a dialog box asking whether you really want to Cancel. Go ahead and click Yes. You won't do any damage by canceling most wizards.

Setting Up Your Display

One of the first things most people do when setting up a new PC is adjust the monitor display to their liking. This makes good sense, when you consider how much time you'll end up staring at the monitor. You might want to take a few minutes now to set the screen size, color depth, and perhaps put up background wallpaper. This section shows you how to do these tasks and also addresses some basics of configuring the Active Desktop, which has changed a little from Windows 95. If you're happy with your display the way it is or would rather adjust it later, go ahead and jump to "Taking a Quick Look Around" on page 74 for a brief tour of some of the new user interface features in Windows 2000 Professional.

Opening the Display Properties Dialog Box

You adjust the display properties in Windows 2000 Professional in the Display Properties dialog box, which you get to either from the shortcut menu on the desktop (see Figure 4-3 on the next page) or from the Control Panel (see Figure 4-4 on the next page). All this is done the same way as it is in Windows 95.

Important

Before doing anything else, make sure you have exited Getting Started, which stays open on the Windows desktop and won't let you see anything else while it's open.

- To open the Display Properties dialog box using the shortcut menu, right-click anywhere on the Windows desktop, and then choose Properties from the shortcut menu.

Figure 4-3

Right-click on the Windows desktop to open the Display shortcut menu.

- To open the Display Properties dialog box from the Control Panel, point to Settings on the Start menu, and then click Control Panel. In the Control Panel, double-click Display.

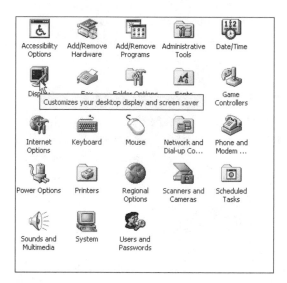

Figure 4-4

Double-click the Display icon in the Control Panel to open the Display Properties dialog box.

Adjusting the Screen Size and Color Depth

This procedure is just like setting the display size in Windows 95. One added feature of Windows 2000 Professional is the Troubleshoot button at the bottom of the Settings tab.

To change the display size:

1. In the Display Properties dialog box, click the Settings tab.

2. Adjust the Screen Area slider to the size you want (see Figure 4-5).

3. Click OK or Apply.

   A dialog box appears telling you that the new desktop settings will be applied and if you don't like them, just wait 15 seconds and the original settings will be restored.

4. Click OK.

   Another dialog box asks if you want to keep the new settings.

5. Click Yes if you like the settings; if you want to return to the current display settings, click No or wait 15 seconds.

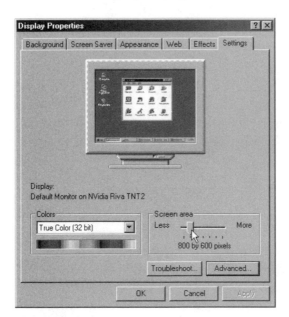

Figure 4-5

Drag the Screen Area slider to set the display size.

Tip

Some programs require you to restart your computer after making display changes. The Advanced button on the Settings tab is the same as it is in Windows 95. It lets you control whether to have your display changes applied immediately (the default), to be warned before changes are put into effect, or to be prompted before the computer is restarted and display changes are applied.

If you have problems with the display settings, you can click the Troubleshoot button just below the Screen Area slider. This brings up the Display Troubleshooter in Windows 2000 Help, a kind of Help wizard that steps you through scenarios of common problems that occur and provides help for those cases.

Tip

Migrating from Microsoft Windows NT 4.0? You'll notice that Windows 2000 Professional is a bit friendlier about applying your desktop settings— it reverts automatically to your previous setting if you do nothing, rather than making you click another button to test the new setting first.

The Display Troubleshooter, shown in Figure 4-6, is fairly straightforward to use; just select an option on each page and click Next. After the first screen, you can click the Back or Start Over button as well as the Next button to navigate through the screens. If you're lucky, your problem will be listed. Unfortunately, the Help file would probably need to be larger than the operating system to cover all the possible troubleshooting scenarios in this manner, so it covers only some of the most common. But when it hits your problem, it's a great help.

If you want to change the font size on the display, you can click Advanced and change the font size from Small Fonts to Large Fonts. Alternatively, you can select Other from the Font Size drop-down list and use the Custom Font Size dialog box to create a custom scaled font. Again, all of this is just the way it's done in Windows 95.

To adjust the color depth (the number of colors shown on the screen), just select one of the available selections in the Colors section of the Settings tab, as shown in Figure 4-7. By default, Windows 2000 uses the lowest color depth when you start (256 colors). If you want to be able to display

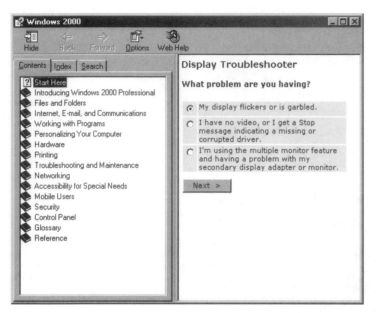

Figure 4-6

The Display Troubleshooter can help you solve common display problems.

graphics as a background you'll need to select at least High Color (16 bit) or better, assuming your graphics card supports this setting.

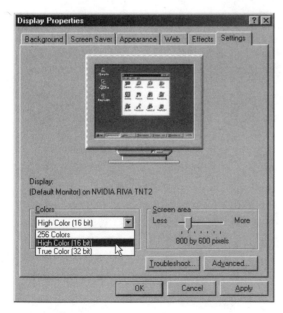

Figure 4-7

Setting a higher color depth shows more colors on the screen.

Putting Up Background Wallpaper

By default, Windows 2000 Professional has no background texture or wallpaper on the Windows desktop. Like Windows 95, you use the Background tab of the Display Properties dialog box to set a background and you get the same general choices for creating desktop backgrounds.

You can put up a tiled bitmap background by choosing one of the tile bitmaps (such as Coffee Bean) and selecting Tile in the Picture Display drop-down list. Figure 4-8 shows this option.

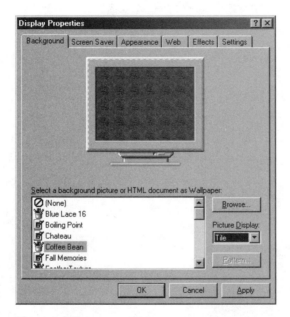

Figure 4-8

You can fill the desktop with an image by choosing a tiled bitmap background.

Alternatively, you can select a full-screen bitmap file anywhere on your hard drive to use as a background. To do this, click Browse, navigate to the folder that contains your bitmap file, and select the file.

Finally—and please read the sidebar on the opposite page before you do this—you can select a Web image file from those presented in the Background tab, or anywhere on your hard drive using the Browse button. A Web image is a JPEG or GIF file, and it can be either a full-screen or tile-size image. You can identify Web images in the Background tab by the icon of a red picture in a gold frame with a blue pen.

Is Your Desktop Active, Passive, or Just Cluttered?

As in Windows 95, to enable displaying Web graphics on your desktop, you'll need to enable Active Desktop, although the mechanism to do this is slightly different in Windows 2000 Professional. When you enable Active Desktop, it assumes you're connected to the Internet and looks for the home page (the address entered in Home Page Address on the General tab in Internet Options, which is *www.msn.com* by default). If you happen to be connected to the Internet when you enable Active Desktop, the page at this address gets loaded onto your desktop; if not, you get an error message on your desktop that covers the entire desktop, so it can be disconcerting.

To select a Web graphic as your background image (and enable Active Desktop):

1. In the Display Properties dialog box, click the Web tab.
2. Select Show Web Content On My Active Desktop and deselect My Current Home Page.

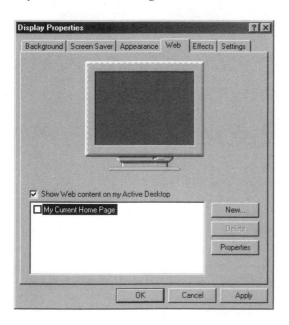

3. Click the Background tab in the Display Properties dialog box.

4. Select one of the Web images from the list, such as Snow Trees or Paradise. Figure 4-9 shows this option.

5. If the image displayed on the sample display screen in the dialog box doesn't fill the screen, select Tile in the Picture Display drop-down list box. Otherwise, you can leave Picture Display at Center. If the image almost fills the screen, you can either select Stretch in the Picture Display list box or click Pattern to choose a wall-paper pattern to fill the screen around the graphic.

6. Click Apply or OK.

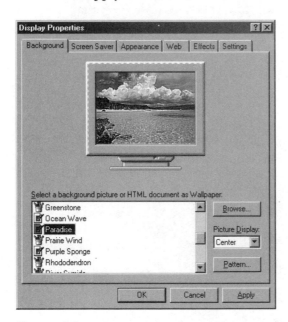

Figure 4-9

The sample display screen shows a full-size Web graphic background.

The steps above show how to enable Active Desktop without requiring an Internet connection. If you set up an Internet connection, you might decide that you want to use a home page instead of the graphic file, in which case you can revisit the Display Properties dialog box, click the Web tab and select My Current Home Page. At any time, you can disable Active Desktop.

To disable Active Desktop:

1. Right-click the Windows desktop to open the shortcut menu.

2. Select Active Desktop to display its cascading menu.

3. Deselect Show Web Content.

    If you have a Web graphic as wallpaper, it will disappear.

Tip

You can also use the Web tab in the Display Properties dialog box to disable Active Desktop. Just clear the Show Web Content On My Active Desktop check box and click OK.

    Without connecting to the Internet, you can't really play too much with Active Desktop, assuming you'd even care to.

A Note about the Screen Saver Password

Setting up a screen saver in Windows 2000 Professional is done in exactly the same way as in Windows 95—on the Screen Saver tab in the Display Properties dialog box. If you select a screen saver and select Password Protected on the Screen Saver tab, you will be prompted for a password whenever you interrupt the screen saver. You use the same password to log on from your screen saver as you use to log on to Windows.

    If you don't have to log on or enter a password to access Windows 2000 Professional, leave the password area blank and click OK—your default account has a blank password assigned. *See "About Your Account" on page 80 for more information about accounts and passwords.*

Taking a Quick Look Around

Here's a quick rundown of what's the same in Windows 2000 Professional and what's different from the Windows 95 and Windows 98 operating systems you're probably familiar with.

The Start Menu – What's Changed?

You'll see all the familiar items on the Start menu in Windows 2000 Professional, including Programs, Documents, Settings, Search (renamed from Find), Help, and Run (see Figure 4-10). Three of these (Documents, Help, and Run) are unchanged from Windows 95; three (Programs, Settings, and Search) have changed slightly; and two items are missing (but you can get them back if you want).

Figure 4-10

The Windows 2000 Professional Start menu looks similar to the Start menu in Windows 95 and Windows 98.

Missing Start Menu Items

You might have noticed that the Favorites and Log Off items are missing from the Windows 2000 version of the Start menu. Windows 2000 Professional tends to keep the Start menu a lot simpler. In fact, it hides menu items you haven't used for a while, unless you disable this feature (see the accompanying sidebar).

If you really want Favorites and Log Off on your Start menu, you can add them using the Taskbar And Start Menu Properties dialog box.

To add Favorites and Logoff to the Start menu:

1. Click Start, point to Settings, and then click Taskbar & Start Menu.

2. In the Taskbar And Start Menu Properties dialog box, click the Advanced tab.

3. In the Start Menu Settings list, select the Display Favorites and Display Logoff check boxes.

4. Click OK.

   These items now appear on the Start menu.

Note

If you add Logoff to the Start menu, be sure to read "About Your Account" on page 80 before you actually log off. Windows 2000 Professional is vastly different from Windows 95 or Windows 98 in this regard.

Disappearing Menus

You can't see one of the innovations in the Windows 2000 Professional user interface when you first begin using it. By default, the operating system monitors your use of the items on the Programs submenu of the Start menu and will start to hide the programs and submenus that you don't use often (you can make them appear again by clicking the down-arrow on the menu). You won't see this start to happen for a couple of weeks, but when you do, you'll see an informational balloon telling you about it.

This feature is called *personalized menus* and it provides much less cluttered access to the programs that you do use. (To disable this feature, click Start, point to Settings, click Taskbar & Start Menu, and clear Use Personalized Menus). Give it a chance before you turn it off though—you might grow to like it.

Although none of the changes in the menus is drastic, you may be looking for a command you can't find, so Table 4-1 is a summary of the commands and submenus that have been moved, removed, or added to the Start menu since Windows 95 and Windows 98.

Table 4-1 Quick Guide to Start Menu Changes

Menu	Removed since Windows 95	Moved/changed since Windows 95	Added in Windows 2000 Professional
Start	Favorites, Log Off		
Start/Settings	Folder Options, Active Desktop, Windows Update		Network And Dial-up Connections
Start/Find	Computer…		
Start/Programs		MS-DOS Prompt is Command Prompt on Accessories menu	
Programs/ Accessories			Accessibility menu (now installed by default), Command Prompt
Accessories/ Accessibility			Narrator, On-Screen Keyboard, Utility Manager
Accessories/ Communications		Dial-Up Networking is now Network And Dial-up Connections (also under Settings)	NetMeeting, Fax
Accessories/ Games			Pinball
Accessories/ System Tools	Drive Space, Disk Compression, Scan Disk, Drive Converter (FAT 32) in Windows 98	Welcome to Windows is now Getting Started	Backup, Character Map

See "Starting with the Start Menu and Taskbar" in Chapter 14 for more information on these changes and how to use the new features of the Windows 2000 Professional Start menu.

Changed Submenus

The three submenus belonging to the Start menu that have changed from Windows 95 to Windows 2000 Professional are these:

- The Programs menu, on which most of the changes are found on the Accessories submenu. Accessories now contains the Accessibility menu by default with an expanded set of commands (Accessibility was an option in Windows 95).

- The Settings menu, which is much simpler now. Gone are Folder Options, Active Desktop, and Windows Update items—these have been moved elsewhere (see the previous table). Added is a new Network And Dial-Up Connections item.

- The Search menu, called Find on the Windows 95 Start menu. Search has been simplified to just three menus. Computer search, as in Windows 95, is no longer available. To search for a computer on a network in Windows 2000 Professional, you double-click My Network Places on the desktop and click the Search button on the Standard toolbar.

New Effects, Pointers, and Tool Tips

Windows 2000 offers some subtle changes to the look and feel of Windows. While these changes may not be important for how you get your work done, they are nevertheless a part of your working environment. To identify them, or get rid of them if they bother you, read on.

The Fade Effect

By default, Windows 2000 Professional menus and tool tips fade in when opened, as opposed to scrolling into view or just popping up suddenly. Some people like this effect, but others like the familiar scroll effect that's in Windows 95, or they prefer no effect at all. You can change the fade effect on the Effects tab of the Display Properties dialog box.

To change the fade effect to scroll:

1. Right-click the Windows desktop and choose Properties to open the Display Properties dialog box.

2. Click the Effects tab.

3. In the drop-down list in the Visual Effects area, select Scroll Effect (or to disable effects entirely, clear Use Transition Effects For Menus And Tooltips).

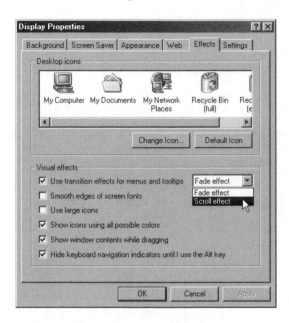

The Pointer Shadow

Notice that the pointer appears to be floating above the screen, casting a shadow on all elements in Windows that it passes over. Many find this a small, but appealing, addition to Windows. If you don't happen to like this effect, you can disable it easily using the Mouse Properties in the Control Panel.

To disable shadowed mouse pointers:

1. Click Start, point to Settings, and then click Control Panel to open the Control Panel.

2. Double-click the Mouse icon.

3. In the Mouse Properties dialog box, click the Pointers tab.

4. At the bottom of this tab, clear Enable Pointer Shadow.

5. Click OK.

Tool Tips Everywhere

Tool tips are those little yellow description boxes that appear when you pause the mouse pointer over some object. They tell you what that object does (Windows refers to them as "pop-up description boxes"). Tool tips are not new to the Windows operating system—they've been around since Windows 95, where they're most noticeable when you pause the mouse pointer over anything on the taskbar, a button on a toolbar, or any entry on the Favorites menu.

In Windows 2000 Professional, tool tips have been extended to items on the Start menu. To see an example, click Start, point to Documents, and then move the mouse pointer to My Documents and pause. You'll also see tool tips when you rest the pointer on icons in the Control Panel and on programs on the Start menu.

After you learn the Windows 2000 Professional interface, you may find that these tool tips get in your way. In Windows 95, Windows 98, and Windows 2000 Professional, you can disable tool tips in the Folder Options dialog box. The main difference is that Folder Options has been moved from the Start/Settings menu in Windows 95 and Windows 98 to the Control Panel in Windows 2000.

To disable tool tips from appearing in the Start menu and in folders:

1. Click Start, point to Settings, and then click Control Panel.

2. In the Control Panel, click Folder Options.

3. In the Folder Options dialog box, click the View tab.

4. At the bottom of the Advanced settings list, clear Show Pop-Up Description For Folder And Desktop Items.

5. Click OK.

About Your Account

Windows 2000 Professional may look a lot like Windows 95 and Windows 98 on the outside. Behind the mild-mannered disguise, however, lies the industrial-strength Windows NT security model. A large part of this security model is based on the concept of user accounts—the fact that a user with an Administrator account can grant different levels of access to other users who log on to the system and thereby limit the vulnerability of data on the computer. Windows 2000 has done a lot to keep this transparent for those who don't want to use it, but there are a few things you should know about the security model even if you never set up additional accounts on your computer.

This section provides a survival guide for most of what you'll need to know about Windows 2000 Professional security if you are the only one using your Windows 2000 Professional computer and it's a stand-alone PC (not linked to others) in a private location. If others will be using your computer, you'll learn about adding user accounts in Part 3.

Shutting Down, Logging Off, and Logging On

As in Windows 95, you can use the Shut Down command on the Start menu to shut down or restart Windows 2000 Professional. The Shut Down Windows dialog box (see Figure 4-11) also contains a Log Off command like the Log Off command on the Start menu of Windows 95. The main difference between the two operating system Log Off commands is this: when you log off Windows 2000 Professional, the computer doesn't shut down. Instead, it leaves the operating system running with nobody at the helm (but with an excellent autopilot on board).

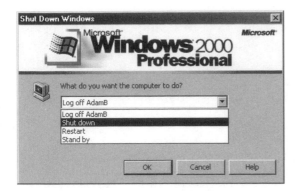

Figure 4-11

You can shut down, restart, or log off Windows 2000 in the Shut Down Windows dialog box.

By contrast, Windows 95 doesn't really require you to log on—after the first time you click Cancel, the Log On screen never appears again. Also, in Windows 95, there's no Log Off menu option in the Shut Down dialog box; it's on the Start menu. So, if you haven't actually logged on to Windows 95, clicking Log Off on the Start Menu just shuts down the computer. If you have logged on to Windows 95—which is likely only if you're attached to a network—then clicking the item labeled Log Off [*your logon name*] on the Start menu is the same as it is in Windows 2000 Professional.

After logging off in Windows 2000 Professional, you are presented with the Log On To Windows dialog box. The last person logged on is shown by default in the Name area, but you can change this to any valid user name and log on, as long as you know the password to enter.

If your computer is attached to a network, logging on to Windows 2000 Professional or Windows 95 automatically logs you on to the network if you have an account on the network with the same name and password as your local account.

Don't Remember Logging On?

You may be wondering how you can log off if you haven't logged on yet. If you've just finished running Setup and don't remember logging on, it's because Windows 2000 Professional makes it easy for you to get going right away.

During setup, you may recall running the Network Identification wizard, which prompted you with this question: "You can require all users to enter a user name and password to log on, or you can have Windows assume the same user will always log on to this computer. Which option do you prefer?" If you checked "Windows always assumes the following user has logged on to this computer:" (which is followed by your user name and a blank password), you aren't required to log on when you boot. If you log off, you'll need to log on with whatever password you entered, or without a password if you didn't enter one.

Changing Your Password

To change your password, and to do a half dozen other security tasks, you use the Ctrl+Alt+Del command (press the three keys Ctrl, Alt, and Del at the same time) to open the Windows Security dialog box. This key sequence is Microsoft's not-so-secret handshake to exiting and troubleshooting the operating system. It's been around since MS-DOS, although it does different things in different versions of the operating system.

To change your password:

1. Press Ctrl+Alt+Del to open the Windows Security dialog box.

2. Click the Change Password button.

3. Fill in the Change Password dialog box by typing your current password in the Old Password box—or leaving it blank if you don't have one yet—and then typing the new password you want in the New Password box. Finally, type your new password again in the Confirm New Password box.

Note

If you are going to be connecting to an existing network at your office, make sure your user name and password match the user name and password you normally use to log on to your network.

4. Click OK. You'll get a message telling you that your password has been changed.

The Windows Security Dialog Box

Take a look now at the Windows Security dialog box on your system. Notice that the first line tells you your logon name. This is good to know, because Windows 2000 Professional provides little indication anywhere else of your logon name—it's easy to forget once you start creating accounts.

Also, notice that besides Change Password, the Windows Security dialog box also contains several other buttons, including the following:

- Shut Down—shuts the computer down.

- Log Off—logs you off the computer and leaves it running.

- Lock Computer button—locks the computer and leaves it running.

- Task Manager—lets you end programs, switch programs, or run programs; also lets you monitor system performance.

You've learned about the shutdown and logoff operations already; here's a little more about the other two features.

The Lock Computer button provides a quick way to lock your PC when you want to leave some application open and running (but secure) while you're not there. For example, you might be working on a salary spreadsheet for your employees and need to step out for a minute; in this case, you don't need to log off—just press Ctrl+Alt+Del and click Lock Computer. To be let back in, just type your password in the Unlock Computer dialog box that appears.

Task Manager performs the same duties that Task Manager in Windows 95 does (letting you terminate wayward programs), but it has many more features. Besides providing a list of running applications, Task Manager has separate tabs that show you system performance and what processes the applications are running (don't worry if you don't know what a process is—you'll never have to use one directly). Task manager also has buttons to switch between programs and to run programs, although this is the least likely place you'd go to perform these operations.

You can click Cancel to exit the Task Manager at any time. If you leave it open without using it, it will close by itself.

Who's This Administrator Anyway?

You'll remember that during setup, you were asked for an administration password. Knowing this password enables you to log on as the Administrator and make system changes. In Windows 2000 Professional, each account has its own level of authority and many system changes can be done only by those with Administrator privileges. A user has Administrator privileges if the user is assigned to the Administrators group.

Your default account (the one with your name on it) belongs to the Administrators group, so you are the Administrator by default, or at least you have all the rights of an Administrator. You might have someone else doing this job, but if you're like most small business operators, this is just one more of the hats you wear. Fortunately, you can get by in Windows 2000 Professional with a minimum of Administrator duties, most of which are covered in Part 3.

If you want to log on as *the* Administrator (as opposed to someone who just has Administrator privileges), you must first log off and log back on with the name Administrator and type the password into the Password area. (You wrote down the password for the Administrator during setup, remember?)

Tip

The Administrator account gives anyone who can access it complete control over settings and other accounts on your computer. So make sure you keep the password in a safe, hidden location. Also, the Administrator password can be changed only by the Administrator. If you forget or lose it, you will need to reinstall Windows 2000 Professional to create a new Administrator password. When you reinstall, you risk losing data and you definitely lose time.

Moving On

Now that you've had a chance to get acquainted with the user interface a little and know the basics of logging off and on, you should feel more at home as you continue to set up your computer with printers, peripherals, connections to the Internet and, perhaps, connections to other computers. If you feel like learning more about user accounts and security right now, you can go ahead and read the chapters in Part 3 now—you can always come back to this section later to install peripherals. If you'd rather stay with the tour bus, the next stop is installing your printer.

Chapter 5

Step Three: Connect Your Printer

Connecting a printer can be almost automatic if you have a plug and play–compatible printer supported by Microsoft Windows 2000 Professional, which supports most current popular brands. Those who have installed printers in Microsoft Windows 95 or Microsoft Windows 98 will find that printer installation in Windows 2000 Professional is very much the same, with a few improvements. So, if you're already comfortable with the process, you might just want to read a couple of sections before you jump in and try it yourself: "Connecting Printers in a Nutshell" to get a bird's eye view of the process and "What's Different in Windows 2000?" to see how Windows 2000 Professional has changed from Windows 95/98.

If you'd like to follow specific steps, this chapter walks you through the entire process and covers the two wizards that Windows 2000 Professional provides for printer installation: the Add Printer Wizard and the Found New Hardware Wizard.

For those who are connected to a network, this chapter also includes a section on connecting to a shared network printer.

> ### Note
> _____
>
> If you need to install a driver instead of using one that Microsoft supplies with Windows 2000 Professional, you must be logged on with Administrator privileges to add the printer to your computer. This is because only members of the Administrator group are allowed to accept *trusted code*, the digital signature that authenticates drivers to Windows 2000 Professional. As you'll recall from the previous chapter, your default logon is a member of the Administrators group.

Connecting Printers in a Nutshell

The short and sweet version of connecting a printer goes something like this:

1. Double-check the hardware and connections.

    Make sure the printer is connected and powered on. If you want to connect to a printer on the network, verify that you've got a working network connection to the computer that hosts the printer and also that printer sharing is enabled on that computer. Also make sure there's paper in the printer.

2. Determine whether you should run the manufacturer's setup.

    Many printer manufacturers provide their own setup software. Read "Should I Run the Printer Manufacturer's Setup?" on page 88 if you need help with this.

3. Run the Add Printer Wizard to see if your printer is plug and play.

    If there's no manufacturer setup (or you want to bypass it because it predates Windows 2000), run the Add Printer Wizard from the Control Panel and let Windows 2000 Professional try to auto-detect the printer and provide its own driver. If it detects a printer, it runs the Found New Hardware Wizard and leads you through the installation process.

4. If the printer is a plug and play model, follow the steps of the Found New Hardware Wizard.

    The Found New Hardware Wizard attempts to locate a built-in driver for the printer it finds. You can supply your own driver on a diskette or CD at this point and tell the wizard where to find it. If you get to this step and don't have a Windows 2000

Professional driver for your printer, you'll need to contact the printer manufacturer and get one. You can often find updated drivers for your printer on the printer manufacturer's Web site.

5. If the printer isn't a plug and play model, the Add Printer Wizard continues as if you had instructed it not to detect the printer.

    At this point you are given the chance to select the printer from a list and then select a built-in driver if Windows 2000 Professional includes one. If the printer is in the list, Windows has a built-in driver that you can use. If the printer isn't in the list, you can enter a name for the printer and you'll need to provide your own driver.

6. Print a test page.

    If you've just finished running the Add Printer Wizard on a local printer, you are prompted whether to print a test page. If you've just connected to a network printer, or you've just run the Found New Hardware Wizard without using the Add Printer Wizard (for example, by rebooting), you'll need to print the test page yourself (*see "Printing a Test Page" on page 107*).

What's Different in Windows 2000?

The main difference between installing printers on Windows 95 and on Windows 2000 Professional is that the latter can often detect printers added to it. Because of this, you can tell Windows 2000 Professional to try to automatically detect your printer in the Add Printer Wizard and, if Windows finds it, the Found New Hardware Wizard runs to finish setting up your printer.

Note

With some plug and play printers, you might have to reboot before the Add Printer Wizard can detect the printer. You might also have to reboot for the printer to be recognized if the Found New Hardware Wizard starts but you cancel it for any reason.

Another difference is that Windows 2000 Professional has many more printer drivers built in than Windows 95 or Windows 98. Chances are you'll have a built-in driver for your existing printer and not have to search for updated drivers on a printer Web site somewhere.

Windows 2000 Professional is also more Web-aware when it comes to printers. It can connect to intranet and Internet printers and it can use the Windows Update site as an installation point when Microsoft adds more supported drivers to the list.

Questions to Consider First

Before you jump in and run the Add Printer Wizard to set up your printer, see if you can answer these two questions. If you answer yes to the first question, you won't have to read the rest of this chapter. If you answer yes to the second question, you'll need to make sure you have a printer driver on hand when you run the Add Printer Wizard.

Should I Run the Printer Manufacturer's Setup?

You need to first determine if your printer has setup software made to run in Windows 2000 Professional. This normally applies only to printers that have come to market since Windows 2000 Professional shipped, but some printer manufacturers might provide updated Windows 2000 Professional installation software for their older printers.

Check whether a CD came with the printer and read the documentation to see if it applies specifically to Windows 2000. If you do have setup software designed for Windows 2000, it's best to use that software, since it often installs other utilities that you might want. In fact, some manufacturers specifically require you to run their installation software and won't install if you try to go through the Add Printer Wizard.

On the other hand, if your printer is supported by Windows 2000 Professional (that is, there is a built-in driver) and you want a quick way to install it without installing the manufacturer's utilities, you can follow the steps in this chapter to install your printer. This is the path to follow if, for example, you bought your printer before Windows 2000 was released, so the installation software doesn't support Windows 2000, but the printer is listed in the hardware compatibility list (HCL), and there is a built-in driver for it.

Do I Need to Supply a Driver?

The next step is to see whether Windows 2000 Professional has a built-in driver for your printer. The easiest way is to run the Add Printer Wizard and see whether it finds a driver when it detects the printer. For the ultimate, definitive answer to this question, though, you can open the hardware compatibility list (HCL) in the Support folder on the Windows 2000 Professional CD-ROM, which lists every printer that Windows 2000 Professional provides a driver for. Or you can find the latest list of drivers on the Web at *www.microsoft.com/hwtest/hcl*, which lists drivers for all released versions of Microsoft operating systems.

Note

It's not necessarily true that the driver provided by Windows 2000 Professional is preferable to one you get from the manufacturer, especially if the manufacturer supplies a more recent version of the driver; if there's a problem with the driver Microsoft provides, be sure to reinstall the printer using your manufacturer's driver.

If Windows 2000 Professional detects the device and finds a driver, you can test the printer and that might be all you need. If it doesn't detect the printer, you still might be in luck if you can locate the printer model in the list of printers provided by the Add Printer Wizard.

If all else fails (that is, if the printer isn't detected and it's not in a list provided by the Add Printer Wizard), you can try to get an updated Windows 2000 Professional driver from your printer manufacturer (drivers are usually available on the manufacturer's Web site) and then run the Add Printer Wizard again using the manufacturer's disk or files you've downloaded containing the printer installation files.

Adding a Printer

This section walks you through the various paths for adding a printer to Windows 2000 Professional. The wizards take you through this process logically and this section describes the various printer installation scenarios so you can follow the one that applies to your printer.

Things to Check First

You'd be surprised at how many installation problems come down to the simplest errors. It's best to avoid the easy ones to begin with. Before running the Add Printer Wizard you should run through this quick checklist:

*   Is the printer plugged in and turned on?

- Is the printer connected to a cable that is connected to the computer?

- Is there paper in the printer feed tray?

- Do you have any installation CDs or diskettes that came with the printer?

If you are connecting to a printer on a network, check the items on this list too:

- Is the network connection working between your computer and the computer whose printer you want to share? See if you can find the network computer listed in My Network Places.

- Is the network printer shared? Look in My Network Places under the computer name—if the printer is shared, it will appear here.

Running the Add Printer Wizard

Here's where just about everyone starts adding a printer. With the Add Printer Wizard, you can test whether your printer is plug and play and try auto-detecting it.

Note

There are at least two cases when plug and play printers will be detected without your having to use the Add Printer Wizard. When you boot the computer after connecting a printer, Windows 2000 detects the printer and, when you log in again, opens the Found New Hardware Wizard. Also, if your printer connects through a universal serial bus (USB) port, just plugging it in causes Windows to detect the printer and run the Found New Hardware Wizard. In either case, you can go directly to "Running the Found New Hardware Wizard," on page 97.

To run the Add Printer Wizard:

1. Click the Start menu, point to Settings, and then click Printers.
2. In the Printers folder, click Add Printer.
   The Add Printer Wizard opens.

3. Click Next.

    The next page of the wizard lets you determine whether to install a local printer (manually or by letting the wizard try to detect your printer) or install a network printer.

4. Click either Local Printer (with or without selecting Automatically Detect My Printer) or Network Printer, and then click Next.

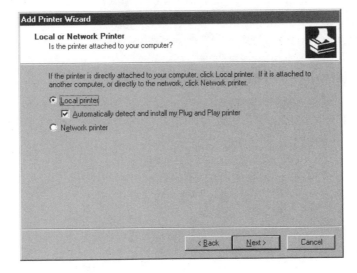

- Local Printer—If you are connecting a printer directly to your computer, choose this option button.

- Automatically Detect My Printer—If you know or suspect the printer is a plug and play model, select this check box. Except when you connect to a network printer, you should try selecting this option at least the first time to see if the printer is detected. If you've just run this wizard and Windows 2000 couldn't detect the printer, you can leave this check box cleared.

- Network Printer—If you are connecting to a printer on a network, select this option.

What happens next depends on your selection at the previous step. If you selected Local Printer and selected Automatically Detect My Printer and the wizard found your printer, the Found New Hardware Wizard appears. In this case, jump to "Running the Found New Hardware Wizard," on page 97, and continue the installation.

If you selected Local Printer and you didn't select Automatically Detect My Printer in the previous step, or if the printer wasn't detected, the next page of the wizard asks you to select a port to which your printer is connected. Continue with the next step in this procedure.

Tip

Not all plug and play printers can be detected without a reboot. If you're sure your printer is plug and play but it isn't detected at this point, you can reboot. It might be faster, however, to simply continue with the Add Printer Wizard and select the printer from the list of printers.

Finally, if you've chosen to install a printer that is on the network, jump directly to step 5 in "Adding a Network Printer," on page 102.

1. Select the port you connected your printer to (probably LPT1 if the computer has only one parallel port) and click Next.

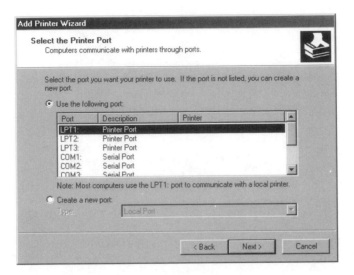

2. Select the printer manufacturer from the Manufacturers list on the left, select the printer model under Printers on the right, and then click Next

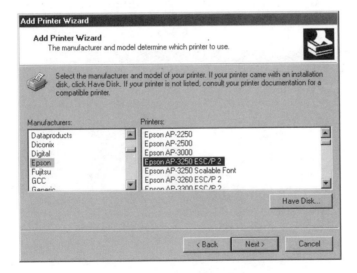

3. Either leave the default name or enter a name of your own for the printer.

4. If you have another printer you'd rather use most of the time, select No under Do You Want Your Windows-Based Programs To Use This Printer As The Default Printer? and click Next.

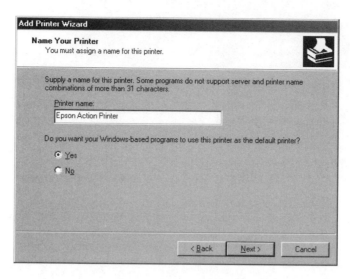

Now you can continue with the Add Printer Wizard by selecting options on the Printer Sharing page.

1. If you want to let others connect to this printer on a network, select Share As and type a name for the printer, and then click Next.

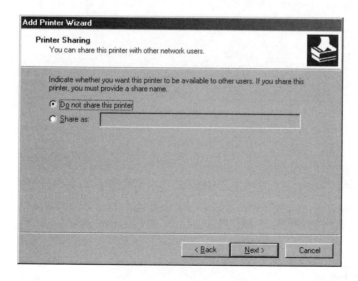

2. If you want to print a test page to check out your installation, click Next. Printing a test page is a good idea.

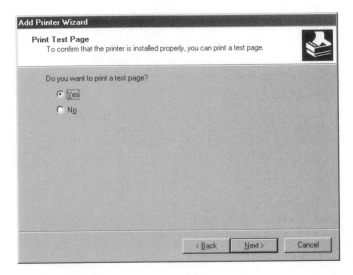

Finally, a summary page shows the properties you've assigned for your printer.

3. If you spot something on this list that doesn't look right, click Back and go back and change it on the appropriate page of the wizard. Otherwise, click Finish to exit the wizard.

Windows copies the files it needs to install the printer and an hourglass appears while the driver is being installed.

If you chose to print a test page, a message appears telling you that a test page is being sent to your printer.

4. Click OK if the page looks fine.

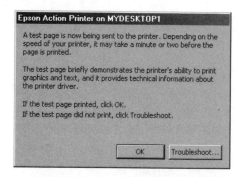

If there's a problem with printing the test page, you can try clicking the Troubleshoot button to get to the Print Trouble-shooter in Help. Select the problem (My local printer won't print, for example) and continue to answer questions and click Next. *See "Troubleshooting your Printer," on page 108, for more help.*

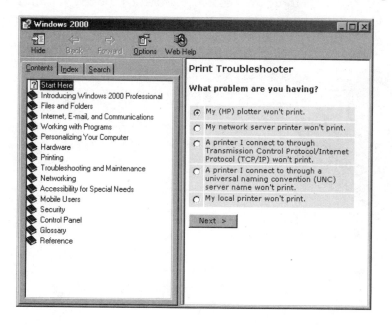

Running the Found New Hardware Wizard

Windows 2000 Professional runs the Found New Hardware Wizard when

- it starts and finds new hardware.

- it's directed to detect hardware with the Add Printer Wizard or the Add/Remove Hardware Wizard. The Add Printer Wizard looks for hardware when you check both Local Printer and Automatically Detect My Printer on the second page.

- a USB printer is plugged in while you are logged on to Windows 2000 Professional (referred to as *hot plugging*).

The first page of the Found New Hardware Wizard welcomes you and tells you to click Next. The second page shows you the device that was found (your printer, hopefully) and lets you select whether you want the wizard to search for a suitable driver or choose one yourself.

Here's the sequence of steps you'll follow through the Found New Hardware Wizard.

1. On the second page of the wizard, leave the default option selected (Search For A Suitable Driver For My Device). If you've been through this once already and no driver was found, select the second option (Display A List Of The Known Drivers…).

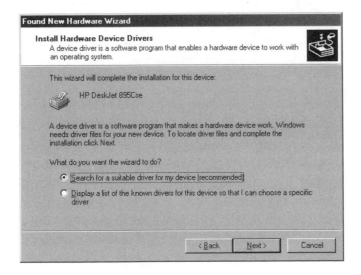

2. Click Next to continue.

What happens next depends on your selection in step 1. If you chose Search For A Suitable Driver, this page appears.

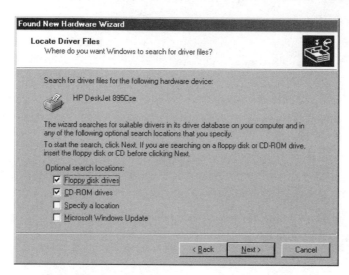

Choose the appropriate search locations, as detailed below, and click Next.

• If you have an installation CD or diskette for the printer, put it in the appropriate drive and make sure to select Floppy Disk Drives or CD-ROM Drives (or both).

• If the driver is in another location (such as on a network drive or in a folder), select Specify A Location. Click Next and go to step 4.

• If you have an Internet connection and you want to see if the driver is on the Microsoft Windows Update Web site, select Microsoft Windows Update.

If you chose to display a list of known drivers in step 2, the next screen enables you to select one of these printers or, if you have a driver from the manufacturer, select Have Disk. You can select Have Disk even if the driver isn't on a disk but you've downloaded it to your hard disk. You'll be able to browse to the folder that contains the driver. Follow the wizard to install the driver. The rest of this procedure doesn't apply to you.

3. Assuming you chose to let the Found New Hardware Wizard search for your driver files, this page shows the driver that the

wizard has found for the printer. Drivers are always associated with a .INF file that tells the installation what files are needed and where they are.

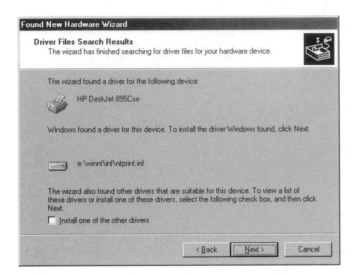

Tip

If other possible drivers are found, you can select Install One Of The Other Drivers, and click Next to get a list of all drivers found—including the recommended one—just to make sure that's the one you want. If you're satisfied with the driver that the wizard found, just click Next.

4.   Click Next to continue.

   The final page of the Found New Hardware Wizard just informs you that the hardware has been installed.

5.   Click Finish to exit the wizard, which either returns you to the Add Printer Wizard or just ends. If it just ends, you should manually print a test page to verify that everything is working as you expect. See "Printing a Test Page," on page 107, for the steps to do this.

   If this wizard was started because you were running the Add Printer Wizard, the following page appears to enable you to print a test page.

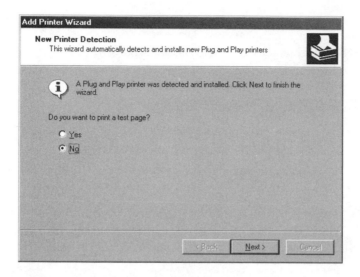

6. Choose Yes.

Finally, the wizard displays a summary of how your printer has been installed.

7. Click Finish to exit the wizard.

If you chose to print a test page, a message appears telling you that a test page is being sent to your printer. If everything looks fine, click OK.

You might notice here that when Windows 2000 detects the printer for you, the printer isn't shared on a network and isn't selected as the default printer for this computer. When you connect a printer manually without auto-detecting it (that is, when you walk through all the Add Printer Wizard steps) you're given the options to share your printer and set it as the default printer. You can still set the printer's sharing properties manually by right-clicking the printer's icon in the Printers folder and choosing Sharing on the shortcut menu. Chapter 16 has more information on sharing printers. You can set the printer as the default printer by clicking Set As Default Printer in the printer's shortcut menu or by selecting the Printer and clicking Set As Default Printer on the File menu in the Printers folder.

If there's a problem with printing the test page, you can click the Troubleshoot button to get to the Print Troubleshooter in Help. Select the problem (My local printer won't print, for example) and continue to answer questions and click Next to get help. See "Troubleshooting Your Printer," on page 108, for more help.

Connecting to a Network Printer

Many small businesses are adding networking to their list of business tools to take advantage of benefits such as sharing printers. Part 4 in this book explains how to connect to an existing network and how to build your own small workgroup network. If you've already established a network for your office and have printers on that network, this section explains how to install those printers on a Windows 2000 Professional computer. It also shows how to install multiple printer drivers on a Windows 2000 Professional computer connected to a printer so that any computer on the network can automatically connect and download the appropriate driver.

Note

Connecting to networks and sharing printers aren't covered until Part 4. You need to be connected to a network before you add a network printer. If you aren't connected yet, read Chapter 16 and connect to your network before continuing here. If you've already connected to a network, you should read that section, or have some knowledge about network connections, before continuing here.

Adding a Network Printer

If you're adding a printer located on a network, you can connect to that printer either by finding the printer on the network or by running the Add Printer Wizard. The first method is quicker, while the second takes you through all the steps.

- Find the printer on the network by navigating from My Network Places to the computer connected to the printer; and then double-click the printer icon.

  If the computer connected to the printer is a Windows 2000 computer, the Printer dialog box opens. From the File menu, choose Connect. The printer connects and Windows installs the proper driver. Otherwise, if the computer connected to the printer isn't Windows 2000 or doesn't have your printer driver, a message box appears asking if you want to install the printer. If you click Yes, the Add Printer Wizard then appears and enables you to select from the list of available printer manufacturers and printers or to provide your own driver. At this point you can jump straight to step 7 in the procedure below to finish.

- Run the Add Printer Wizard to connect to a network printer:

1. On the Start menu, point to Settings, and then click Printers.

2. In the Printers folder, click Add Printer. The Add Printer Wizard appears.

3. Click Next.

4. Select Network Printer and click Next.

   The next wizard page gives you two option buttons and three ways to identify the network printer.

Tip

If you're connected to a domain network with a Windows 2000 Server implementing Active Directory, you're also given a choice of searching for the printer in the Active Directory. In this case, see your network administrator for help with questions about using Active Directory, or see the Windows 2000 Professional Help.

Here are the three ways you can identify your network printer on a workgroup network:

- If you don't remember the name of your printer, you can make the computer look it up. Select Type The Printer Name but leave the Name area blank; then click Next and continue with step 5 below.

- If you happen to know the Universal Naming Convention (UNC) name of the printer, select Type The Printer Name. Then type a location for your printer in the format *computer_name*\ *share_name*; for example, type *MYDESKTOP1*\ *HP895Cse* if you shared a printer with the name HP895Cse on a network computer named MYDESKTOP1. Then click Next and go to step 6.

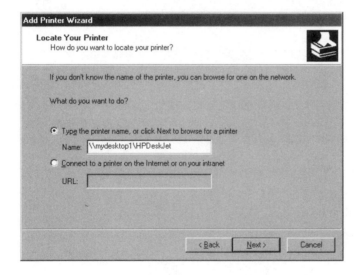

- If you have an intranet set up on your network or know of a printer on the Internet you can connect to, enter the URL in the format *www.addressofmycorporateintranet.com/printername* and continue with step 7.

5. If you didn't enter a printer name and clicked Next, the Browse For Printer page appears. After a few minutes, it shows you the name of the workgroup or domain that it found on the network. Click the workgroup to display a list of computers on the network, find the computer with the printer, and then click the printer.

Internet and Intranet Printing

Implementing an intranet requires that one of the computers on the network run a Web server. You can install a Web server on any Windows 2000 Professional computer by adding the Microsoft Internet Information Services (IIS) component using Add/Remove Programs in Control Panel. When you run the Web server and share the printer, the printer becomes available on the intranet—as simple as that. This book doesn't cover intranets or Web server components, but if you wish to set up an intranet, the documentation for IIS is excellent.

Its UNC name will appear in the Printer area at the top of the panel. Click Next to install this printer and continue with the next step.

6. If the printer on the network is on a computer that doesn't have the Windows 2000 Professional printer drivers (for example, if it's connected to a Windows 95 or Windows 98 computer), a message box appears asking if you want to install the drivers on your local computer. Click OK and continue with step 7. If you don't see this message, your printer drivers were found on the computer attached to the printer and will be used—you can skip to step 8.

7. Select the name of your printer in the Manufacturers list and the specific printer in the Printers list and click OK.

    If the printer doesn't appear here, you'll need to provide your own Windows 2000 Professional drivers (available from the manufacturer); click Have Disk and follow the instructions to finish installing your printer.

    Congratulations, you're almost done!

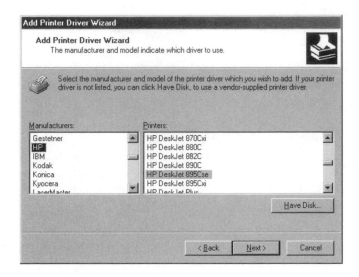

8. Click Finish on this page after reviewing the information it provides.

Tip

If this page shows that the printer is now the default printer and you don't want it to be, go to your Printers folder, right-click a different printer icon and select Set As Default Printer from the shortcut menu. This removes the default printer check mark from the network printer you've installed.

9. Finally, you should print a test page to verify that your printer connection is really working. This is described on page 107.

Adding Network Printer Drivers

Although many of the network and network printing capabilities of Windows 2000 were created with network administrators in mind, this section covers adding network printers because it can be implemented easily on a simple, peer-to-peer network, which is appropriate for many small businesses. If you have more than a few computers on a network using shared printers, however, you might want to leave this feature to your network administrator.

When a printer is shared on the network, available for use by all the other computers on the network, the computer is said to be a *print server* to other computers on the network. One big advantage of Windows 2000 Professional is that the Windows 2000 printer server has the added capability of storing and providing the correct printer drivers for different Windows platforms on the network.

For example, suppose you have an HP LaserJet printer connected to your new Windows 2000 Professional computer and you want to share it with other computers in your office, two that are running Windows 95 and one that is running Microsoft Windows NT 3.1. Windows 2000 Professional enables you to install the Windows 95 and Windows NT 3.1 drivers for the LaserJet directly onto the print server, so that when someone connects to that computer's shared printer from a Windows 95 or Windows NT 3.1 computer, the correct printer driver is downloaded and installed.

This feature makes life much easier for the administrators of large corporate networks, in which one printer might serve twenty or more computers that use a variety of operating systems. While it's probably not as important for a small business office, you might find it useful to enable this feature because once you've installed the drivers on the print server, you never have to worry about which computers will or won't need to access the printer. If you don't have the appropriate drivers, it's probably best to install the printer as a network printer on each of the computers in your office that will use the shared printer.

Note

If your printer's manufacturer doesn't supply an .INF file and the printer can be installed only through the manufacturer's setup program, this procedure won't work.

To add additional drivers for other platforms to a Windows 2000 network printer:

1. In the Printers folder, right-click the icon for the printer and click Properties.

2. Click the Sharing tab and click Additional Drivers.

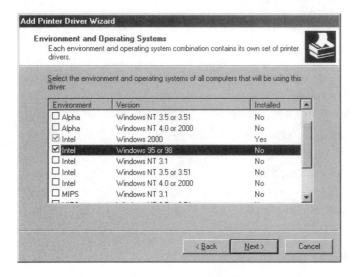

3. Select the printers you want to add and click OK.

4. You'll be prompted to insert the Windows 2000 Server disk. The computer is looking for the .INF file that contains the drivers you've specified. Just click OK. The next dialog box prompts you to enter the location of the drivers. You'll need to supply the drivers on a CD, floppy disk, or network location; enter that path at this time and click OK. Just remember to use the same driver files you'd use if you were installing the drivers on the non–Windows 2000 computer.

5. Continue following any prompts that appear to finish installing the driver.

Printing a Test Page

One difference between adding a printer using plug and play and stepping through all the steps of the Add Printer Wizard is that, for local printers anyway, the Add Printer Wizard has a much nicer finish and ends by giving you an option to test your printer.

The Found New Hardware Wizard is a more generic wizard and it doesn't try to test the hardware it installs. When the Add Printer Wizard launches the Found New Hardware Wizard, it picks up again after that wizard exits and gives you the chance to print a test page. However, if you install a printer by rebooting or hot plugging a USB device, you actually need to "plug and test" before you get to play. This is also true if you've just connected to a network printer—you need to manually test the printer connection first.

To print a test page:

1. On the Start menu, point to Settings, and then click Printers.

2. In the Printers folder, right-click the name of your new printer and choose Properties from the shortcut menu.

3. In the Properties dialog box for your printer, click Print Test Page at the lower right corner. A message appears telling you that a test page is being sent to your printer. If everything looks fine, click OK. If everything doesn't work correctly, try clicking the Troubleshoot button to get to the Print Troubleshooter in Help. See "Troubleshooting your Printer," next, for more help.

Troubleshooting Your Printer

The Windows 2000 Professional Help Troubleshooter provides a good place to start when you want to fix printer connection problems. Just open Help and look for troubleshooters in the index. Here are more troubleshooting tips.

General Troubleshooting Guidelines

The first thing to do when troubleshooting just about anything is to divide the problem in half. When you're installing a printer, this means determining if the problem is the printer or the computer. This works best in cases where you're getting no print output from the computer and you're getting no feedback, such as an "out of paper" error.

First, try to determine if the printer and cable are functioning. For example, install the printer on another computer in your office. If you've been using it with another computer, make sure you use the same printer cable when connecting it to the Windows 2000 Professional computer. If the printer works fine on another computer, see if the Windows 2000 Professional computer works with another printer connected to the same port.

Another way to break the problem in half is to see if you can print to a file. This tells you if the application is printing. To print to a file, select Properties for your printer, and on the Ports tab, select FILE:. Then open Notepad, type a sentence and print it. When the dialog box comes up asking for the file to print to, type any name (*PFILE*, for example).

Although you won't be able to tell if the document is formatted correctly, you can tell if the job completes and creates a file of some size. Printer files are typically quite large. If printing to a file works, see if you can then make a directory listing from a command prompt to your printer (for example *DIR > LPT1*). Finally, see if you can copy the printed file to your printer (for example *COPY /B PFILE > LPT1*).

Printing Garbage Characters

When your printer is outputting something that's unintelligible, you might have the wrong driver attached to your printer. Go to the Printers folder, delete the printer object you've just created, and run Add Printer again, choosing a different driver. If you let Windows 2000 Professional choose a Windows driver and you have a manufacturer's driver, or vice versa, try using the other driver. You can also specify that you want to select from a list of drivers when you run the Add Printer Wizard—so try using another driver from this list if nothing else is working. Often, just reinstalling the original driver works, especially if you took a wrong turn in one of the wizards.

When a Plug and Play Printer Is Not Recognized

Some printers require that you reboot with the printer connected in order for it to be detected. If you're sure the printer is plug and play but it isn't recognized in the Add Printer Wizard when you choose to automatically detect the printer, try rebooting. If it's detected when Windows starts, the Found New Hardware Wizard will appear when you log on so that you can finish installing.

Network Printing Problems

If you don't have enough disk space and memory on the computer that is connected to the printer, you might encounter performance problems when you print to the printer on a network. Printing large documents creates extremely large files on the print server and this can be compounded by the number of computers accessing the printer. If you're experiencing print problems, you might consider dedicating as the printer server a single computer that isn't used on a full-time basis by any employee.

Now that you've connected your printer to your Windows 2000 Professional computer, you might want to add another external device such as a scanner, or perhaps some internal card that you didn't add before running Setup. The next chapter, "Step Four: Hook Up Your Other Hardware," covers the details for adding all types of hardware to your Windows 2000 Professional computer.

Chapter 6

Step Four: Hook Up Your Other Hardware

In the previous chapter you connected your printer, so you've already been through one example of hooking up hardware. Now is a good time to add the other hardware that you didn't have connected before running Setup. This includes external devices such as scanners, digital cameras, and external hard drives, and internal devices such as add-in cards.

About Plug and Play

In the simplest terms, plug and play enables you to quickly and easily install hardware devices—ideally, you just plug in the device and it works. More technically, plug and play is both a hardware specification and a service running on Microsoft Windows 2000 Professional called the Plug and Play

Manager (you won't actually see this label anywhere). The specification helps hardware vendors build devices that the operating system can detect and install.

The Plug and Play Manager in Windows 2000 Professional does more than meets the eye. While it can detect and install a hardware device, it also manages the resources used by each device, such as memory and interrupts. It dynamically allocates resources as new devices are added or removed. In addition, it manages power states for devices that can be placed in low-power modes.

Plug and play support has two levels: complete plug and play support and plug and play driver support. If a device has complete plug and play support, the device is detected when you plug it in and when the device has a plug and play driver. If a device isn't plug and play compatible, it won't be detected automatically; however, it can still have plug and play driver support provided by either Microsoft or the manufacturer of the device. A plug and play driver lets the device be managed by the plug and play service so that its resources can be dynamically assigned along with all other devices.

If you have a non–plug and play device without a plug and play driver, you'll need to configure your device manually. Unless you have the knowledge to do this and the time to spend figuring it out, it's often worth buying a newer device that's fully plug and play compatible. Using devices in the hardware compatibility list (HCL) is the safest and easiest way to go.

Adding a Hardware Device

Most new devices are plug and play compatible. If you're installing a device that isn't plug and play compatible, or if you're not sure whether it is, plug in the device and see if Windows 2000 Professional recognizes and installs it. If the device you're adding is listed in the hardware compatibility list, it probably will work.

Tip

Microsoft lists drivers for all released versions of Microsoft operating systems on its Web site at *www.microsoft.com/hwtest/hcl*.

Before you add a new device, you'll need to determine whether to power down the computer and in what order to power things back up. Your device's documentation is the best place for this information. In general, however, you can plug in most USB and IEEE 1394 (also known as Fire-Wire) devices without turning off the computer. You can also plug in most PC Cards in portable computers. Read "Installing a Device While Powered Up," on page 114, for more information. Most other external devices and, of course, all internal cards require that you shut down Windows and turn off power to the computer first. Read "Powering Down to Install a Device," on page 115, for specific steps on adding these devices.

If the device you want to add isn't plug and play compatible, or if it doesn't seem to be working after you've installed it, you'll need to trouble-shoot. Read "It's Plugged In But It's Not Playing," on page 116, for an overview and then see "Running the Add/Remove Hardware Wizard," on page 116, for details about installing or troubleshooting a device.

The Installation Process

Windows 2000 Professional needs information about any device that you add. It needs to know what device has been added and what port it's connected to, if any. The system needs to find the appropriate driver for the device—the software that allows the device to communicate with the operating system. Finally, it needs to configure the driver to make sure the resources used by the device don't conflict with resources used by other devices. Resources are finite computer elements such as memory addresses that are linked to each device.

In the best case, Windows 2000 detects the new device, finds a built-in driver, and configures the driver. You won't need to know anything about any of this and you won't even have to reboot.

In other cases, Windows 2000 detects your hardware but needs some help in selecting a driver. Or it might not detect the hardware, in which case you'll have to select the hardware from a list and then let it suggest a driver or use one provided by the manufacturer.

In the worst case, your hardware won't be detected, you'll need to provide the manufacturer's driver, and the driver you end up installing will require manual configuration. (Fortunately, this worst-case scenario is by far the exception rather than the rule and it's very unlikely if you have newer hardware.)

Installing a Device While Powered Up

For most USB, IEEE 1394, and PC Card devices, you can just connect the device to the computer or plug in the PC Card, and that's about all there is to it. Here's what you do in this case, and what to do if the device doesn't seem to work as it's supposed to.

To install a plug and play device while the computer is powered up:

1. If the device doesn't get its power from the computer, make sure it's connected to power and turned on.

2. Log on to the computer.

    It's best to be logged on with Administrator privileges in case you need to troubleshoot the installation. If you haven't set up the computer to require a logon, just start the computer—you'll have Administrator privileges automatically.

3. Plug one end of the cable into the device and the other end into the computer, or plug the PC Card into the card slot on the portable.

4. Watch the computer display to see if a message appears showing that the device has been detected.

    Figure 6-1 shows the message that appears after you simply connect a Hewlett-Packard USB scanner to a computer. If you see the message and nothing else appears, test the device. If the device works, you're done.

Figure 6-1

Windows 2000 displays a message when you connect a new USB device.

If the Found New Hardware Wizard appears, the device was detected, but you'll need to select which driver to use; follow the wizard steps to select or install a driver and then test the device. If it works, you're done.

If no message appears, or if the device doesn't work when you test it, read "It's Plugged In But It's Not Playing," on page 116.

Tip

Plug and play works quickly and it's easy to miss the message that the device was detected. Also, when it's successful, it doesn't really give you any indication that the device has installed correctly. Before troubleshooting a device, test to see whether it works. You might be surprised!

Powering Down to Install a Device

Many device manufacturers require that you turn off the computer before you connect a cable to their external hardware because this avoids unnecessary electrical problems. The computer also must be powered down before you can install an internal card. Here are the steps for installing a device in this case and what to do if the installation doesn't go exactly as you expected.

To install a plug and play device while the computer is powered down:

1. Shut down Windows and turn off the computer.

2. If you're installing a card, open the computer case and plug the card into an available slot. Or, if you're connecting an external device, connect the device to the bus (make sure the device is turned off when you do this).

3. Power up the computer and the device in the order specified by the device's documentation.

4. If you've set up Windows 2000 Professional to require a logon, log on as someone with administrator privileges (you'll need these privileges to troubleshoot the installation). If you aren't required to log on, you have administrator privileges by default.

5. Watch for the Found New Hardware Wizard when Windows starts. If you don't see it, the device is probably installed.

6. Test the device. If it works, you're done.

    If the Found New Hardware Wizard does appear, follow the wizard steps to select a driver or install the driver that comes with the device. If the device works when you test it, you're done.

It's Plugged In But It's Not Playing

While plug and play devices should install easily, they sometimes don't. This can happen for a number of reasons. The device might require resources that the system can't provide. Or maybe the card needs a nudge (figuratively speaking) to be detected. Or maybe the card just isn't plug and play. In any case, you can find out what's wrong or add a non–plug and play device by running the Add/Remove Hardware Wizard.

The Add/Remove Hardware Wizard handles the following possible scenarios:

- If your device is plug and play compatible but wasn't detected, running this wizard will cause the system to try to find your hardware and select a matching driver.

- If your device isn't plug and play compatible, you'll use this wizard to install the device and driver.

- If the device was detected but has some other problem, this wizard will direct you to a Help Troubleshooter to help resolve the problem. The wizard also will let you choose another driver for the detected device.

See "Running the Add/Remove Hardware Wizard," on page 116, for the steps to get the system to look for a plug and play device or to install a non–plug and play device. See "Testing and Troubleshooting Hardware Installation," on page 122, for information about using the Add/Remove Hardware Wizard to troubleshoot your device.

Running the Add/Remove Hardware Wizard

The Add/Remove Hardware Wizard enables you to force detection of a plug and play device, to check the status of installed devices and add a non–plug and play device, or to see whether the device has already been detected by the system but has a problem. In the first two cases, you're installing a device; in the third, you're troubleshooting a device you've installed—this wizard is multipurpose.

The wizard also allows you to uninstall and unplug or eject devices. To learn about that, see "Removing and Unplugging Devices," on page 121.

Note

You must be logged on as a member of the Administrators group to access the Add/Remove Hardware Wizard in the Control Panel.

Adding and Checking Installed Devices

To add or check an added device, you should run the Add/Remove Hardware Wizard.

To check a plug and play device or to install a non–plug and play device:

1. Click Start, point to Settings, click Control Panel, and then double-click Add/Remove Hardware. The Add/Remove Hardware Wizard welcome screen appears.

2. Click Next.

3. Select Add/Troubleshoot A Device, and then click Next.

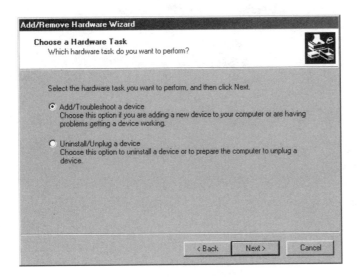

The wizard now attempts to detect any new hardware in the system. If it finds previously undetected plug and play hardware, the wizard installs it. If the Found New Hardware Wizard appears, follow the steps in this wizard to finish installing the device. After the Found New Hardware Wizard finishes, return to the Add/Remove Hardware Wizard and click Cancel.

If no new hardware is found, the next screen provides you with the option of either troubleshooting a hardware device that the system already recognizes or installing a new device.

4. If you know your device is not plug and play compatible, select Add A New Device and click Next. If you're not sure whether your device is plug and play compatible, but you've plugged the device in and it doesn't work, look for your device in the Devices list. If you don't see it there, it isn't plug and play; select Add A New Device and click Next.

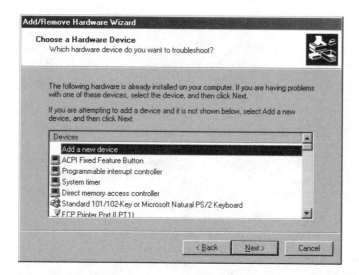

Regardless of whether it's plug and play compatible or not, if you see the device in the Devices list but it has a yellow exclamation mark icon, it isn't working; select the device, click Next, and continue to step 4 in "Troubleshooting Your Device," on page 122.

5. You can now let the wizard detect new non–plug and play hardware. To do so, select Yes, Search For New Hardware and then click Next. The wizard will take a few minutes to search for new hardware in your computer.

If you'd rather select from a list of known, supported hardware, or you have a .INF file and driver files for the device, select No, I Want To Select The Hardware From A List.

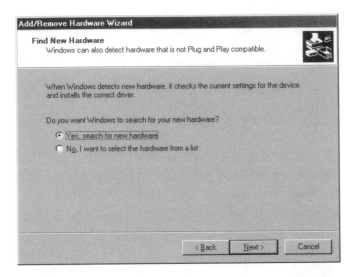

6. If the wizard finds your device, follow the steps of the wizard to finish installing your device. If the device wasn't found, this message appears: Windows Did Not Find Any New Devices On Your Computer. Click Next.

7. Select the manufacturer of the device in the left column and the specific model of the device in the right column, and then click Next. If your device isn't in the list and you have a .INF file and driver available, click Have Disk and enter the location of the files.

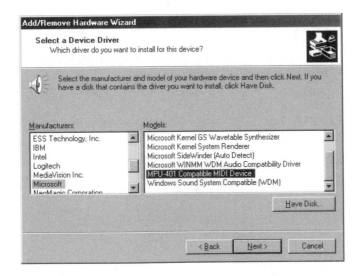

8. Click Next on the next page, which tells you that the wizard is about to install the drivers for the device you selected in the previous step.

   The wizard screen that appears now depends on what device you chose in the previous step. In many cases a screen similar to the following appears informing you that the device has been installed.

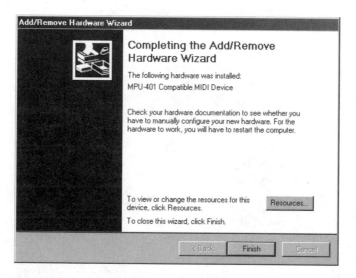

Tip

Be sure to click the Resources button if one is present to check the resources for the device. If there's a problem in allocating resources, this might be the only way that you'll know (that is, until you find that the device doesn't work and start troubleshooting it).

In other cases, such as when you install a modem, the wizard has more steps for you to complete before you're done. Another wizard might also appear. For example, if you're adding a scanner or camera, the Scanner And Digital Camera Wizard appears so that you can select the port for the device or have it selected automatically for you.

There are so many non–plug and play device types available that listing all of the paths the Add/Remove Hardware Wizard can take would be impractical. The wizards steps aren't difficult to decipher, however, so you'll either have a successful installation or the wizard will give you a specific error that will help you troubleshoot the installation. If you find that you must resolve resources for the device, see "Resolving Problems Using the Device Manager," on page 123, to learn how to view the system resources and how to set the resources used by your device.

Removing and Unplugging Devices

The Add/Remove Hardware Wizard enables you to uninstall, unplug, or eject devices. You should use this wizard to uninstall any device that you've physically removed and will not be using again, such as an internal card.

Some devices that you remove only temporarily need to be unplugged or ejected before you physically remove them. Usually, PC Cards must be unplugged, for example, and some docked portable computers must be ejected. To determine which devices you need to unplug or eject, run the Add/Remove Hardware Wizard, as described below, and see what devices show up in the list in step 5.

Tip

If you use a portable computer, check to see if Eject is on the Start menu; if so, you can use the Start menu to eject your docked portable.

To uninstall, unplug or eject a device:

1. Click Start, point to Settings, click Control Panel, and then double-click Add/Remove Hardware. The Add/Remove Hardware Wizard welcome page appears.

2. Click Next.

3. Select Uninstall/Unplug A Device, and then click Next.

4. Select Uninstall A Device or Unplug/Eject A Device, and then click Next.

5. If you selected Uninstall A Device in the previous step, select the device from the list and click Next, and then select Yes, I Want To Uninstall This Device and click Next.

    If you selected Unplug/Eject A Device in the previous step, select the device you want to unplug or eject from the list and click Next. (If you just wanted to see what devices you need to eject, click Cancel now.) Click Next to verify that you want to unplug the device.

6. Click Next again to finish the wizard. You might need to restart the computer.

Testing and Troubleshooting Hardware Installation

After you install a device, you should test it immediately. Unlike using the Add Printer Wizard, which lets you print a test page after installing a printer, you'll have to figure out your own way to test devices that aren't printers. Typically, to test a device you can just find an application that uses the device and try to get it to work. For example, if you've installed a scanner or a digital camera, you can use the Imaging tool (under Programs/Accessories on the Start menu) to acquire an image from the device.

If you don't have an application to check the device, the next best thing is to run the Add/Remove Hardware Wizard again and check the device you've installed to see if it's listed as working (see "Troubleshooting Your Device," on page 122). Alternatively, you can look up the device in the Device Manager to see if it's shown as working. See "Resolving Problems Using the Device Manager," on page 123, to learn how.

Troubleshooting Your Device

Here are the steps to running the Add/Remove Hardware Wizard when you want to verify that a device is working and troubleshoot the device if it isn't. When the device has a yellow exclamation mark icon, it isn't working. A question mark icon means that the device is of unknown origin. If a device has both exclamation mark and question mark icons, it's both not working and unknown.

To troubleshoot a device:

1. Double-click Add/Remove Hardware in the Control Panel and click Next on the opening page of the wizard.
2. Select Add/Troubleshoot A Device and click Next.
   The next panel shows a list of the devices installed.
3. Find your device in this list.
4. If the device has an exclamation mark icon, select it, and click Next.

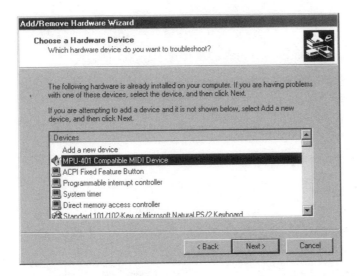

5. The final screen of the Add/Remove Hardware Wizard gives you an indication of the problem that was found. Click Finish to exit this wizard and jump to the Help Troubleshooter.

6. Follow the instructions given in the Troubleshooter to resolve the problem.

Resolving Problems Using the Device Manager

The Plug and Play Manager in Windows 2000 Professional resolves all resource problems for plug and play devices. If you've installed a non–plug and play device, you might need to make some adjustments to the resources assigned to the device to get it working. To view the resources assigned to a device and open a Properties dialog box to edit them, use the Device Manager.

Caution

Setting resources requires advanced knowledge of computer hardware settings and, if you're not careful, you can end up with a bigger problem than the one you started with. You should attempt to set resources only if you've successfully done this before in other Windows operating systems. Do not change resources associated with any other device or you risk disabling a working device.

To open the Device Manager and check resources:

1. In the Control Panel, double-click the System icon.

2. In the System Properties dialog box, click the Hardware tab.

3. Click Device Manager.

    You'll see all of the devices installed, listed by type. You can also view the devices listed by resource. There are four resource categories:

    • Direct Memory Access (DMA)

    • Input/output (IO)

    • Interrupt request (IRQ)

    • Memory

    If you view the category listed by resource, you need to expand the resource category to view all the devices. Otherwise, if the devices are listed by type, just find the device in the list.

4. Double-click the device to open its Properties dialog box and set its resources. After setting resources, you'll be prompted to restart the computer.

Tip

You can also open the Device Manager by double-clicking Administrative Tools in the Control Panel, double-clicking Computer Management in the Administrative Tools folder, and then selecting Device Manager in the left column.

Having finished with the hardware part of setting your Windows 2000 Professional computer, you're probably eager to load some software and finish setting up your computer. The next chapter, "Step 5: Install and Test Your Programs," helps you handle that task and concludes the setup part of this book.

Chapter 7

Step Five: Install and Test Your Programs

This chapter will help you determine whether your current programs are compatible in Microsoft Windows 2000 Professional and also to install and test new programs. Because you might need to install older programs that are untested in Windows 2000 Professional, it also gives you some tips on what to watch out for when installing legacy applications.

Determining Whether Your Programs Are Compatible

Windows 2000 Professional is compatible with a huge number of programs, including programs designed to run on earlier Windows platforms as well as those certified to install and run in Windows 2000 Professional.

Windows 2000 Distributed Installation

Windows 2000 Professional is designed to work well as a stand-alone system, in a small office network environment, or in the distributed network environments of larger businesses. The Active Directory service on a network computer running Microsoft Windows 2000 Server enables network administrators to remotely install applications by "publishing" applications in the Active Directory so they can be installed on demand (this is called "just in time installation"). Because this book is aimed at small business owners who want to avoid the complexities of large networks and network administration, the topics of client/server networking and using the Active Directory are outside the scope of this book.

The Microsoft Compatibility List

It's a good rule to buy upgrades to your existing software that specifically comply with Windows 2000. Microsoft has done much of the legwork for you in testing the compatibility of applications and compiling a list of Windows 2000–compatible applications, which can be found at *www. microsoft.com/windows/professional/deploy/compatible*. Applications in that database are given one of three rankings, as listed in Table 7-1.

Table 7-1 Application Compatibility Rankings

Ranking	Description
Certified	The application has met all standards in the Application Specification for Windows 2000 and has passed all Windows 2000 compliance testing by both the independent software vendor (ISV) and VeriTest, an independent testing organization. This is the highest level ranking for Windows 2000–compatible applications.
Ready	The ISV has tested the application for Windows 2000 compatibility and will provide Windows 2000–related product support.
Planned	The ISV has committed to delivering a Windows 2000–compatible version of this application in the future and has indicated that it will be Ready or Certified level.

Microsoft's compatibility database on the Microsoft Web site can save you time because you can look up your applications to see if there is a Windows 2000–compatible version released or about to be released. The database provides compatibility information based on the Application Specification for Windows 2000, a detailed document that spells out what applications must do to install, work well in Windows 2000, and uninstall if required. This is the requirement for displaying the important Windows 2000 logo on the product. Any new or updated applications that you purchase should have that logo on the box. The Web site provides more information on what the specification means, so you can read more about it if you want.

What to Do if Your Program Is Not Listed

If your program is not listed, you should first contact the software vendor and see if a Windows 2000 version is available or planned for a near release. Also ask them if there are any known issues with running your current version of the software on Windows 2000. Two good sources for this information are the software vendor's Web site and its product technical support. If an update for Windows 2000 is coming out soon, it's probably worth waiting for. If no update is available, but they tell you it runs fine on Windows 2000, you can at least install it with some confidence.

But what if your favorite software company hasn't provided an upgrade yet, or perhaps the software is no longer supported? Fortunately, Windows 2000 Professional does a good job of installing and running legacy software, so chances are still good that your application will work well in Windows 2000 Professional. In this case, you can try installing and testing the application yourself.

Caution

If the application is critical to your business operation, test it first on a Windows 2000 Professional installation before removing it from the computer on which it's currently running. Software backward compatibility is important to Windows 2000 Professional but not at the risk of reducing stability and reliability, so your legacy application might not work if it threatens the reliability of the operating system.

What Kinds of Programs Will Run in Windows 2000 Professional?

Windows 2000–certified programs are your first choice, either new applications or upgrades of your current software. Windows 2000 Professional will also run the majority of "well-behaved" applications specified to run on Microsoft Windows NT, Microsoft Windows 98, Microsoft Windows 95, Microsoft Windows 3.1, MS-DOS, OS/2 (versions 1.x and 2.x) and POSIX.

What's a well-behaved application? This is hard to describe without going into more technical description than most people care about. However, the two most common characteristics of badly behaved applications are

- Programs that write to hardware devices directly
- Programs that overwrite system DLLs upon installation

Windows 2000 prohibits applications from accessing the hardware directly and won't run any applications that do so. This applies mostly to MS-DOS programs, but it can apply to any program; the largest percentage of these are graphics-intensive programs such as video games. Your small business probably doesn't depend on running video games but there might be other graphics-intensive software that you use for computer-aided design (CAD) work, graphing business data, scientific instrumentation, creating computer graphics, desktop publishing, customer kiosks, and so on.

Some installation programs attempt to overwrite system DLL files. DLLs are *dynamic-link libraries* that are often shared between applications. It was common in previous versions of Windows for applications to install their own updated versions of DLLs over the DLLs that the system maintained. During installation you were usually prompted to determine if you wanted to overwrite the existing file (usually giving you a queasy feeling after you click Yes, since you didn't really know what it was replacing or why). Windows 2000 Professional, however, doesn't allow applications to overwrite its system DLLs with updated versions—if an application attempts to overwrite a DLL, Windows 2000 Professional will replace the updated version of the DLL with the original version. So your application might not work if it depends on its own specific version of a system DLL. Applications can, as always, copy their DLLs to their own installation directories, which is the preferred solution. Microsoft has committed to maintaining the latest system DLLs in updates, making vendor updates unnecessary.

Installing and Running Programs

Programs that are designed to run in Windows 3.0, Windows 3.1, Windows 3.11 and MS-DOS are called 16-bit applications, whereas anything that was written for Windows 2000, Windows NT, Windows 98, or Windows 95 is called a 32-bit application and is based on the Win32 application programming interface (API).

Windows 32-bit applications are designed to be easily installed, run, and uninstalled in a 32-bit operating system. To add a 32-bit program, you can use Add/Remove Programs in the Control Panel or just run the setup program that comes with the application. These applications have the benefit of registering themselves in the Windows 2000 Professional registry so that they can be removed. Only 32-bit applications will show up in the Add/Remove Programs dialog box after they're added so that they can be changed or removed.

Programs that are 16-bit applications run in special subsystems in Windows 2000 Professional that emulate the computers for which the programs were originally written. In fact, the emulation modes often do a better job than the original computers because things like extended memory can be emulated in memory and are not subject to hardware limitations.

To add 16-bit programs, you can use the Add/Remove Programs dialog box or you can just run the setup program. Most Windows applications install easily. MS-DOS programs might take a little more work to install if they modify the MS-DOS configuration files.

Before You Install Legacy Applications

Before you begin to install and test legacy applications in Windows 2000 Professional, make sure you are prepared in case something goes wrong. The following checklist should help make sure you're ready for any unexpected surprises and steer you away from programs that could cause you grief or lost time.

- Make sure you have an emergency repair diskette (ERD). If you didn't create an ERD during setup, do it now. It's unlikely that installing a program will trash your system but it's best to be prepared before adding anything to your hard disk. To learn how to create an ERD or recover your system using the ERD, read Chapter 10.

- Make sure you know how to shut down misbehaving applications using the Task Manager (*see "Using the Task Manager to End a Program," on page 145*).

- Avoid installing any kernel-mode applications (virus checkers for example) that aren't specifically listed as Windows 2000 compatible. These programs are given greater access to hardware, such as disk drives, and can be harder to recover from when they don't work. This also applies to programs that do disk defragmentation, partitioning, and so forth.

- Avoid installing any Windows 95 programs that use virtual device drivers (VxDs) to share hardware between programs. Windows 2000 Professional doesn't support virtual device drivers. (You might not know that the program uses VxDs until after you've installed the software, unfortunately.)

- Avoid programs like screen savers or any program that locks your display, unless it's specifically Windows 2000 compatible.

- Avoid video games unless they're listed as compatible. Older video games are often the worst offenders when it comes to accessing hardware directly because, before Microsoft invented DirectX, direct access was the only way for games to get good performance from video cards.

Adding Windows 32-bit Applications

Using the Add/Remove Programs utility in the Control Panel, you can install and remove applications certified for Windows 2000 Professional or designed to run on Windows NT 4.0, Windows 98, or Windows 95. This utility contains options to add programs, remove programs, change components in the program (if the program supports this), and add or remove Windows Components. When you add a program using this utility, you're actually just running the setup program on the CD or floppy disk, but this utility presents a single location for accomplishing those tasks.

You can also install a program by running the setup program on the CD or floppy disk. You can use any means you like to do this, such as double-clicking the setup program in Windows Explorer. Also, most programs are on CD and many CDs have an autorun file that causes the setup program to start as soon as you insert the CD—if the setup program appears when you insert the CD, you can go ahead and run it. However, here's the official way to install an application.

To use the Add/Remove Programs utility to add an application:

1. In the Control Panel, double-click the Add/Remove Programs icon. The Add/Remove Programs utility opens with the Change Or Remove Programs option selected.

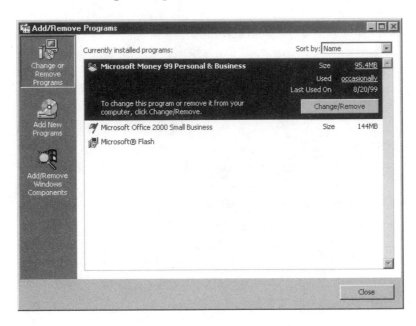

2. Click Add New Programs on the left.

3. Click the CD Or Floppy button. The Install Program From Floppy Disk Or CD-ROM Wizard appears.

4. Insert the CD or first installation floppy disk and Click Next.

    If the wizard finds a program named SETUP.EXE or INSTALL.EXE on either the floppy disk drive or the CD-ROM drive, it will appear in the Open box. Otherwise, you can click Browse and search for the correct installation program file to run. You can also click Browse if the application is somewhere else, such as downloaded from theWeb onto your hard drive.

5. Click Next to run the setup program, and follow the instructions provided by the setup program.

6. Test the program if it isn't certified to run on Windows 2000.

Adding Windows 16-bit Applications

Programs written specifically to run in Windows 3.0, Windows 3.1, or Windows 3.11 are often referred to as Windows 3.x or Win16 programs and are generically referred to as Windows 3.1 applications in this chapter. They differ from Windows 32-bit applications in a few significant ways when it comes to installing and testing them:

- They aren't supported in the Add/Remove Programs utility. While you can use this utility to run the setup program for a Windows 3.1 program, the program won't be listed here after you install it, so you can't remove it using this utility. Windows 3.1 programs don't know about the registry so they can't register information that allows them to be uninstalled.

- They don't use long file names, so all file names with more than eight characters in Windows 2000 Professional are truncated. For example, the folder Documents and Settings, which contains user information in Windows 2000 Professional, appears as DOCUME~1 when viewed from a Windows 3.1 application.

- They don't use the common dialog boxes for saving files, opening files, or browsing so they don't provide the new features of these dialog boxes that come with Windows 2000 Professional.

Installing Windows 3.1 Applications

To install a 16-bit Windows-based application, you run its setup program in Windows using any method you like, such as double-clicking the setup program in Windows Explorer. You can use the Add/Remove Programs utility to add a Windows 3.1 program but the utility won't help you remove the program after it's installed. Here's how to use the Run command to install a Windows 3.1 application.

To add a Windows 3.1 application from the Run dialog box:

1. Insert the setup disk in the A: drive. Or, if it's on CD, insert the CD-ROM.

2. Click Start and then click Run.

3. Type *A:* (or the drive letter of the disk or CD-ROM that contains the installation program followed by a backslash) and select the appropriate file (usually SETUP.EXE or INSTALL.EXE) from the

drop-down list box that appears. You can also use the Browse button to search for the setup program if it's on some other medium, such as a network drive or your hard disk.

Note

If a Command Prompt window appears at this point, the program is an MS-DOS application. Close the window by clicking the Close button in the upper right corner. If an End Program dialog box appears informing you that Windows can't end this program, click End Now. Then go to "Adding MS-DOS Applications," on page 135.

4. Follow the instructions to install the application.

5. Test the application to make sure that it's working correctly.

Setting Properties of Window 3.1 Applications

You might want to edit the properties of a Windows 3.1 application after it's installed for these reasons:

• To run the application in a separate memory space. By default, all Windows 16-bit applications run together, sharing the same memory and input queue, just as if they were running on a Windows 3.1 computer. If there are conflicts between applications (your program hangs when you run another Win16 program, for example), you can run the programs in different memory spaces—similar to running them on different computers.

- To assign a shortcut key to run the application, such as Alt+Ctrl and any key.

- To define how the application appears when it first starts (in a normal window, maximized, or minimized).

- To force a Run As Other User dialog box to appear when the program is run, enabling you to run the program with the permissions granted to another user.

To edit a Windows 3.1 program's properties, you need to edit the properties of the shortcut to the program file. The shortcut is on the Start menu in the folder created as a Program Group. You might also have created a shortcut on the desktop, which you can also change.

Note

Remember to edit the properties of every shortcut to the program you make if you change any of them.

To change the properties of a Windows 3.1 application shortcut:

1. Find the program on the Start menu, right-click the program, and then choose Properties from the shortcut menu. If you've created a shortcut somewhere else, such as on the desktop, locate that file in Windows Explorer, right-click it, and then choose Properties from the shortcut menu.

    The dialog box that appears has two tabs but you'll need to use only the Shortcut tab.

2. Change settings on the Shortcut tab.

    If you need more help on a feature, click the question mark button at the top right of the dialog box and then click the element that you want help on.

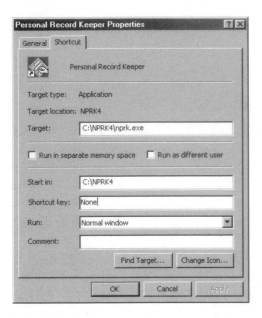

3. Click OK when you're done setting properties.

Adding MS-DOS Applications

MS-DOS programs can run in Windows 2000 Professional as long as they don't access hardware devices directly or load drivers not supplied by the system. MS-DOS applications run in their own subsystem inside Windows 2000 Professional called the NT virtual DOS machine (NTVDM). The NTVDM emulates a 16-bit operating system, complete with its own version of the configuration files CONFIG.SYS and AUTOEXEC.BAT familiar to MS-DOS users. These are called CONFIG.NT and AUTOEXEC.NT and they're located in the WINNT\System32 folder.

Note

In Windows NT parlance, the *system root* is the directory in which you installed Windows 2000 Professional (for example C:\WINNT if you installed on the C: drive). When the system directory is referred to in files such as CONFIG.NT and AUTOEXEC.NT, it is denoted by %SystemRoot%.

The process of installing an MS-DOS application isn't difficult, but it can require several steps, the shortest of which is actually running the setup program. You encounter the extra steps because MS-DOS applications often modify the configuration files and you need to detect what is modified and then move that information into the appropriate .NT configuration files. You'll also need to create a shortcut to the application and, if necessary, configure how it runs in the MS-DOS environment.

Handling Changes to Configuration Files

MS-DOS programs often modify the MS-DOS configuration files to add their own commands and settings. Most often they will modify AUTOEXEC.BAT to add their program directory to the Path command and set environment variables using the Set command. They might also modify CONFIG.SYS to set variables or load drivers. You'll need to take any information written to those files and place it in the appropriate .NT file in the system root folder (for example, C:\WINNT\System32).

First, however, you have to capture that information. If the MS-DOS setup program is well written, it'll prompt you for the names of the files in which to store this information. More often, it'll just add its information to the existing AUTOEXEC.BAT and CONFIG.SYS files. In this case, you can see what was added in a couple of ways. One way is to create backup copies of these files and then run the program installation. After installation, you can compare the new files with their backup copies. However, you might sometimes find it difficult to spot the changes added by the installation program if the configuration files already contain information, particularly in cases where configuration files are complex or where parameters are added to existing lines (such as the Path variable).

Another approach, useful when your configuration files are complicated, is to create blank configuration files as follows:

1. Make backup copies of the configuration files (for example, copy AUTOEXEC.BAT to AUTOEXEC.BAK and CONFIG.SYS to CONFIG.BAK).

2. Remove the contents of the original configuration files so they are blank. (Later, you'll restore the backup files you've made.)

3. Install the MS-DOS program.

4. Open these MS-DOS configuration files and copy the contents into the appropriate .NT file (see detailed steps next).

Caution

If you alter the original configuration files by removing their contents, make sure you remember to restore them to their original state as described at the end of the next procedure.

Here's how to copy the information added to the MS-DOS configuration files into the .NT files:

1. Open the C:\AUTOEXEC.BAT file by right-clicking it and choosing Edit from the shortcut menu. (Don't double-click the file or you'll run it—it's a batch file.)

2. In Windows Explorer, navigate to the WINNT\System32 folder, locate AUTOEXEC.NT and make a copy of it (named AUTOEXEC.NTB, for example). The copy is just to be safe if you want to quickly return to the previous working version.

3. Open AUTOEXEC.NT it by right-clicking it, choosing Open With, and selecting Notepad.

4. Now, copy and paste the information added by the program from AUTOEXEC.BAT to the AUTOEXEC.NT file and save it.

Note

You might need to understand a little about MS-DOS here. For example, there can be only one path variable, so if there is an existing path command in AUTOEXEC.NT (for example, path=c:\), and you have a path in AUTOEXEC.BAT to add (say, path=c:\dosapp), you'll need to add the new path to the end of the existing path after adding a semicolon (path=c:\;c:\dosapp).

5. Open the C:\ CONFIG.SYS file by right-clicking it, choosing Open With from the shortcut menu, selecting Notepad, and clicking OK. (If you get a warning that CONFIG.SYS is a system file, go ahead and click Open With).

6. In Windows Explorer, navigate to the WINNT\System32 folder, locate CONFIG.NT and make a backup copy (named CONFIG.NTB, for example).

7. Open CONFIG.NT by right-clicking it, choosing Open With, and selecting Notepad.

8. Now, copy and paste the program's configuration information from CONFIG.SYS to CONFIG.NT file and save it.

Note

You'll have to apply some MS-DOS knowledge to this operation. For example, if there is already a line in CONFIG.NT that says *files=20* and your CONFIG.SYS has a line *files=40*, replace the former with the latter—don't create two separate lines with *files* = in them. (The files variable sets the maximum number of files an application can have open at one time.)

There are restrictions about the drivers you can load in CONFIG.NT. For example, do not load EMM386.EXE, SMARTDRV.SYS, RAMDRIVE.SYS, DBLSPACE.SYS, or any hardware or network drivers. In general, it's safe to use a driver in CONFIG.NT if you can find it in the %SYSTEMROOT%/ System32 directory (for example HIMEM.SYS).

Tip

If you've used the blank configuration file method to capture the program's configuration information, your MS-DOS configuration files now contain unique information pertaining to your program. Save these files to your program's directory before continuing to the next step. This way, you'll maintain a record of what your MS-DOS program installed.

9. Restore the original MS-DOS configuration files to the C:\ directory from the backup files you made (for example, copy AUTOEXEC.BAK over AUTOEXEC.BAT and CONFIG.BAK over CONFIG.SYS). Some legacy Windows 95 programs still put information they use in these files.

Installing an MS-DOS Program

You can run the MS-DOS installation program in several ways. Here's how to use the Run command to add an MS-DOS Program:

1. Insert the MS-DOS setup disk in the A: drive. Or, if the setup program is on CD, insert the CD-ROM.

2. Click Start and then click Run.

3. Type *A:* (or the drive letter of the disk or CD-ROM that contains the installation program followed by a backslash) and select the appropriate file (usually SETUP.EXE or INSTALL.EXE) from the drop-down list box. A Command Prompt window opens and the setup program for the application runs.

4. Follow the instructions in the Command Prompt window to install the application. When setup has finished, the window should disappear. If the program asks you what to do with the AUTOEXEC.BAT and CONFIG.SYS information, save it with different names, something like AUTOEXEC.001 and CONFIG.001, for example.

Creating a Shortcut to the MS-DOS Program

Now you need a convenient way to run the program, and the easiest method is to add it to the Start menu. You might also need to set up the MS-DOS environment that the program runs in, which is done in a shortcut file (in Windows 3.1 this was done in a .PIF file). By adding the program to the Start menu, you create a shortcut, which you can then modify as you wish to set the MS-DOS environment.

Note

If you don't want to add an MS-DOS program to the Start menu, just locate the program file (.EXE or .COM) in Explorer, press and hold the right mouse button, drag it to some destination, such as the desktop, release the button, and then select Create Shortcut(s) Here.

To create a program shortcut and add it to the Start menu:

1. Click Start, point to Settings, and then click Taskbar & Start Menu. The Taskbar And Start Menu Properties dialog box appears.

2. Click the Advanced Tab and click the Add button. The Create Shortcut Wizard appears.

3. Follow the wizard steps to create a shortcut on the Start menu.

Tip

In the first step, you can click the Browse button to locate the program.

Editing the MS-DOS Shortcut Properties

Now you can finish up by setting the MS-DOS properties in the shortcut file. If you've installed the program on the Start menu, right-click the program on the Start menu and then click Properties. If you've created a shortcut somewhere else, such as on the desktop, locate that file in Windows Explorer, right-click it, and then choose Properties from the shortcut menu.

The Properties dialog box that appears has several tabs in which you can set properties. This dialog box is very similar to the MS-DOS Properties dialog box in Windows 95.

Probably the most important properties to set now are those on the Memory tab. The documentation for your MS-DOS program will tell you how much extended or expanded memory your program needs to run. Set these values in the Expanded (EMS) Memory and Extended (XMS) Memory drop-down lists, respectively.

Set any other properties you want, and then click OK.

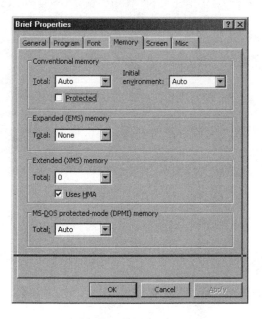

Running Your Programs

As with every other version of Windows, you can start an application in countless ways. If you're familiar with Windows, you undoubtedly have your own favorite. Most of these methods are the same in Windows 2000 Professional. For example, you can start a program by

- Clicking its icon on the Start menu.

- Typing (or browsing for) the program's name (and usually its directory path) in the Start menu's Run command and clicking OK.

- Typing the program's name, and path if required, in a Command Prompt window. It's similar to the MS-DOS box in Windows 95, except that it doesn't run MS-DOS but rather it runs a command-line interface to Windows 2000 Professional, which looks much like MS-DOS.

- Associating a document type with the program and then double-clicking the document either in the Start menu's most recently used document list (under Documents) or by opening My Documents and double-clicking a file.

Note

To associate a document type with a program, select the document file in Windows Explorer, click Open With on the File menu, select a program from the list, and select Always Use This Program To Open These Files. Then click OK.

- Double-clicking any document in Windows Explorer that has an associated program.

- Double-clicking the actual program file or a shortcut to it in Windows Explorer.

- Double-clicking a shortcut to the program on the desktop.

- Double-clicking a shortcut to a document on the desktop that has an associated program.

Windows 2000 Professional adds two new methods of running a program, both associated with double-clicking a document to run the associated program. You can use the History explorer bar in Windows Explorer to open a document you've accessed before. Or you can set up the

My Documents folder to expand on the Start menu so that all its documents and subfolders appear as menu items and require only a single click to open. (*See "Direct Browsing From the Start Menu," on page 259 in Chapter 14, for information about configuring the Start menu.*)

Removing Programs

Perhaps you've tested your application and it isn't working as you want it to, or you simply want to remove it for some other reason. Removing Windows 32-bit applications is straightforward because they're registered and have uninstall programs. Removing 16-bit programs is more involved.

To remove a Windows 32-bit program:

1. In the Control Panel, double-click Add/Remove Programs.

2. Click the Change Or Remove Programs button on the left (this is the default when you open Add/Remove Programs).

3. Select the program you want to remove.

4. Click Change/Remove or just Remove if the program has both a Change and a Remove button.

Windows 3.1 and MS-DOS programs are a little different because they aren't actually registered when installed so they don't show up in the Add/Remove Programs utility. This means you can't remove them by using the Add/Remove Programs utility the way you can with 32-bit programs. Here's how you remove 16-bit programs and fix the Start menu.

To remove a 16-bit application:

1. Open Windows Explorer, find the folder that holds the program, and delete it.

2. Remove any program group or shortcut from the Start menu. To do this, click Start, right-click the program or folder shortcut, and then choose Delete from the shortcut menu.

3. Remove any shortcut from the desktop or any other folder.

4. If this is an MS-DOS application, remove any additions you made to the configuration files (CONFIG.NT and AUTOEXEC.NT) when you installed the program.

Note

If you're deleting a folder, you'll see a message that tells you that modifying this folder will affect all users who log on to this computer and asks whether you want to continue. What does this mean? By default, all folders added to the Programs menu on the Start menu are saved as folders in the Documents and Settings/All Users/Start Menu/Programs folder. This means they will appear on the Start menu of all users with accounts on the computer. Deleting the folder on the Start menu deletes this folder on the hard disk, thereby removing it from everyone's Start menu. If you're actually deleting the program, click Yes.

Testing and Troubleshooting Programs

After installing programs that aren't certified to run on Windows 2000 Professional, you should test them thoroughly. You should take a methodical approach to try and cover the most common operations. If you encounter problems when testing the program, you'll need to troubleshoot them.

While there isn't sufficient space here for a detailed description of troubleshooting legacy programs, there are good troubleshooters for programs in Windows 2000 Professional Help. You can also contact the software vendor's technical support, search the Web for information on your program, browse Internet newsgroups for help from others who've encountered similar problems, or perhaps live with the incompatibility if it's insignificant and doesn't affect your business data.

If worse comes to worst, you should still have a copy of the program running on an older operating system in your office and you might have to maintain that system until your software is updated to Windows 2000 specifications by the manufacturer or you find newer software to takes its place.

Testing Your Applications

Here are some guidelines to help you get started testing your applications.

Testing Startup Behavior

You'll often see the biggest problems when you first run the program. This is when the program looks for drivers it needs and does most of its configuration; if you make it past this step, you're usually most of the way home. Here are a couple of things to check:

- Run the program from the Start menu or a shortcut to see that it starts up without a hitch. Is there anything unexpected about the startup? Does it tell you there are any files missing or report any other errors?

- Open a file and see if the data is displayed as you'd expect to see it.

- If it's an MS-DOS application, does it work in full-screen mode? Does it work when not in full-screen mode? Does the mouse work as you expect it to?

Making Sure You Can Save and Load Data

Accessing the hard disk to save and load data is the next big troubleshooting step. Try running some of these tests on your program:

- Modify the data and save it as a temporary file (that is, with a different name). Then close the temporary file and reopen it. Can you save and open files?

- Add new data to the temporary file, save it, close the file, and then open it again. Check to see that everything is as you saved it.

- Close the program and double-click the data file you just saved to see if it opens your program. If no association is made, make one in Windows Explorer (using the Open With command on the File menu) and then try opening the document again.

- Run other programs at the same time. If it's a Windows 3.1 program, run other Windows 3.1 programs you might have installed. If there are performance problems, try running one or both the programs in their own memory space.

Testing All Components of the Program

Although every program is different, you'll need to approach the task of examining the user interface in an organized fashion. Use the menu bar, since it usually contains all of the program's functionality. Try following these steps in your program:

- Visit every screen that you can in the program. Start at the left end of the menu bar and work your way to the right end, visiting every dialog box and program mode that you can. This includes setting different preferences, such as colors and fonts.

• If there is a macro language that you have macros written for, load a few and run the program to make sure they work.

• If your program uses a database, and you are moving a database from another computer, make sure you can read from it and write to it from the installed program on the new computer.

Test Hardware Connections

Try out every hardware device that the program can use. For example, make sure you can print from the program. If the program uses audio, make sure you can hear sounds; if the program uses devices you've installed, such as a scanner, test those functions as well.

Using the Program Troubleshooter

Windows 2000 Professional Help provides some good troubleshooting tips for debugging your program installation. Here are the steps to look up the troubleshooters for programs:

1. Click Start and then click Help.

2. In the left pane of Windows 2000 Help, click Troubleshooting And Maintenance.

3. Click the topic Windows 2000 Troubleshooters.

4. Click one of the program troubleshooting links such as MS-DOS Programs or Windows 3.1 Programs.

Using the Task Manager to End a Program

Occasionally, you'll run into a program that loses its way. Fortunately, Windows 2000 Professional prevents it from bringing down your system, but if the program won't allow you to exit, you might need to close it in the Task Manager.

To shut down a program in the Task Manager:

1. Press the three keys Ctrl+Alt+Del simultaneously. The Windows Security utility appears.

2. Click Task Manager. The Task Manager appears.

Tip

You can also open the Task Manager by right-clicking the Taskbar and choosing Task Manager from the shortcut menu.

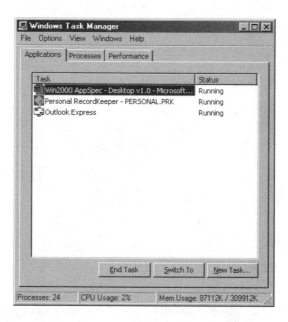

3.   Select the program you want to end and click End Task.

4.   Click Exit Task Manager on the File menu to close the Task Manager.

   Now that you've finished installing the operating system, hardware, and programs on your computer, you should be all set to put the computer and Windows 2000 Professional to work. The remainder of this book will help you learn how to get the most out of Windows 2000 Professional, whether it's used as a stand-alone computer, is connected to the Internet, or is part of a local area network in your office. If you're setting up your computer to be used by more than one person or you want to learn about safeguarding your data or backing up your data, read the chapters in Part 3, "How to Create Accounts and Keep Your Data Safe," next. Otherwise, you can continue on with Part 4, "Connecting Your Computer Online," to learn about getting connected to the Internet, setting up e-mail, and using the built-in fax services of Windows 2000 Professional.

Chapter 8

Ten Easy Ways to Protect Your Data

Owners of small businesses are well aware that they need to keep their business data safe. Because you're changing to a new operating system, now may be a good time to reevaluate your current scheme for keeping your business data safe and secure, especially in light of the security features built into Microsoft Windows 2000 Professional. Here are ten steps you can take to make sure you don't lose the important business data on your Windows 2000 Professional computer.

The Top Ten List

While this list certainly doesn't cover everything you can do to protect your data, it offers tips you can follow to make your data much more secure.

- Enable Mandatory Logging On
- Change Your Default Logon Password
- Change the Name of Your Administrator Account
- Create Separate Accounts for All Users
- Make a Habit of Logging Off or Locking Your Computer
- Use a Screen Saver
- Don't Give Out Your Password to Anyone
- Disable or Delete Unused Accounts
- Use NTFS Permissions on Folders
- Back Up Your Files Regularly

Note

This list is not in order of priority; you should probably do them all but if not, you'll have to decide which work best for your business.

Enable Mandatory Logging On

During setup, Windows 2000 Professional gives you the option to establish yourself as the sole user of the computer rather than set up the computer for multiple users. If you choose to set up the computer just for yourself, you can run Windows 2000 Professional without requiring a logon prompt. In this case, Windows logs you on automatically.

Many people like to bypass the security of using a logon prompt, especially when nobody else in the office should use the computer. However, consider carefully whether the computer contains critical or private information about your small business or your customers. Also consider what would happen if the computer were accessed when you weren't around and your computer's files were destroyed. You might have backed up your data before you left; but more often than not, you didn't.

To make sure that a logon prompt requires any user to log on after the computer boots, perform the following steps:

Note

You'll need administrator privileges to enable mandatory logging on, which you'll have with your default account.

1. Click Start, point to Settings, and then click Control Panel.

2. Double-click the Users And Passwords icon.

3. Select Users Must Enter A User Name And Password To Use This Computer.

4. Click OK.

Change Your Default Logon Password

If you enable a mandatory logon prompt, as described in the previous step, you should also remember to change your default logon password, which by default is blank. To create a password for yourself, press Ctrl+Alt+Del to open the Windows Security dialog box, click Change Password, and fill in the form that appears.

Change the Name of Your Administrator Account

It's a good idea to rename the administrator account to something other than Administrator. This adds an extra level of security to your system because nobody will know the name you've chosen even if they successfully guess the password. It's very important to guard access to this account because it gives absolute power over the operating system to anyone logged on as Administrator. See "Renaming User Accounts," on page 163 in Chapter 9, to learn how to rename any account, including the administrator account.

Create Separate Accounts for All Users

You may be tempted to forgo the whole business of setting up user accounts, particularly when you know, and probably trust, all the people who will be using your computer. (They're a critical part of your small business, right? Why shouldn't you trust them?) What some overlook are the benefits you receive from maintaining separate user accounts, and the peace of mind you'll have when you take steps to keep your data safe. Chapter 9 presents an overview of user accounts and points out why using them is a good idea; be sure to read that section before deciding whether to create separate accounts.

Make a Habit of Logging Off or Locking Your Computer

Even if you enable mandatory logging on, you won't necessarily log off your computer when it's time to leave. It's easy to forget to log off, especially if you've been using unsecured computers on a day-to-day basis in your small business. Remind yourself with a note stuck to your monitor or, if you have scheduling software, use a reminder that pops up and reminds to you go home! (And to log off!)

A good way to make logging off easier is to put the Log Off command on the Start menu, as it is in Microsoft Windows 95. This also reminds you that you're logged on every time you open the Start menu. On the Advanced tab of the Taskbar And Start Menu Properties dialog box, you can choose to display the Log Off option on the Start menu. See "Optional Start Menu Items," on page 257 in Chapter 14, to find out how to use the Taskbar And Start Menu Properties dialog box.

If you don't log off, you should lock your computer, instead. If you don't want to disturb a program that is running, or if you've shared a modem using Internet Connection Sharing (see Chapter 18), you might need to leave your computer running when you leave work so others can still use the Internet connection. It's easy to lock your computer, and the security provided is equivalent to logging off. The only downside is that nobody else will be able to log on to the computer until you unlock it. (While someone with administrator privileges can unlock a computer, this automatically closes the account and any data not saved before the computer was locked will be lost—so it's best to log off if someone else will need to use the computer before you return.)

To lock your computer:

1. Press Ctrl+Alt+Del to open the Windows Security dialog box.

2. Click Lock Computer. An Unlock Computer dialog box appears with your name.

    To unlock the computer, just type in your password and click OK.

Use a Screen Saver

Screen savers have built-in password protection that you can enable. The password you use for a screen saver is the same as the one you use to log on. Screen savers can be a benefit, especially if you get called away from your computer regularly and find that you aren't logging off or locking it. But a password-protected screen saver can be a nuisance when it starts too frequently. You'll have to experiment to find the best timing for you.

To set up a screen saver and enable password protection:

1. Right-click the desktop and choose Properties from the shortcut menu.
2. Click the Screen Saver tab in the Display Properties dialog box.
3. Select a screen saver from the drop-down list.
4. Select Password Protected.
5. Set the Wait period to a value that makes sense for you.
6. Click OK.

Don't Give Out Your Password to Anyone

If you need to grant someone access to your system, even for just a few minutes, provide access to a Guest account and change the password regularly on this account. If someone absolutely needs administrator rights, create a Guest administrator account and change its password after it is used. Even if you trust the person to whom you've given your password, that person might still let it slip or jot it down where someone else might discover it.

If you make temporary users enter through their own accounts, you can also track who logs on to your system (although auditing is an advanced feature). So if any damage occurs, you'll have a better idea if a temporary user did it. Finally, by giving out your password, you are often also giving out information about how you remember passwords, since most people have a theme they use to remember (favorite hobby, pet, date, and so on). So if you give out your password, even if you change your password after it's used, you might have given someone a good chance at guessing what your next password will be.

Disable or Delete Unused Accounts

It's easy to create an account for a temporary employee or contractor and then forget to remove the account when that person leaves. This can cause a security hole in your system that's comparable to leaving the key to your office with a contractor.

If the user of an account is not coming back, delete the account. Even if that person does come back, you can create a new account. If you know that the person is likely to need access to your computer in the future, you can just disable the account. In Chapter 9, see "Deleting User Accounts," on page 162 and "Disabling an Account," on page 168 for specific steps.

Use NTFS Permissions on Folders

The only way to absolutely protect data on your computer is to set permissions on the folders and files that contain the data. Only the NTFS file system enables this feature. If you didn't choose to format your hard drive as NTFS during setup, you might still want to consider formatting a free partition or a separate hard drive with NTFS and keeping your most critical data there. Setting permissions on a folder or file lets you selectively permit others to access it. See "Setting Security Permissions on Files and Folders," on page 170 in Chapter 9, to learn how to set permissions.

Back Up Your Files Regularly

Backing up your data is probably the most important thing you can do to make sure it remains safe. No amount of user account administration can prevent a hard disk crash. Windows 2000 Professional provides excellent backup and recovery tools.

With your move to a new operating system, you'll need to take another look at your backup plans. Chapter 10 will help you tailor a backup plan for your small business computers that run Windows 2000 Professional and it will show you how to use the Windows 2000 Backup and Recovery Tools.

Now that you've had a chance to consider where to focus your efforts in securing your computer and its data, you can move on to the next two chapters in this part, which will help you implement these steps.

Chapter 9

Setting Up and Managing User Accounts

If more than one person will be using the Microsoft Windows 2000 Professional computer you're setting up, you'll want each person to have a separate user account on the computer. User accounts enable you to keep the data on the computer safe, particularly when you use them in conjunction with NTFS file permissions. They also help you keep other users from modifying the computer in ways you might not have intended. Besides, if you have a network in your office or are planning one, you'll need to set up user accounts anyway to access the network.

This chapter describes why you'd want user accounts in Windows 2000 Professional and what you'll need to know when creating and managing user accounts. "Working with User Accounts and Groups" covers the benefits of users and groups and the tasks required to set up user accounts. Separate sections cover common and advanced tasks. "Setting Security Permissions on Files and Folders" shows how to set permissions in NTFS-formatted partitions; this task is described in this chapter because it's one of the best reasons for establishing individual user accounts on your computer.

Working with User Accounts and Groups

User accounts provide the primary benefit of controlling access to both individual and networked computers by enforcing logons and passwords. Groups provide a means of granting users predefined levels of access to the system and managing access to files, folders, and resources on your computer in an organized manner.

Overview of User Accounts

User accounts control access to individual computers and to those connected to a network. The term *local account* generally refers to an account on an individual computer that a user logs on to (whether it's connected to a network or not). The term *domain account* refers to the user account used to access a network that's connected to a server, such as Microsoft Windows 2000 Server. Typically, if you're using a domain network (also called a client/server network), you'll have a network administrator who sets up the domain account for you. The process of connecting to that domain account creates a local account on your computer with the same name and password (*for details, see "Running the Network Identification Wizard" on page 309 in Chapter 16*). Therefore, from the viewpoint of an individual user, both local and domain accounts work the same—except that the domain account allows access to a server in addition to an individual computer. To simplify matters, this book refers to all accounts as user accounts and uses the term domain accounts only where it's important to note the difference.

User Accounts and Local Access

You can enable more than one person to log on to your local computer whether you're connected to a network or not. User accounts provide several benefits:

- Local system control—user accounts enable you to control access to the operating system. Your default account provides complete access to your computer, allowing the addition of hardware devices, configuring the system, and so on. You probably don't want everyone who uses your computer to have this much control. Even if you think other users wouldn't do anything harmful to the computer on purpose, why take the risk that they could do something by mistake? When you create new user accounts, you define the level of access users have (also called user rights) to modify the system. Typically, you do this by assigning the user to a group that has predefined user rights (*for more information about groups, see "What You Need to Know About Groups," on page 158*).

- Local access to data—user accounts enable you to control access to files and folders. If you are using the NTFS file system, you can specify exactly which users have permissions to files and folders and exactly what rights those users have. For example, if you have a folder on your computer containing personnel data, including salaries and other private information, and your employees have access to your computer, you probably want to select who can open that folder.

- Local user environments—user accounts enable users to have their own desktop settings and to maintain separate documents folders. For example, Jim can set up his display at 1280 by 1024 pixels with a picture of his dog in the background, and you can have your 800 by 600 pixel display (so you don't have to squint to read your e-mail) and keep your favorite Web site as an Active Desktop background. Also, individual accounts have separate My Document folders, so users can keep their data separate. By using permissions on their My Document folders, as described above, users can keep their data private as well as separate.

Tip

If several people log on to a computer to run a single application, such as a cash register or inventory program, create a separate user account for that program and then put the program in the Startup menu of that account. For example, when users log on as cashreg, the cash register program would open. If "Log Off cashreg" is on the Start menu, users can quickly log off the account. Chapter 14 describes working with the Start menu.

User Accounts and Network Access

If you have a network in your office or are considering creating one, you'll need user accounts for everyone who wants to access it. User accounts on networks provide a number of benefits.

- Access to network resources—user accounts enable people to access shared resources (such as files, folders, printers, and Internet connections) on other computers on the network. Creating a user account name for a person in your small business is like providing a special key. You can create a user account on any computer connected to the network; when the user logs on to that computer, the user has access to that user account and also to any shared resource on the network that the account has permission to access.

- Control of shared resources—when you share a resource such as a folder or printer on your computer, you have the option of selecting who can access it over the network. As an example, you might be the sole user of your computer and want to share a folder containing some confidential files with a business partner. You can easily share the folder and then set the folder's share permissions to contain just your partner's account name. You can set share permissions to read, read and change, or not read or change. You can also selectively deny share permissions to individuals or groups (read on to learn more about groups).

What You Need to Know About Groups

A group provides a means to specify common access rights for a collection of user accounts. All members of a group receive the permissions granted to the group. Groups make it easier to organize the access of users to resources like files, folders, and printers. In larger corporate network computing environments, administrators use groups to help them manage activities like remotely deploying applications and files, configuring computers, and restricting access to resources.

For small businesses, working with groups is infinitely simpler; typically, you need to be concerned only with how to restrict the access of users logged on to your computer. The primary way you do this is by assigning users to built-in groups when you create the user accounts. Built-in groups give users predefined capabilities and restrictions on the computer. For example, assigning users to the Administrators group gives them full access to every aspect of the system, whereas assigning users to the Guests group lets them operate and shut down the computer but make no changes to the system.

You can also create your own groups for organizational purposes. For small businesses, the biggest benefit here is that you can enable or deny permissions to a group of users as opposed to listing individual users. This applies whether you're setting permissions on a local file or folder or on a shared resource file, folder, or printer on a network.

Windows 2000 Professional provides two types of pre-defined groups: built-in local groups and built-in system groups (Windows 2000 Server has two additional built-in groups for domains). You'll use the built-in local groups to set access rights to the local computer. Built-in system groups are maintained by the system (you can't add users to them or delete users from them). For example, the built-in system group *Everyone* contains all users on the system—you'll see the Everyone group a lot if you look at or set permissions on any file or folder or shared resource, because it's the group given access by default. You won't need to use system groups much, but you might encounter them from time to time, so you'll want to know what they are. Except for two (Everyone and Authenticated Users), system groups use all capital letters, such as SERVICE, DIALUP, and so on.

Table 9-1 shows the built-in local groups used by Windows 2000 Professional (a sixth group, Replicator, is available for file replication on a domain network but we can ignore it here).

Table 9-1 Built-In Local Groups

Local group	Description
Administrators	Members can perform all administrative tasks. The administrator account is a member of this group as is the default user account established during setup.
Power Users	Members can create and modify user accounts and share resources on a network.
Users	Members have limited access but can run programs and create their own desktop environments.
Guests	Members have limited rights; they can't make changes to their desktop environment.
Backup	Members can use the Windows Backup utility to back up the computer.

Common Account Management Tasks

Your administrative duties in the area of user accounts can, for the most part, be quick and painless. Basically, you'll need to know how to create a new user account or remove an account that's no longer used. You'll also need to know how to change the name on an account and you'll probably want to know how to change someone's group assignment. For more exotic tasks like disabling users or creating new groups, see "Advanced Account Management Tasks," on page 164.

Creating New User Accounts

Before you create new user accounts, you'll want to do a little up front planning to consider a naming convention to use and how you want to deal with passwords.

Naming Conventions

Usually, you choose naming conventions to avoid name collisions, particularly in organizations with many network users. For small businesses, naming conventions are less of an issue but it's still good to be consistent and plan ahead for when your business grows. Just remember that users will need to type the names you pick every day, so keep the names short. A first name or a nickname might work if you have very few employees. It's often good to include the first initial of the last name as well (such as philb and heatherm) in case you eventually have two employees with the same first name. Also, if you create accounts for temporary or contract employees, it's often a good idea to put a letter at the front of the name (for example t-johnh) to make it easier to spot those names. You don't have to put all the letters together either; you can use spaces and capitalization (such as Heather M). Capitalization, however, isn't acknowledged by the system (the user could type heather m) and spaces aren't commonly used unless you're using the full name (such as Heather Mitchell).

Password Considerations

When you create a user account, you're given the opportunity to set a password for the user. You can provide a temporary password that you'll give the user (or leave the password blank) and ask the user to change the password at the first logon. One problem with leaving the password blank is that anyone who knows that person's user name can log on without a password until that person sets a password.

Note

You must log on as an administrator (a member of the Administrators group) to open the Users And Passwords dialog box. If you aren't logged on as an administrator, you can still access this feature by entering the administrator account password when you click on Users And Passwords in the Control Panel and are prompted for the password.

Creating a User Account

Here are the steps for creating a new user account:

1. In the Control Panel, click Users And Passwords.

2. Make sure Users Must Enter A User Name And Password To Use This Computer is selected.

3. Click the Add button.

4. The Add New User Wizard appears.

5. Fill in the User Name (this is the name used to log on), the full name of the user, and a description, and click Next.

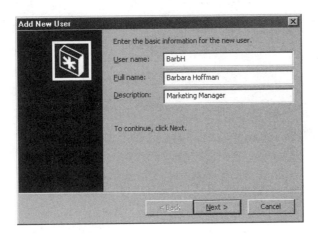

6. In the Password and Confirm Password fields, type a temporary password that you'll give the user, and click Next.

7. Choose a level of access you want to provide the user by choosing a group for the user. See Table 9-1, on page 159, for more information on group access levels. Click Finish when you're done. You should see the person you've added appear in the User Name list.

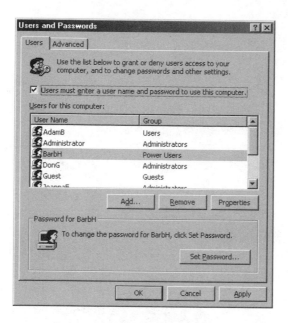

Deleting User Accounts

When someone leaves your business, you'll want to remove his or her account from your computer. If you think the employee will be returning, it's better to simply disable the account, which is described in "Disabling an Account," on page 168.

To delete a user account from your computer:

1. In the Control Panel, click Users And Passwords to open the Users And Passwords dialog box.

2. On the Users tab, select the name of the user you want to delete.

3. Click Remove.

4. Click Yes in the dialog box that appears asking you to confirm that you want to remove the user. The user account is removed.

Note

If the user you've removed had permissions on local shared resources, the user's name, but not the user's ID (a very long number), will be removed from that object's Security properties. Even If you recreate an account with the same name, the new number will be different, so after you delete a user, you should remove the old number by opening the Properties dialog box for a file, folder, or shared resource, clicking the Security tab, selecting the number, and clicking Remove.

Renaming User Accounts

Renaming a user's account name is extremely easy. The password doesn't change in this case, just the name that the person uses to log on.

To rename a user account:

1. In the Control Panel, click Users And Passwords.

2. In the Users tab, click Properties.

3. In the User Name field, enter a new user name.

4. Click OK.

Changing a User's Password

A user's password can be changed in two ways. As an administrator, you can change the password from the Users And Passwords dialog box. Users with fewer rights than those of an administrator can change their own passwords when logged on by pressing Ctrl+Alt+Del to open the Windows Security dialog box, and then clicking the Change Password button. This opens a dialog box in which they can enter a new password.

You can require users to change their password the first time they log on (*see "Advanced Account Management Tasks," on page 164*).

To change a user's password:

1. In the Control Panel, click Users And Passwords.

2. In the Users tab, click Set Password.

3. A Set Password dialog appears. Enter the password in both fields, and click OK.

Changing a User's Group Membership

You assign a user to a group when you create the user account, but you might want to change the user to a different group later. Here's how to do that.

To change a user's group membership access level:

1. In the Control Panel, click Users And Passwords.

2. In the Users tab, click Properties.

3. Click the Group Membership tab.

4. Select the group access level you want to change to.

5. Click OK.

Other Ways of Getting at Users and Group Properties

The Users And Passwords option in the Control Panel is the quickest and safest way to create new users, remove users, and assign group access levels to users. It's quick because it's one click from the Control Panel and it's safe because it requires administrator logon. However, you can also access both user and group properties from the Computer Management Console in the Administrative Tools folder, where you'll find Local Users And Groups under System Tools in the console tree in the left pane. This snap-in is described later in this chapter. (*Chapter 20, "Using the Computer Management Console" describes this administrative tool.*) This method of accessing user and group properties doesn't require administrator privileges—however, users who use this procedure are restricted to performing only the activities allowed in their group. For example, a user assigned to the Users group can create another user account but can't give that account more permissions than the Users group has. Also, non-administrator users can delete or modify only accounts that they have created themselves.

Advanced Account Management Tasks

The most common administrative tasks are performed in the Users tab of the Users And Passwords dialog box. When you want more control, you can make more advanced changes to user accounts and groups, such as setting password properties or disabling users. You might also need to create new groups if you want to assign to groups permissions to files, folders, and shared network resources rather than to individual user accounts.

In Windows 2000 Professional, you perform advanced administrative duties in the Local Users And Groups snap-in, which you can most easily access by clicking the Advanced tab in the Users And Passwords dialog box and then clicking the Advanced button (see Figure 9-1).

The Local Users And Groups snap-in actually provides another way to do everything you can do from the Users And Passwords dialog box plus a few more tasks, described next. Some things work a little differently here, however. For example, when you create a new user account in the Users And Passwords dialog box, you click the Add button and run the Add New

Figure 9-1
Click the Advanced button on the Advanced Tab of the Users And Passwords dialog box to open the Local Users And Groups snap-in.

User Wizard. In this case, the new user doesn't need to change the assigned password at the first logon. In the Local Users And Groups snap-in, you create a new user by clicking New User on the Action menu and filling in the New User dialog box that appears. In this case, however, the default behavior is to force the user to change the password at first logon.

Changing Password Properties

For each user account, you can set three password options, described in Table 9-2.

Table 9-2 User Account Password Options

Option	Description
User Must Change Password At Next Logon	Users will be prompted for a new password when they next log on.
User Cannot Change Password	Disables password changes (used for low-priority or temporary users).
Password Never Expires	Disables the password timeout, which requires users to change their password after 42 days.

What Is a Snap-In?

Windows 2000 Professional consolidates most advanced administration chores into a single user interface called the Microsoft Management Console (MMC). You can think of MMC as a sort of tool holder into which you snap different tools for different jobs. The MMC itself is just a shell that works very much like Windows Explorer— a panel on the left shows the console tree (an expandable hierarchy like the folders in Windows Explorer) and a panel on the right displays or lets you edit the contents of whatever is selected in the left panel.

What's cool about MMC is that it enables you to use a single user interface to access any administration task in Windows 2000 Professional. Each tool or service is provided as a snap-in, presenting its data in the same way as every other tool or service. Plus, the MMC can be configured with any number of tools and services. Many of the common administrative tools come preconfigured as snap-ins in an existing MMC; for example, if you double-click Computer Management in the Control Panel's Administrative Tools folder, you'll see an MMC configured with several snap-ins. Another example is the Local Users And Groups snap-in (shown in Figure 9-2) accessed from Users And Passwords in the Control Panel, among other places.

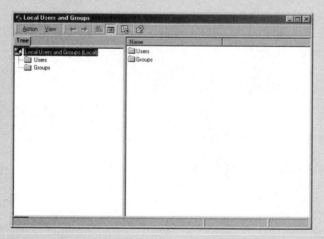

Figure 9-2

The Local Users And Groups snap-in lets you manage accounts.

> ### What Is a Snap-In? (*continued*)
>
> You can create your own custom consoles by adding to an MMC just the snap-ins you use, and you can even distribute custom consoles—if you can find anyone who'd want such a thing (administrators will love this). Chapters 20 and 21 in "Part 7, Advanced Administrative Tasks," cover more details of using the built-in MMC tools and creating your own consoles.

To change password properties:

1. In the Control Panel, click Users And Passwords, click the Advanced tab, and click the Advanced button. A console with the Local Users And Groups snap-in appears.

Tip

You can also access the Local Users And Groups snap-in by clicking Administrative Tools in the Control Panel, clicking Computer Management, and then expanding Local Users And Groups under System Tools.

2. In the console tree in the left pane, click Users to view all of the local users on the system.

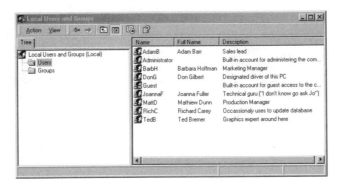

3. Double-click a user account in the right panel to open the Properties dialog box for that user.

4. On the General tab, select one or more of the first three password property check boxes (note that some options are mutually exclusive). You can click the question mark button and then click on the check box to get more information about any of these options.

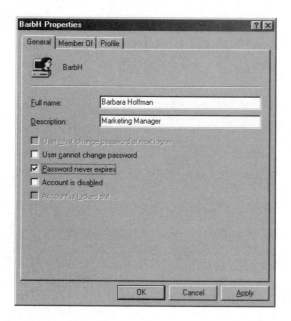

5. Click OK.

Disabling an Account

You can disable an account in the user account Properties dialog box in a similar manner to changing the password properties.

To disable an account:

1. In the Control Panel, click Users And Passwords, click the Advanced tab, and click the Advanced button. An MMC with the Local Users And Groups snap-in appears.

2. In the Tree pane on the left, click Users to view all of the local users on the system.

3. Double-click a user account in the right pane to open the Properties dialog box for that user.

4. On the General tab, select the Account Is Disabled check box.

5. Click OK.

Creating a New Group

Typically, you'd want to use groups for setting permissions on files and folders or network resources. It's easier to add groups to security permissions than to enable or block individual users, mostly because it's easier to manage groups than individual accounts when users change organizational roles, leave your business, or are hired on.

To create a new group:

1. In the Control Panel, click Users And Passwords, click the Advanced tab, and click the Advanced button. An MMC with the Local Users And Groups snap-in appears.

2. In the Tree pane on the left, right-click Groups and choose New Group from the shortcut menu.

3. Fill in the Group Name and Description fields.

4. Click Add to add a user or another group to this group, select the name in the upper panel of the Select Users Or Groups dialog box, click Add to add the name to the lower panel, and then click OK. After a few minutes, you should see the name you've selected appear in the Members area of the New Group dialog box.

5. Click OK.

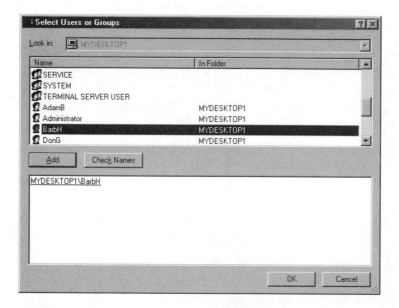

6. Repeat the previous step for all users you want to add, and then click Create to create the group.

7. Click Close to close the dialog box. Check to see that the new group you created appears in the right pane of the Local Users And Groups dialog box.

Setting Security Permissions on Files and Folders

The best way to protect data from being accessed on your computer and changed by other users is to use the NTFS file system and restrict access to specified users or groups. You cannot enable permissions on FAT or FAT32 file systems.

You grant permissions to access a file or folder by adding one or more user or group names to the Security tab in the file or folder's Properties dialog box. Then for each name you add, you can adjust permissions for activities you will allow that person or group. Permissions include activities such as reading, writing, or executing files, and listing folder contents.

Setting permissions is easy to do; the only part that can be complex is understanding how inheritance of permissions works. The sidebar on page 174 provides more information about this.

Some Considerations

You can set permissions for files or folders by adding groups or individual users. If you expect only one person in your business to access the file or folder, use that person's user name. When more than one person needs access to the files or folders, groups make this much easier to manage. As an example, if you have a folder that contains information that you want only your accounting staff to access, you can create a group called Accountants and then add to that group everyone who needs access to the folder. (In your small business, that might be only you, your partner, and the accountant who visits you, but you get the idea.) In this example, you can set permissions on the folder so that only the Accountants group can access the folder. That way, if someone leaves the group or is added to it (if you change accountants), you only have to make changes to the group, which is quite simple.

Also, while you can set permissions on individual files, it's more sensible to set the permissions at the folder level. When you set the permissions of a folder, all files and folders within that folder inherit the permissions of the folder, as do folders within those folders, and so on.

Setting Permissions

Here are the steps for setting permissions on a file or folder on your NTFS-formatted partition in Windows 2000 Professional. The example screen shots show changing the permissions on a folder called Keep Out to allow only members of the Administrators group full access to the files and folders it contains. Everyone else (as specified by the Everyone group) will be able to list the folder's contents and read files but not edit files or run programs in the folder.

To set permissions on a file or folder:

1. In Windows Explorer, locate the file or folder for which you want to set permissions.

2. Right-click the file or folder and choose Properties from the shortcut menu.

3. Click the Security tab. Notice that, by default, the built-in system group Everyone is assigned Full permissions on this file or folder.

171

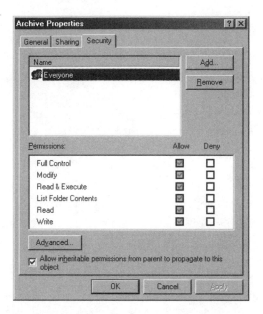

4. Clear Allow Inheritable Permissions From Parent To Propagate To This Object.

5. A Security dialog box appears asking you to decide whether you want to copy permissions from the parent folder or remove all permissions and start from scratch. You can choose either, but click Copy if you're not sure—that way nothing's lost.

6. Now you can either remove the Everyone group or change its permissions. To remove Everyone, select it and click the Remove button. To modify its permissions, select Everyone and select just the permissions in the Allow column of the Permissions area that you want to grant.

7. For each user or group you want to add, click Add, scroll the list box and select the name of the user or group, click Add, and then click OK.

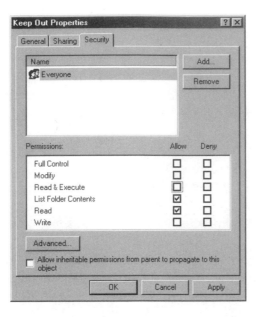

8. Set the permissions for each user or group by selecting the user or group and selecting the permission check boxes.

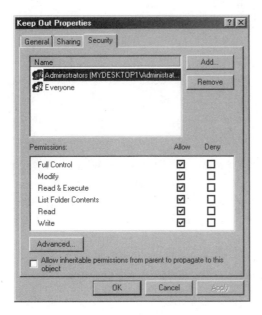

9. Click OK to close the Properties dialog box.

Permissions and Inheritance in a Nutshell

Each file or folder that you create automatically inherits the permissions of the folder or partition in which it is created. The built-in system group Everyone, which contains all users on the system, is assigned Full permission on every partition, and this is inherited by default every time you create a folder. So, by default, every user on the system has Full permission on every folder created on the partition. To restrict users, you must either remove the Everyone group from that file or folder or modify the permissions of the Everyone group for that file or folder. For example, you might change the permissions of Everyone to just a single Read permission or maybe to some combination, such as Read and List Folder Contents.

Here's the important part: You can't both modify permissions and inherit permissions. So, you must first break the link with the parent folder to stop inheriting its permissions. To do this, clear the Allow Inheritable Permissions From Parent To Propagate To This Object check box. When you do this, you're asked if you want to copy the existing permissions from the parent or remove all permissions. It's usually easiest to copy the existing permissions to the folder and then make modifications to the copy.

To summarize, you need to do three things when assigning permissions: first, break the inheritance link from the parent drive or folder; second, delete Everyone or reduce the permissions for Everyone; and third, add a user or group to the file or folder, granting the user or group Full permissions.

This chapter has covered a lot of ground, to say the least, and perhaps not all of it applies to the computers in your business. If you've read this far, however, you've learned enough about accounts and permissions to handle most tasks you'll encounter in configuring Windows 2000 Professional computers for multiple users. If some of this still seems vague, it's probably information overload—it'll be much clearer once you've set up a few accounts using the procedures described in this chapter. When you're ready to tackle the next step in securing your data, continue on to Chapter 10, which describes using the Windows Backup program.

Using Windows Backup to Keep Your Data Safe

When it comes to securing your data and operating system from harm, backing up is the ultimate safety net you can employ. Operating your small business without a working plan for backing up your computers is a gamble that's simply not worth taking. Disaster can strike in many ways when it comes to damage to files on hard disk drives—a virus, disk hardware failure, vandalism, or operator error. Fortunately, Microsoft Windows 2000 Professional provides a built-in solution to help you avoid needless loss of data: the Windows Backup utility, which makes the actual task of backing up and restoring backed up files relatively simple.

This chapter describes how to use Windows Backup to protect against losing computer files that contain your data, applications, or operating system. It includes information about creating an emergency repair disk so you can recover from an operating system that won't start, creating backups to secure the files on your computer, and scheduling those backups to run automatically. You'll also learn what to do to recover from a disaster and restore your system to a recent state.

Planning Your Backups

Planning your backups is probably the most important part of backing up. Let's face it—the only reason to back up is in case you have to restore some day and you don't want to discover the inadequacies of your backup plan when the time comes to restore. To that end, this chapter spends considerable time up front, considering the "what," "where," and "when" issues, before jumping into the "how" of backing up and restoring files.

When to Back Up

When you decide how often to back up your data, you'll need to pick an interval that works into the normal routine of your business. Breaking the process down into smaller, more frequent backups is a good way to do this. A common approach is to implement a dual backup scheme, in which you perform a major backup of everything—say, once a week—and perform intermediate backups of your data files in between—say, daily. This provides a good trade-off between ensuring the safety of your data and efficient use of your time and resources. You'll need to pick a timetable that works for your small business, but daily and weekly are good intervals to start with and they're easy to remember. You can schedule these backups to run automatically so you'll only have to remember to insert the backup medium, such as a tape.

Some small businesses might not keep enough information on their computers to warrant daily backups. On the other hand, if you have crucial data that changes drastically during the business day, you might consider backing up more than once a day—at least backing up those files that have changed since the last backup. With scheduling, you can automate the backups, but you can't back up while someone is using the data because Windows Backup won't copy open files. Unfortunately, it's usually the case that the files that you want to back up most often are the files that are open the most during the day.

What to Back Up

The easiest and safest approach is to back up everything on all of your hard disks. This takes quite some time and usually requires swapping out tapes or other media, so it isn't something you'll want to do often. You can perform smaller backup operations when you want to make sure you have the most important data on your computer safe and secure and don't want to spend the money for a robotic changer or don't want to stick around yourself to swap out tapes. Here are the smaller backup operations you should undertake, listed in order of importance. You'll learn how to accomplish these later in the chapter.

- Create an emergency repair disk (ERD) and include the registry information on that disk. This makes it possible to regain access to your computer in case of a hard disk crash or a damaged system file that won't let you start Windows.

- Back up the system state, which includes the registry, COM+ Class Registration database, and system boot files. This makes possible regaining your most recent operating system state. Back up the system state after installing applications or devices, since this option backs up drivers and registry entries they've installed.

- Back up all data files on your computer. Back up data files you haven't used for a while to a separate archive location. Devise a plan to regularly back up files you use often. If you store all your data files in folders under the My Documents folder, you'll find it easier to separate documents from the applications you used to create and edit them.

- Back up application files. Since you can reinstall applications, you can just keep the application installation disks in a safe place (preferably off-site) instead of backing up applications in between complete system backups.

Where to Back Up

You can back up your data on several types of media—tapes, removable media, other hard disk drives, or any of those same media on another computer on the network. If Windows Backup recognizes the medium, you can back up to it. While it's difficult to predict what media Windows 2000 Professional will support in the future as new storage hardware and drivers are developed, here are some of the most popular backup media today.

Good Old Dependable Tapes

For many years, tape has been the de facto standard medium for backing up computer systems. When you need to back up a lot of data (on the order of several gigabytes), tape still provides the easiest solution.

NT Backup, the Microsoft Windows NT 4.0 predecessor to Windows Backup, supported only tape. The price, capacity, speed, and availability of other media are starting to erode the popularity of tape as a backup media choice. Windows 2000 Professional reflects this trend by including the ability to back up to files on other media, in addition to tape. Nonetheless, tape backup is still cost effective when you compare dollars per gigabyte and, when you use long tapes and built-in compression hardware, it still provides the largest single media sizes. Some tapes hold as much as 24 gigabytes, enough to back up almost any hard disk drive without changing the tape. With a single tape, you can set the backup going and leave for the night—or schedule the backup to run while you're not around—without having to worry about someone being there to swap out media. If you need to back up a large database daily, you'll probably be relying on tapes.

The downside of tape drives is that they are slow, not only to back up to but also to recover from if you're looking for a single file that was mistakenly deleted. And tape is notoriously short-lived, with a guaranteed life span of around two years, so it's not good for archiving data.

Removable Media

Some examples of removable media are the Iomega Zip and Jaz drives and the ORB removable hard disk drive. The proliferation of removable media in recent years has brought about 250 MB Zip drives and removable hard disks with capacities of more than 2 gigabytes. Unlike tapes, removable media don't degrade for decades and are therefore excellent for archiving data as well as for making routine backups.

Compared to tapes, removable media are more expensive and might require an operator to swap media during backup, depending on the size of the removable media. If you're backing up an entire hard disk, you might need many removable disks and the storage cost per gigabyte is greater than it is with tape.

On the other hand, the longer life of disks might help offset the long-term cost. Another advantage of removable media over tapes is that you can use the media for more than backing up—for example, to give files to someone else who has the same hardware.

If your business data can fit on a removable disk drive, or you can delegate someone in your business to swap media during backups, removable media provide an excellent alternative to tapes. Most of the time, the data that's been changed in one day on any individual workstation running Windows 2000 Professional will fit on a 100 MB or 250 MB Zip drive, unless it contains huge files such as digital video or audio files. You might want to dedicate a removable disk just for daily backups and run or schedule a backup of your My Documents folder that runs every night before you go home.

A Second Hard Disk Drive

If you have an extra hard disk drive in your computer, you might consider simply backing up daily from your main hard drive to the secondary hard drive. If you do this, you'll want to back up the secondary hard disk to some other storage medium at least once a week. One advantage of this scheme is that you can be working on the files on your primary disk while the weekly backup of your secondary disk runs, as long as you don't open files on the secondary disk (Windows Backup won't copy an open file).

A Network Location

If you use a network in your office, you can choose a shared folder or removable disk drive on a computer on the network as the backup destination, or you can back up shared drives or folders on a network computer to a backup medium on your computer. However, there are some exceptions to this—system state data can only be backed up locally, for example. And although you can back up a remote computer's files to your tape drive, you can't control a remote computer's tape drive from your computer.

Using a network is a good way to back up files from computers that don't have large enough storage media to back up individually but have a network connection. In many cases, it's worth the price of the network hardware just so you can back up your older computers onto the backup medium you use for your new Windows 2000 Professional computers.

About Backup Markers and Backup Types

Each time you back up, you can choose a backup type, which determines whether the operation will copy all files and folders you've selected or only those that have changed. A default backup type, called Normal, always copies everything you've selected to back up regardless of what's changed since the last backup, so you don't have to worry about backup markers or types. For major backups, the Normal type is the best to use anyway, because you perform it less frequently and it includes everything. For intermediate backups (for example, every night), the Intermediate type is a good choice.

It's to your advantage to familiarize yourself with the backup types because using the right backup type and being selective about what gets backed up between major backups can save you time and backup media. To fully understand backup types, you need to know a little about the backup markers that some of them use.

What Are Backup Markers?

Every file in the file system contains an Archive attribute, which you can see at the bottom of the Properties dialog box when you right-click the file and choose Properties from the shortcut menu. This attribute, called the backup marker, is used by backup programs like Windows Backup. Whenever the file is modified—such as when you open it, work on it, and save it again—the backup marker is set; that is, the Archive attribute is selected in the Properties dialog box. When the backup operation runs, this marker is examined or ignored, depending on the backup type you've chosen. The Normal (default) backup type ignores markers and backs up everything you've selected, but other backup types back up only modified files. Also, depending on the backup type, the backup operation can clear the backup marker after backing up a file or leave it alone (the Normal type clears the marker). Thus, there are four possible ways a backup operation can deal with the backup marker and a backup type for each of these possibilities. When you select the appropriate backup type, a backup operation can

- Read the backup marker and clear it after backing up the file (Incremental).

- Ignore the backup marker and clear it after backing up the file (Normal).

- Read the backup marker and leave it alone after backing up the file (Differential).
- Ignore the backup marker and leave it alone after backing up the file (Copy).

Understanding Backup Types

Windows Backup provides five backup types—four corresponding to the four ways of handling the backup marker, and one that ignores the marker and uses a time stamp to determine what to back up. You can select any of these when creating a backup rather than use the default backup type. Table 10-1 describes these backup types.

Table 10-1. Backup Types in Windows Backup

Backup Type	Action	Backup Marker Read?	Backup Marker Cleared?
Copy	Copies selected files and folders regardless of markers. Used for major or intermediate backups, but copies everything and shouldn't be used in conjunction with backup types that rely on backup markers.	No	No
Daily	Copies selected files and folders changed that day, regardless of markers. Used for intermediate backups and shouldn't be used in conjunction with backup types that rely on backup markers.	No	No
Differential	Copies selected files and folders that have markers set but doesn't clear markers. Preferred for intermediate backups but not for major backups.	Yes	No
Incremental	Copies selected files and folders that have a marker set and clears the marker. Used for intermediate backups but not for major backups.	Yes	Yes
Normal	Copies selected files and folders regardless of the markers and clears all markers. Preferred for major backups but not efficient for intermediate backups.	No	Yes

So how do you make sense of these backup types when it comes to devising a backup plan? If you're using a dual backup approach—that is, doing a major backup periodically and intermediate backups in between—you'll want to choose a major backup type that clears the markers so that intermediate backups can determine what's been modified since the last major backup and back up only those files. The two backup types that clear markers are Incremental and Normal. Normal is typically used for major backups, since it grabs everything regardless of backup markers.

Which type should you use for intermediate backups? Since these backups are meant only to pick up changes between major backups, using Normal for intermediate backups would be overkill. Daily is a good option, but only if you're sure that it's performed every day (if you miss a day, you could lose data). Copy also works for intermediate backups but it ends up copying everything, not just what's changed, so it makes for larger backups than necessary. Incremental works well since it copies only what has changed each day. The problem here is when you want to restore—you first need to restore the last major backup, and then you have to restore in order every Incremental backup since the major backup. If it's been four days since the last major backup, this could be a lot of tedious work!

That leaves the Differential type, which is generally the best to use for intermediate backups. Differential copies only what has changed since the last backup that cleared the markers (which would be the last major backup if you used the Normal backup type). If you need to restore, you just restore the last major backup and the last Differential backup. The only downside is that Differential backups are redundant—that is, a file changed on Monday is backed up every day until Friday's major backup clears the marker.

How to Perform a Backup

You can perform a backup immediately or schedule a backup job for later, using the Backup Wizard or the options on the Backup tab. The Backup Wizard takes you through all of the steps in a prescribed order, but using the options on the Backup tab is just about as easy.

Backing Up Using the Backup Wizard

The Backup Wizard leads you through the steps of creating a backup job. To schedule the job, complete these steps and continue on to "Scheduling Automated Backups," on page 188.

To create a backup using the Backup Wizard:

1. Click Start, point to Accessories, point to System Tools, and click Backup. The Windows Backup utility appears.

2. Click Backup Wizard to start the wizard, and then follow the steps. The wizard walks you through the steps of determining what to back up. You can choose to back up everything, selected files, or the system state data.

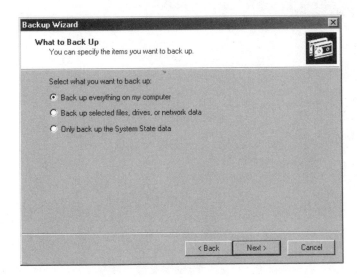

If you choose to back up selected files, you'll be able to select the drives, folders, and files or network data that you want to back up. Note that if you choose to back up only system state data, this will take over 200 MB of storage (you can't back up just part of the system state data using the wizard). The wizard will then ask you where to back the data up (if you don't have a tape drive, the default will be File) and you'll select a backup medium or file name.

Tip

If you use Windows Backup to back up files from another computer on the network, make sure the folders or drives that you want to copy from are shared with Full access on the other computer. By default, Windows Backup will clear backup markers after backing up the file and it needs at least Write access to do this.

---

3. When you reach the page titled Completing The Backup Wizard you can click Finish to start the backup or click Advanced to select more options.

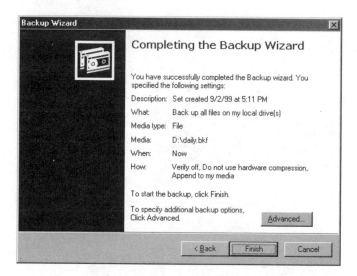

Here are the reasons to click the Advanced button before clicking Finish:

- To change the type of backup. The most important thing to select in Advanced is the type of backup, if you want a type other than the default.

Note

While Windows Backup deems selecting a backup type an advanced task (that is, under the Advanced button), it's something you should do if you're performing intermediate backups and want to be efficient.

- To set Backup to verify what was backed up or to enable hardware compression if your tape drive supports it. Both of these are good ideas—although verifying a backup takes time, it's better to know ahead of time if the backup is not good. Also, using compression on a tape gives you more storage per tape and requires less tape swapping.

- To replace the current backup rather than append the backup to the current backup. Usually you'll want to replace the backup set in a tape only for major backups and only every other backup at most.

Important

You should rotate media every other week so that you don't overwrite your only backup copy each week. Keep a tape labeled Odd Week and one labeled Even Week.

- To change the labels placed on the backup set you're producing or the backup medium you're creating or over-writing. The default labels give you a description such as "Set created 3/22/00 at 11:00 PM," but you'll probably be better off with a name that's more descriptive, such as "Set of Daily Backups: My Documents". The media label is used only if you're creating the backup the first time or overwriting an existing backup file. You can also give media labels more recognizable names such as "Daily Backups on Even Weeks."

- To schedule a backup for later. *See "Scheduling Automated Backups," on page 188, for more on this.*

4. Click Finish to start the backup or to exit the wizard if you've scheduled a backup job for later.

Backing Up Using the Backup Tab

While the Backup Wizard walks you through the backup process, it's really not complicated to go right to the Backup tab and run the Backup utility directly. The following procedure sets the same backup properties as the Backup Wizard.

To create a backup using the Backup tab:

1. Open Windows Backup and click the Backup tab.

2. Select the check boxes next to the drives, files, or folders you want to back up. To back up everything on the computer, expand My Computer and select every check box next to every drive under My Computer. To back up the system state, select just the System State check box. By default, backing up the system state requires over 220 MB of storage space (unless you disable System Protected Files—see step 7).

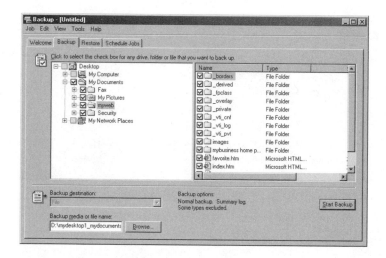

3. Select the backup destination and backup medium or file at the bottom of the window.

4. If you want, you can save your backup job by clicking Save Selections As on the Job menu and choosing a name for the backup job. You'll need to save the job if you want to schedule it, although you'll be prompted to save later if you forget.

Tip

It's a good idea to save backup jobs you've created even if you don't want to schedule them, so you can easily recall them later using Load Selections on the Job menu and run them at any time.

5. Click Start Backup to start the backup. The Backup Job Information dialog box appears.

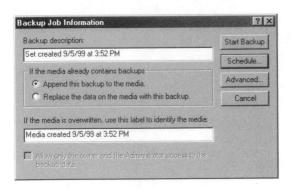

6. At this point, you can change the backup description, which is placed on the backup set, to something that describes your backup, or you can keep the default that's provided. You can also change the default media label if you're creating a new backup or overwriting an existing backup.

7. Click Advanced if you want to modify the backup type, verify the data after backing up, back up data in Remote Storage (a library and media management service), or enable compression if it's supported by your tape drive. (These are the same options as in the Advanced part of the Backup Wizard.) If you've selected System State as part of your backup, click Advanced to choose not to back up System Protected Files (the operating system files) with the system state. Click OK in the Advanced Options to accept changes you've made.

Note

Backing up the System Protected Files with your system state can add to the backup over 200 MB of files from your %SystemRoot% folder (WINNT/ System32). This option is selected by default, but you can clear it in the Advanced Backup Options dialog box. It can't be cleared when you run the Backup Wizard, however.

8. Click Start Backup to immediately begin the backup, or click the Schedule button to schedule a backup for a future time. *See "Scheduling from the Backup Tab," on page 188, for the steps to do that.*

Scheduling Automated Backups

One of the biggest improvements over the NT Backup utility in Windows 2000 Professional's Backup is the addition of scheduling. Setting up a scheduled backup is easy and, once it's set up, you can view your schedule in a calendar on the Schedule tab.

Scheduling a Backup

When you want to perform a backup at a specified time, either once or repeatedly, Windows Backup makes it easy to schedule the backup.

Note

Any tasks that you schedule in Windows 2000 Professional show up in Scheduled Tasks in the Control Panel. Use the Scheduled Task Wizard in that folder for scheduling other programs but use Windows Backup to schedule backups.

Scheduling tasks has no wizard—if you're running the Backup Wizard, just click Advanced at the last page and continue until you get to the When To Back Up page. Then click Later and click the Set Schedule button. If you're not using the wizard, you create a backup, click Start Backup, and then click the Schedule button. Both of these paths lead to the same Schedule Job dialog box, where you set the schedule.

Scheduling from the Backup Tab

To schedule a backup without using the wizard, follow the steps in "Backing Up Using the Backup Tab," on page 185, save the backup job by clicking Save Selections As on the Job menu, and then follow these steps:

To schedule a backup job from the Backup tab:

1. Click Start Backup.

2. When the Backup Job Information dialog box opens, click Schedule. The Scheduled Job Options dialog box appears. (If you haven't saved your job, as previously suggested, you'll be prompted to do so and you'll be provided with the Save Selections dialog box.)

3. Enter a Job name.

4. Click Properties. The Schedule Job dialog box appears. Follow the steps in "Setting the Job Schedule," on page 190, to complete the schedule.

Scheduling from the Backup Wizard

To schedule a backup, you can simply run the Backup Wizard and create a backup job. Then, at the final page, click Advanced and continue through the wizard pages until you reach the When To Back Up page. Follow these steps to set up a schedule at this point.

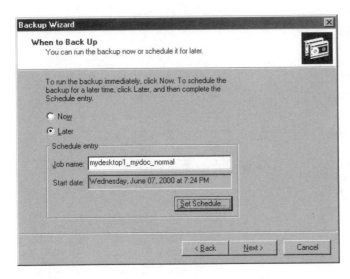

To schedule a backup job from the Backup wizard:

1. On the When To Back Up page of the Backup Wizard, click Later.

2. Enter a job name.

3. Click Set Schedule. The Schedule Job dialog box appears. Follow the steps in "Setting the Job Schedule," next.

Setting the Job Schedule

The Schedule Job dialog box appears when you click the Set Schedule button in the Backup Wizard. It also appears when you click Start Backup on the Backup tab, click the Schedule button, and then click Properties.

1. From the Schedule Task drop-down list box, choose when you want the task to run. In most cases, after you select a schedule task option, the section in the dialog box below the Schedule Task list box changes so you can select more options.

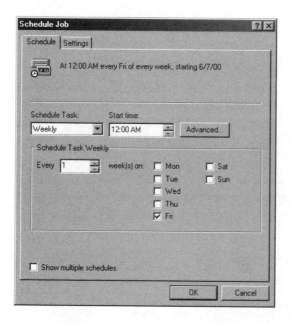

Table 10-2 describes the options in the Schedule Task list and the kinds of controls that become available when you select those options.

Note

If you need to run a backup more often than once a day or only for a specified period of time, click the Advanced button. Here you can fill in the start and end dates for the task and how often to repeat it daily, if at all.

Table 10-2. The Schedule Task Options

Schedule Task Option	Description
Weekly	Runs the job on selected days of the week and at a selected interval measured in weeks.
Monthly	Runs the job on selected months on the specified day of the month.
Once	Runs the job once at a specified date.
At System Startup	Runs the job when the computer starts.
At Logon	Runs the job after a logon.
When Idle	Runs the job when the computer has not been used for a selected number of minutes.

2. Below the Schedule Task drop-down list on the Schedule tab, select the options for the task you chose in the previous step. It's best to pick a time when files will be closed and nobody will be working with them. Make sure all programs that open files you are backing up are closed before any scheduled backup.

3. Click the Settings tab if you want to make any adjustments. On this tab, you can

    •   Have the job delete the task after it's run once if it's not scheduled to be run again.

    •   Have the job stop the task after it has run for a specific period of time (for instance, you might want it to time out if a problem occurs).

    •   Specify how many minutes to wait when the computer is idle before starting a backup.

    •   Specify whether to stop the backup if someone starts using the computer after it's been idle.

    •   Specify Power Management options for backing up, such as whether to prohibit the backup when a portable is running on batteries or stop the backup if it switches to battery mode. Also, if the computer is in sleep mode, specify whether to wake the computer so the backup can run.

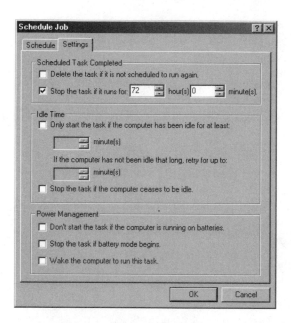

4. Click OK when you're finished setting the schedule. If you were running the Backup Wizard, this returns you to the wizard, where you click Next and then Finish. If you're setting up a schedule on the Backup tab, this returns you to the Schedule Job dialog box. Click OK and the scheduled job will be created.

5. Click the Schedule Jobs tab to view on a calendar the schedule you just created.

Note

When you schedule a backup, make sure all the files on the computer you're backing up are closed before the scheduled time arrives. If you schedule the job to run after you leave, make sure you tell anyone else using that computer to be sure to close all files and, preferably, log off.

Viewing Scheduled Jobs

To view all the scheduled backup jobs in a calendar (see Figure 10-1), click the Schedule Jobs tab in Windows Backup. You'll see an icon for a backup task on every day that you've scheduled it to occur. Normal backups are marked with an N, Differential backups are marked with a D, and so on. If you scheduled the backup to run based on a system event, such as during idle time or when logging on, the icon will be labeled System Event and it will appear at the lower right.

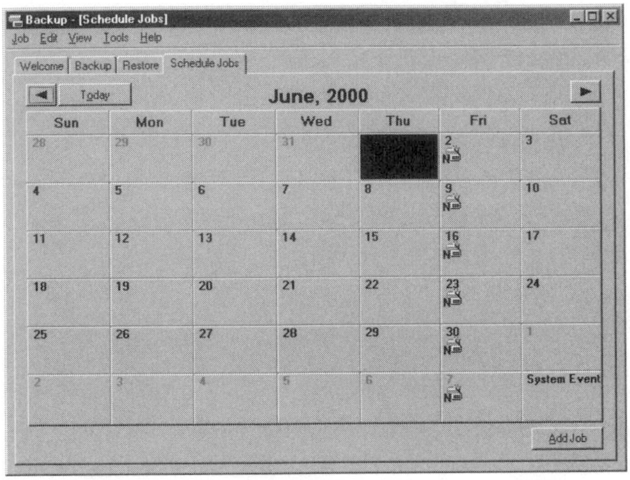

Figure 10-1

Icons for backup jobs appear in the Schedule Jobs Calendar.

If you let the mouse pointer hover on an icon in the calendar, you'll see the name of the job. If you click the job, a Scheduled Job Options dialog box appears where you can

- Rename or delete the job.

- Click the Backup Details tab to view a description of the job, including all of the options you've chosen for it and the location of the backup file you'll be backing up to.

- Click Properties to open the Schedule Job dialog box and change the schedule or the settings (these are the same controls you originally used to set up the schedule). One extra tab appears here; it enables you to run virtually any task, not just a backup. This is fairly advanced, however, and not likely to be used by most users.

Creating an Emergency Repair Disk

One of the most fundamental safeguards is to create an emergency repair disk (ERD) in the event that you suffer damage to the operating system and can't boot. An ERD takes only a few minutes to create and it can save you immeasurable grief in recovering your Windows 2000 Professional system if system files are damaged and you can't run Windows.

To create an emergency repair disk:

1. Insert a blank, formatted floppy disk in the A: drive.

2. Click the Emergency Repair Disk button in the Welcome tab of Windows Backup.

    In the Emergency Repair Diskette dialog box, you can select the check box if you also want to back up the registry. The registry contains information about your installed devices and programs and it's a good idea to back it up.

Note

You'll also back up the registry when you back up the system state, so be sure to restore the last system state you backed up after you recover the system to retrieve your latest registry settings.

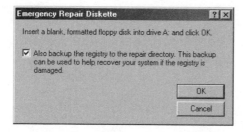

3. Click OK and wait for the files to be copied to the ERD.

4. When prompted, remove the diskette, date it, and label it "Emergency Repair Disk." Be sure to indicate which computer it belongs to and keep it in a safe, secure location, preferably off-site.

Restoring Backups and Recovering Your System

Restoring lost data is sort of like calling your insurance agent after the house has burned down—you won't do it until you have to and you hope at that time that you picked a good insurance plan. If you've created an emergency repair disk and you've been backing up your entire system once a week and your data every day, you should be in good shape if disaster strikes.

Unlike backup operations, which offer several backup types, there is only one type of restore operation, whether you run the Restore Wizard or perform the restore operation manually from the Restore tab. The basic procedure is to select the files to restore, start the restore, and sit back and watch your data come back to you.

What to Restore

You might need to restore files for a couple of reasons. If you've mistakenly deleted a document or folder, you can usually selectively restore that data by going to the last intermediate backup of the data folder if the backups were made as Daily, Copy, Normal, or Differential backup types. If your intermediate backups were made as Incremental backup types, you'll need to poke around a bit to find when the deleted file was actually backed up (an Incremental backup would have backed up the data after it was last altered and then cleared the backup marker so it would not appear in subsequent backups).

When you restore files after a major calamity, such as a hard disk crash, what you restore depends on whether you lost your operating system and your data, or your data alone. If both your operating system and data are gone, follow the steps outlined in "Restoring Your Operating System," in the next section, and then follow these steps to recover your data.

To recover your data:

1. Restore the last weekly backup you performed.

2. If the last weekly backup didn't include the system state, restore the last system state you backed up.

3. If your intermediate backups are of the type Incremental, restore every backup in order since your last weekly backup. Otherwise, if your intermediate backups are any other type, recover only your last intermediate backup.

Restoring Your Operating System

Follow these steps to recover your operating system in the event that you can't run Windows.

1. Insert the Windows 2000 Professional Setup disk in your CD-ROM drive and turn on your computer. The Setup program on the CD-ROM will start if you have a bootable CD-ROM drive.

Tip

If your CD-ROM drive doesn't boot, you'll need startup disks for setup. If you don't have them, you can create startup disks using another computer by following the steps under "Setting Up a New System," on page 48 of Chapter 3. Then insert the setup boot disk, start your computer, and follow the instructions to insert the remaining disks. Finally, continue with step 2.

---

2. Press Enter when asked by Setup if you want to continue installing Windows 2000 Professional.

3. When asked if you want to repair a damaged or corrupt system, press R for Repair.

4. When asked if you want to repair your system using the Recovery Console or emergency repair process, press R for the emergency repair process (the Recovery Console is for very advanced users).

5. Choose the Fast Repair option, unless you're an advanced user.

6. If you're using a CD, Insert the ERD in drive A: and leave the Windows 2000 Installation CD in the CD drive. (If you don't have an ERD, just leave the CD in place; however, recovery is less likely to be more successful without an ERD.) Then restart your computer.

Note

If you used startup disks, press Enter at this point if you have an ERD or press L if you don't have an ERD and follow the steps provided.

The emergency repair process will attempt to fix your system and reinstall the registry (if the registry was included on the ERD).

Restoring Files Using the Restore Wizard

Nothing about having to restore your data is painless, since accidents like losing data always seem to come at the worst times. But there's comfort in knowing your data is backed up and using the Restore Wizard makes retrieving your data at least a relatively painless process. Use the Restore Wizard to recover full or intermediate backups or just to find a single file you might have mistakenly deleted.

Tip

If you just deleted a file that you want to retrieve, remember to look in the Recycle Bin first. If it's not there, use the Restore Wizard to find it on your backup media and retrieve it.

To recover files using the Restore Wizard:

1. Place the medium from which you want to restore in the media drive.

2. On the Welcome tab in Backup, click Restore Wizard, and click Next at the Welcome screen.

3. In the What To Restore dialog box, find the media label that contains your backup sets. For example, if you labeled media for daily data backups "Daily Data Backups" and you're recovering something you've deleted, click the + symbol to expand this media name to see the sets of data backed up.

Tip

If you don't see the media name you want when restoring from a file, you can click Import File to open the Backup File Name dialog box and select a different backup file. Also, if this dialog box appears at any point asking you to enter the name of the backup file you want to catalog, just click OK unless you want to select a different backup file to restore from.

4. If the backup set name has an icon with a question mark, you can catalog it by double-clicking it. For example, when you restore from a file, the Backup File Name dialog box appears; just click OK. If the backup file name doesn't match your backup set, click Browse and find the backup file name that does match.

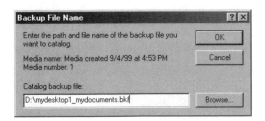

5. Select the check boxes next to the folders and files you want to restore and click Next.

6. Look at the final screen of the Restore Wizard to confirm where you're restoring from and whether existing files will be replaced if encountered. If you want to change the destination location, overwrite existing files with the backed up files, or restore from a Removable Storage database (a very advanced option) click Advanced and follow the wizard. Otherwise, click Next to begin the restore process.

Restoring Files Using the Restore Tab

While you can use the Restore Wizard to restore files, the Restore tab provides everything in one place and it's about as easy to use.

To restore a backup using the Restore tab:

1. Click the Restore tab in Windows Backup.

2. In the area on the left, find the media label that contains your backup sets.

3. If the backup set has an icon with a question mark, you need to catalog it to examine the contents, which you can do by double-clicking it.

Note

When restoring from a file, a Backup File Name dialog box appears with the name of the last file cataloged (not necessarily the one you just double-clicked!). If the backup file name doesn't match your backup set, click Browse and find the backup file name that does—it will be on the backup media. Click OK. The contents of the backup file should appear.

4. Select the check boxes next to the folders and files you want to restore.

5. Under Restore Files To, select where you want to restore the files to. If you select anything but Original Location, an Alternate Location box appears. Enter the location you want to restore to, either by typing it or by clicking the Browse button to locate it.

6. On the Tools menu, click Options. On the Restore tab of the Options dialog box, select how you want the restore operation to treat files that it encounters when restoring. The default is to not overwrite files, but you can choose to replace files if they are older than the restored version, or to always replace files. Click OK to close the Options dialog box.

7. Click Start Restore. In the Confirm Restore dialog box, click OK. (Click Advanced only if you understand this option and you're using the advanced Removable Storage feature.)

Other Backup Topics

You can find more information about the following topics in Windows Backup Help. These subjects require advanced administration knowledge, and they're most often used by businesses running client/server networks:

- Using the Removable Storage service to manage multiple sets of removable media.

- Backing up files to Microsoft Exchange Server.

- Using the ntbackup command to perform backup operations from the command line.

- Setting permissions and user rights for backing up files.

- Understanding the implications of restoring NTFS data on a FAT volume (losing information).

- Examining Backup Reports.

- Setting Backup Options.

With your data secured against catastrophe, you're done with a crucial part of keeping Windows 2000 Professional running and you'll sleep better for having taken the time to back up your data. If you've read the other chapters in this part, you've also taken the important security steps of setting up user accounts. Now you can move on to the next part of this book, which helps you get connected to the Internet and use the e-mail and fax services built into Windows 2000 Professional.

Part 4

Connecting a Computer Online

Step One: Connect to Your Internet Service Provider

The first and most important step you'll take in connecting to the Internet is connecting your computer to an Internet service provider (ISP). You might already have an existing ISP connection in your office and only need to transfer that account to your Microsoft Windows 2000 Professional computer. Or you might be signing up for the first time, choosing a new ISP, or wondering what broadband connection types are available, such as ISDN (Integrated Services Digital Network), DSL (Digital Subscriber Line), or cable modem.

This chapter describes the types of connections you can make to the Internet and details the steps of setting up a connection, whether you use a phone-line dial-up connection or connect to an ISP through a local area network. If you're using a dial-up connection, you should verify that your modem is working and then run the Internet Connection Wizard to set up the connection to your ISP. The Internet Connection Wizard sets up all dial-up accounts for an Internet connection and also enables your Internet e-mail accounts. While this chapter describes the dial-up connection setup, Chapter 12 describes the e-mail portion of this wizard, which you can run independently or as an extension of setting up your Internet account.

Choosing an Internet Connection

Internet service providers link customers to the Internet by routing digital information between customers' computers and computers on the Internet. As a customer you have many choices for connecting to an ISP, depending on factors such as the type of physical wiring you use (phone line or cable), how fast you need to connect, what level of security you need, and how much you want to spend.

Data travels both downstream and upstream on an Internet connection. Downstream flow occurs when you browse Web pages. Upstream flow occurs when you send e-mail, for example. Each connection type offers a different speed (or *bandwidth*); the downstream speed is typically the more important of the two unless you're hosting a Web site, which requires data going equally fast in both directions.

The following sections describe the common types of Internet connections available for businesses today. Not all are supported by every ISP, so you'll need to shop around.

Phone-Line Dial-Up Connection

This is the ubiquitous dial-up connection employed by most home users and many small businesses that have modest Internet requirements. A dial-up connection uses a standard, copper wire phone line and modem to connect with a service provider. When you want to connect to the Internet, you dial the ISP and validate a user name and password. Downstream speeds peak at 56 Kbps (normally slower than this however, due to line noise and other factors) and upstream rates are 33.6 Kbps at best. Most of this chapter deals with configuring phone-line dial-up connections—the other types are usually installed by the ISP or require specific instructions from the ISP to install.

ISDN Connection

ISDN uses copper wire phone lines to provide voice and data transmission at speeds of either 64 or 128 Kbps for basic rate service, with higher speeds available through PPP (Point-to-Point Protocol) multilink dial-up connections (an advanced configuration). Many ISPs offer compression to double the lower bandwidth basic service. This service is provided by an ISP in conjunction with the local phone company.

Downstream and upstream transmission speeds are equivalent on an ISDN connection and, although this is technically a dial-up service, the connection is made almost instantaneously with authentication taking just a few seconds, so it's similar to a constant connection. Connections to the ISP are made through an ISDN adapter and network terminator and typically require an additional telephone line. The Windows 2000 Professional hardware compatibility list contains several ISDN adapters, many of which are plug and play. As a technology, ISDN is the oldest digital network service and it's installed worldwide. While there's some debate about DSL replacing ISDN, it'll likely be around for quite a while.

Tip

You can find an excellent tutorial on ISDN on the Web at *www.microsoft. com/windows/getisdn/*.

DSL Connection

DSL (Digital Subscriber Line), also known as xDSL, ADSL, HDSL, SDSL, VDSL, IDSL, and others, uses a standard copper phone line with a splitter to provide telephone and Internet access at the same time. This service is provided by an ISP in conjunction with the local phone company. The DSL line connects to a modem, which connects to a network interface card (NIC) in your computer.

Transmission speeds for DSL vary depending on the acronym: ADSL is capable of downstream speeds from 1.5 Mbps up to 8 Mbps and upstream speeds of up to 1 Mbps; HDSL provides downstream traffic at up to 1.5 Mbps but has much lower upstream rates; SDSL is a symmetrical service, meaning that downstream and upstream transmissions are equally fast (from 144 kbps to 1.1 Mpbs), which is great if you're hosting a Web site from your office.

A DSL connection maintains Internet access at all times—you don't need to dial up. Unlike cable modems, the DSL network connection isn't shared by other users in your area so transmission speeds don't decrease with added subscribers, and your computer isn't vulnerable to outside computers' gaining access to shared resources. If you're connected to a network in your office, you'll need a second, dedicated NIC for your DSL connection.

Cable Modem Connection

Provided by the local cable company, or a cable company in conjunction with an ISP, this service uses television cable to offer upstream speeds of up to 2.56 Mbps and potential downstream transmission speeds of up to 30 Mbps (although more realistically in the range of 1 to 3 Mbps, depending on factors such as the cable operator, the modem brand, and the number of users). A cable connection is essentially a (local area network) LAN connection, so you'll need a NIC in your computer connected to a cable modem that, in turn, connects to a LAN in your neighborhood. This neighborhood LAN provides a proxy (also called a firewall) to connect to the larger cable network and eventually to the Internet. The proxy server provides security against users outside the neighborhood and also caches Web pages so that Web pages previously downloaded by anyone on the neighborhood LAN are accessed faster from the proxy server. This is exactly the same way many large companies set up their network access to the Internet.

Unfortunately for small businesses, this arrangement lacks security because any files shared on your computer or office network can be exposed to anyone on the neighborhood network unless they are password-protected. If you have a network in your office, you can avoid exposing shared files on your network by using a separate NIC for your cable modem connection rather than plugging the cable modem directly into the hub, and by using a proxy or NAT firewall solution. Also, because Internet access is shared through a single point by all users in your neighborhood LAN, the transmission speed for individual users decreases as more users are added to your neighborhood.

PPP Multilink Dial-Up Connections

Windows 2000 Professional supports multiple device dialing for dial-up connections. If you have multiple modems or ISDN adapters installed and your ISP supports PPP Multilink connections, this feature enables you to achieve much wider bandwidths for Internet connections by increasing upstream and downstream transmission speeds.

Verifying that Your Modem Works

Before you create a dial-up connection to your ISP using a phone-line - modem, it's a good idea to be sure your modem is actually working and can dial out.

Try Registering Windows 2000 Professional

One easy way to check your modem is simply to register your copy of Windows 2000 Professional on line. Because online registration doesn't rely on dialing rules and uses a known-good toll-free connection, it provides a great opportunity to check the basic setup of your modem and phone connection—not to mention getting your computer registered at the same time! If this works, you'll know that your modem is recognized by the system and working, and also that the phone-line connection is working. If you encounter any problems with connecting to your ISP later, you can rule out basic modem setup errors, which comprise the majority of communication configuration problems.

You might already have registered your computer because Windows 2000 provides a Register Now button in the Getting Started application that runs at startup. If so, you can skip the rest of this troubleshooting section and move on to running the Internet Connection Wizard. If you haven't registered yet, try it now. To open Getting Started and register on line, follow these steps.

To register your copy of Windows 2000 Professional:

1. Click Start, point to Programs, point to Accessories, point to System Tools, and then click Getting Started.

2. Click Register Now in Getting Started. The Microsoft Windows 2000 Registration Wizard appears.

3. Follow the wizard steps and enter the information required. You will eventually come to a step labeled Connect To Microsoft.

4. Click the Connect button and your modem will attempt to connect and register.

5. When it has finished registering, the Completing The Microsoft Windows 2000 Registration page will appear with a message that indicates you have successfully registered. If the message at this point tells you that registration wasn't successful, it will also offer some explanation of the problem.

Troubleshooting Your Modem

Troubleshooting a modem is no different from fixing any other problem—use the "divide and conquer" method to track down the problem and solve it. Starting at the wall phone jack, the problem could be in the phone line, in a device such as a splitter or fax machine that shares the phone line, in the connection to the modem or, if it's an external modem, in the cable from the modem to the COM port or USB port. Most of these connections are easy to verify and, if they check out, you can place the problem in the modem, thereby separating cabling problems from modem or configuration problems.

Note

If you're using an external modem, did you remember to install it first? (This might seem like an all too obvious hint, but it's quite easy to forget this!) If not, run the Add/Remove Hardware wizard from the control panel to install the modem and try to register your computer again.

If you see a message indicating that there is no dial tone when you try to register, you'll need to troubleshoot the phone line connection (*see* "*Checking the Phone Line,*" *on page 209*). On the other hand, if you get a dial tone and the modem dials but the wizard reports a modem problem, read "Verifying the Connection Problem," below, to make sure that this is truly your problem and not a connection problem on the other end.

Verifying the Connection Problem

If you've tried to register and failed due to a reported modem problem, you should check whether you really do have a modem problem that will affect your Internet connection. To verify this, follow the instructions in "Signing

Up With a New Service Provider," on page 213. If your connection is working, your modem will dial the Microsoft Internet Referral Service and download a list of ISPs. At this point you can click Cancel to end the Internet Connection Wizard unless you want to sign up for a new ISP, of course. (If you click Cancel, you'll get a confirmation message asking if you're sure you want to close the wizard—click Yes.) If connecting to the Microsoft Internet Referral Service failed but you are getting a dial tone at the modem, skip to "Checking Out the Modem," below.

Checking the Phone Line

First, perform a visual check of all of your connections. If you find nothing obviously wrong, try unplugging the telephone line from your modem and connecting it to a standard telephone to see whether you have a dial tone. If you do have a dial tone, the problem is in the modem, or in the cable or port if it's an external modem. If you don't have a dial tone, continue to check for a dial tone down the line (for example before a splitter, if you have one) until you hear a dial tone. Then work backwards, replacing or reconnecting phone lines until you discover where the problem is.

Checking Out the Modem

If the problem is in the modem, it might be a configuration problem or a hardware problem. Try running diagnostics on the modem.

To check the modem configuration and run diagnostics:

1. In the Control Panel, double-click Phone And Modem Options.

2. Click the Modems tab. Notice the port that the modem is connected to. You might need to troubleshoot this port.

3. Select the modem and click Properties.

4. Click the Diagnostics tab.

5. Click Query Modem.

You'll see a series of modem commands that have been sent to the modem in the Command column (such as AT12) and the response from the modem for each command (such as OK) in the Response column. If you don't see responses, you know that the modem isn't communicating—because of configuration problems, cable problems, port problems, or a defective modem.

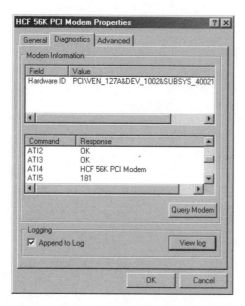

Tip

You can also use the HyperTerminal program to send individual modem commands to the modem. To do this, open the HyperTerminal program (it's on the Communications submenu under Accessories), cancel the Connection Description dialog box, and simply type each command in the connection window and press Enter. You won't see your commands unless you open Properties from the File menu, click ASCII Settings and check Echo Typed Characters Locally. The AT command should cause the modem to respond with OK, the ATH1 command should cause the modem to pick up the line so you hear a dial tone, and the ATH command should cause it to hang up.

If you can't communicate with an external modem using the modem diagnostics or HyperTerminal, try to rule out a COM port or cable problem by switching the cable to another port and or using a different cable.

If you're not getting responses from the modem, check the COM port that's associated with your modem on the Modems tab of the Phone And Modem dialog box. To examine COM ports on your computer, open the Device Manager and look at the COM port properties.

To examine COM ports in the Device Manager:

1. Double-click System in the Control Panel, click the Hardware tab, and then click Device Manager.

2. Click the plus sign next to Ports (COM & LPT) to expand the list of ports and look for the port your modem is connected to.

3. Right-click the port and click Properties on the shortcut menu to open the Port Properties dialog box.

Does the Device Status box in the General tab indicate that the device is working? If not, it could be a device driver or some other problem. Click Troubleshooter to see if the Help troubleshooter has any solutions. If the Device Status area in the Properties dialog box indicates the COM port isn't working, try clicking the Port Settings tab, clicking Restore Defaults, and then clicking OK. Keep trying the diagnostics or HyperTerminal modem commands to see if any of those fixes have worked.

Connecting to the Internet

No matter which ISP you choose, you use the Internet Connection Wizard to establish a dial-up or LAN-based connection. When you finish running the wizard you'll see an icon for your connection in the Network And Dial-Up Connections folder. Double-click that icon to start your connection.

Note

If you're setting up an ISDN, DSL, or cable connection, you should have an expert help you because broadband services typically require more expertise in configuring.

The Internet Connection Wizard (see Figure 11-1 on the next page) is almost identical in operation to its counterpart in Microsoft Windows 95 and Microsoft Windows NT 4.0.

In the spirit of making your computer an extension of the Internet, Windows 2000 Professional makes it hard to avoid the signposts to the Internet Connection Wizard when you first set up your computer. You're given the opportunity to run this wizard during the actual setup and as an option in the Getting Started application that appears at startup. Also, this wizard pops up whenever you try to run Internet Explorer until you've made a connection. If you miss these launch points, you can run the - Internet Connection Wizard at any time in a number of ways:

- Click Start, point to Programs, point to Accessories, point to Communications, and click Internet Connection Wizard.

Figure 11-1

The Internet Connection Wizard establishes your connection to an ISP.

- Click Start, point to Settings, point to Network And Dial-Up Connections, double-click Make New Connection, click Next, select Dial-Up To The Internet, and click Next.

- Click Start, point to Settings, click Control Panel, double-click Internet Options, click the Connections tab, and click Setup.

Depending on your situation, you can run the wizard to contact the Microsoft Internet Referral Service (IRS) and set up a new dial-up account on your current computer, or transfer an existing dial-up account if it's supported by IRS. Or, if you've signed up for a dial-up connection, you can use the wizard to enter information from the ISP and let it create a dial-up connection for your modem. Or you can use the wizard to connect your computer to the Internet through a local area network (LAN); this is the path you'll take if you have a network in your office with a computer serving as a gateway to the Internet.

Note

After setting up the dial-up connection, the Internet Connection Wizard steps you through the process of hooking up your e-mail. If you have any problems or questions about this, you can wait until you've read Chapter 12, which describes setting up Internet e-mail.

Signing Up With a New Service Provider

If you're using a regular modem and want to choose from a list of service providers offered by Microsoft Internet Referral Service, follow these steps:

1. Run the Internet Connection Wizard (click Start, point to Programs, point to Accessories, point to Communications, and then click Internet Connection Wizard).

2. On the Welcome page, click I Want To Sign Up For A New Internet Account. (My Telephone Line Is Connected To My Modem).

3. Click Next. The wizard dials the Microsoft Internet Referral Service and you can follow the steps to selecting a provider and plan from the list.

Connecting to an Existing Service Provider

It's quite probable that your business has already signed up with a dial-up ISP and is accessing that account from another computer. If so, you'll need to determine if that service provider's software is compatible with Windows 2000 Professional. There are really two types of dial-up services: Internet service providers, which simply provide access to the Internet, usually combined with e-mail and news (USENET) access, and online services, such as America Online and CompuServe, which provide a host of services, one of which is an Internet connection.

Windows 2000 Professional is designed to work with most ISPs. Online services, on the other hand, usually require installing a client application on your computer to enable access. If your online service or ISP (such as MSN) uses its own application and was originally installed without using the Internet Connection Wizard, check with the service to see whether the application is compatible with Windows 2000 Professional and, if so, how to transfer it to Windows 2000 Professional.

If you've already signed up with a dial-up ISP, you have two options for using the Internet Connection Wizard to create a connection: automatic or manual configuration. Manual configuration will work in any case; automatic configuration works only if your ISP is supported by the Microsoft Internet Referral Service. Before beginning, make sure you have the following information from your ISP:

*   The telephone number to dial to connect to the Internet. When you choose from a list of possible telephone numbers provided

by your service provider for your area, choose one that isn't long distance if possible and be sure to check whether you need to dial the area code first.

Tip

You can save time by testing the dial-up connection numbers before connecting your computer. Using a standard telephone, dial the number and see if it requires a long distance or area code prefix. When you hear the high-pitched modem squeal, you'll know you have the right number and the right prefixes.

- The user name you use to sign in. This name is usually the same as your e-mail name and sometimes contains the domain of the service provider preceding it, separated with a forward slash.

- The password you use to sign in.

Configuring Your Connection Automatically

If you think your service provider might be associated with the Microsoft Internet Referral Service, you can easily determine if there is an automatic configuration provided for you. While automatic configuration is only offered by a few ISPs, it might be worth checking because the wizard leads you on to the steps for manual configuration if automatic configuration is not provided.

To transfer an existing account using the Microsoft Internet Referral Service:

1. Run the Internet Connection Wizard.

2. On the Welcome page, click I Want To Transfer My Existing Internet Account To This Computer. (My Telephone Line Is Connected To My Modem).

3. Click Next. The wizard dials the Microsoft Internet Referral Service.

4. When the list of ISPs is downloaded, look for your ISP in the list to see if your service provider and plan are listed and, if so, select them. Your wizard will contact your service provider and configure your system if your service provider supports automatic configuration.

If your service provider isn't on the list, or if it is but it doesn't provide the automatic configuration service, click Next and the wizard will lead you through the manual configuration steps.

Configuring Your Connection Manually

This is the route taken by most people who have an existing dial-up Internet service provider and it's the way to go if you're fairly certain there isn't an automatic configuration or if you'd rather just do it manually.

To manually configure a connection to your service provider using the Internet Connection Wizard:

1. Start the Internet Connection Wizard.

2. On the Welcome page, click I Want To Set Up My Internet Connection Manually, Or I Want To Connect Through A Local Area Network (LAN), and click Next.

3. Click I Connect Through A Phone Line And A Modem, and then click Next.

4. Enter the area code and telephone number and choose the country or region name and code.

5. Select Use Area Code And Dialing Rules if you need to use the area code or if you need to dial some other number to access an outside line. (Dialing Rules are similar to the Windows 98 feature of the same name.) Click Next.

6. Enter your User Name and Password, and click Next.

7. In Connection Name, enter the name for this connection that you want to appear in the Network And Dial-Up Connections folder, and click Next.

8. You can continue with the e-mail portion of the wizard now by clicking Yes or you can click No to finish the wizard if you want to wait to set up your e-mail.

When the wizard ends, it attempts to connect to the Internet unless you clear that option on the final page. By default, the Dial-Up Connection dialog box appears (see Figure 11-2 on the next page) with your name and password. Click Connect and watch the connection status in the dialog box as the wizard attempts to connect.

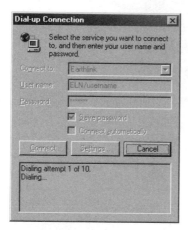

Figure 11-2

The Dial-Up Connection dialog box appears when the wizard tries to connect to the Internet.

Note

The Dial-Up Connection dialog box is provided by the system whenever an application such as Internet Explorer or the Internet Connection Wizard needs to make a connection. When you double-click a connection icon in the Network And Dial-Up Connections folder, you get a different Dial-Up Connection dialog box. The main difference between these is that, with the application-generated connection (as shown in Figure 11-2), you have the ability to work off line or configure it to connect automatically when it's needed.

If you have problems connecting to your ISP, you might have entered an incorrect telephone number or password, or you might be using dialing rules incorrectly. To make changes to your ISP account information, open the Internet Properties dialog box by following the steps that follow.

To check or change the telephone number or other properties of your dial-up connection:

1. In the Control panel, double-click Internet Options.

2. In the Internet Properties dialog box, click the Connections tab and select the dial-up connection.

3. Click the Settings button to open the Connection Settings dialog box. Here you can change the user name, password, and domain.

4. Click Properties to change the telephone number and enable or disable dialing rules. To add, modify, delete, or change the order of alternate phone numbers, click the Alternates button.

5. Click OK to close the dial-up connection's Properties dialog box, and then click OK to close the connection's Settings dialog box.

Configuring Multiple Device Dialing

If your ISP supports connecting through multiple devices and you have multiple modems or ISDN adapters, you can use the PPP Multilink dialing feature in Network And Dial-Up Connections to manage these devices and increase your connection bandwidth. This is an advanced feature, but implementing it isn't complicated.

To set up Multilink, you'll need to manually configure the dial-up connection by right-clicking the connection icon in Network And Dial-Up Connections and clicking Properties on the shortcut menu. If you've selected multiple modem or ISDN adapter devices on the General tab, Multiple Devices will be enabled on the Options tab. You can then choose when you want multiple devices dialed by clicking one of these options:

- Dial Only First Available Device—dials only one device for the connection.

- Dial All Devices—dials all devices at the same time.

- Dial Devices Only As Needed—monitors the activity level of the connection and dials or hangs up extra lines as needed. If you choose this option, you should click Configure and set the Automatic Dialing and Automatic Hang-Up properties to tell the system at what level of activity you want to engage or disengage additional devices.

Connecting to the Internet Over a Network

You can use the information in this topic if you are connected to a network in your office and one of the computers is acting as a gateway to an Internet connection. That computer might be another Windows 2000 Professional computer (or a Microsoft Windows 98 Second Edition computer) using Internet Connection Sharing. Or it might be another computer using third-party gateway software, such as Wingate (*www.wingate.deerfield.com*), an example of a gateway that uses proxy technology, or SyGate (*www.sybergen.com*), which, like Internet Connection Sharing, uses a technology called network address translation (NAT).

Note

This procedure doesn't address the specific steps you'll need to install and configure a DSL modem or cable modem. Although both of these use a NIC in addition to a modem and they're technically LAN Internet connections, the connection is typically installed and configured by the ISP or requires specific documentation from the ISP to configure.

To configure a connection to your service provider using a LAN connection:

1. Run the Internet Connection Wizard.

2. On the Welcome page, click I Want To Set Up My Internet Connection Manually, Or I Want To Connect Through A Local Area Network (LAN), and then click Next.

3. Select I Connect Through A Local Area Network (LAN), and click Next.

4. You now have a choice of automatic or manual configuration. In most cases you'll select Automatic Discovery Of Proxy Server. If your network is connected to the Internet through Internet

Connection Sharing or proxy software on another computer, this should be all you need to do. Select Use Automatic Configuration Script only if your network administrator has set this up for you. Clear both options under Automatic Configuration and select Manual Proxy Server if you know the proxy address and port number to use. Click Next. Go to step 6 if you're using automatic configuration.

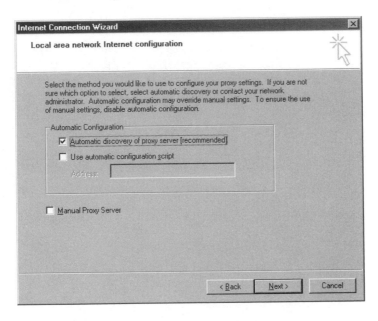

5. If you chose Manual Proxy Server in the previous step, enter the proxy server address and port number for each of the Internet services. This page enables you to set different proxy addresses and ports for different Internet services, but that's a highly unlikely scenario—you can probably just fill in the top one and select Use The Same Proxy For All Protocols. Click Next.

6. Choose whether to set up your e-mail.

Using Your Internet Connection

Most of this chapter has concentrated on getting connected to the Internet in Windows 2000 Professional. How you actually use the Internet is mostly dependent on the programs you choose to use when you're on line.

Windows 2000 Professional comes with many built-in Internet tools as part of Internet Explorer 5.0, including the Internet Explorer Web browser itself, the Outlook Express e-mail editor, the NetMeeting communications program, and others. Microsoft Press provides several good books that cover these tools, including *Quick Course in Microsoft Internet Explorer 5* and *Running Microsoft Internet Explorer 5*. Of course, programs to access the Internet are plentiful these days, so you have a wide selection to choose from if you don't want to use the built-in solutions.

Because e-mail is an important tool for small businesses, the next chapter describes the basics of connecting with and using Windows 2000 Professional's built-in e-mail program, Outlook Express.

Chapter 12

Step Two: Hooking Up Your E-Mail

E-mail is one of the best reasons for using the Internet. While e-mail use has been prevalent in large-scale businesses for quite some time, primarily for internal communication, small businesses have been slower to embrace the technology. However, now that e-mail accounts have become as common as cellular telephones, many small businesses are using e-mail as an efficient way to communicate with vendors, customers, employees, consultants, potential hires, and many other business contacts. E-mail is also useful for keeping current by subscribing to mailing lists that provide periodic, up-to-date information on specific fields of interest.

Microsoft Outlook Express is the component in Microsoft Windows 2000 Professional that handles e-mail (technically, it's part of Microsoft Internet Explorer 5.0). Outlook Express has far too many features to cover in a single chapter, so this chapter will concentrate on just the basics to get you up and running and using e-mail on your Windows 2000 Professional computer. You'll learn

- How to set up e-mail accounts, including importing existing e-mail and address books into Outlook Express.

- How to set up multiple e-mail accounts on a single computer.

- How to use Outlook Express for basic e-mail services to read, reply, forward, compose, and send e-mail messages.

- How to create and use contacts and the Address Book.

Configuring Outlook Express

You'll first need to configure Outlook Express to use your e-mail account. This assumes that you've already signed up with an ISP and have an e-mail account name (if not, see Chapter 11). If you have multiple e-mail accounts, you'll also need to set those up with Outlook Express, as described in this section.

Setting Up a Single Account

If you've already run the Internet Connection Wizard to set up a dial-up ISP account (see Chapter 11), you'll recall that the wizard asked if you wanted to set up e-mail. If you declined to set up your e-mail account then, you can set up the account now.

Note

If your ISP provides a setup program that is specified to work with Windows 2000 Professional, use that program to set up your e-mail instead of using the following procedure.

Before starting, you will need the following information from your ISP (typically they will have setup instructions that include this information):

- Your e-mail address. This address is composed of a name (with no spaces), followed by the "at" sign (@), followed by the domain name of the ISP. For example, a typical entry might be something like joeuser@myispoffersfreeemailtousers.com.

- The name of your incoming mail server. This will be something like mail.myispoffersfreeemailtousers.com.

- The type of your incoming mail server (whether it's POP3 or IMAP). IMAP servers maintain e-mail on the server and POP3 servers download it to your computer.

- The name of your outgoing mail server. This might be the same name as your incoming mail server.

- The account name provided for you by your ISP for your e-mail. This will often be the same as the first part of your e-mail address (joeuser, for example).

- The password provided for you by your ISP for e-mail (we'll use the password apple99 as an example).

- Whether your ISP requires you to log on using Secure Password Authentication (SPA).

With all of this information in hand, you can now run the Internet Connection Wizard to set up Outlook Express.

To configure Outlook Express as your e-mail program:

1. Start Outlook Express (click the Outlook Express icon on the Quick Launch toolbar, or click Start, point to Programs, and then click Outlook Express). This will start the Internet Connection Wizard if your computer has not yet been configured for e-mail. Click Next.

2. On the Your Name page, type your name in the Display Name box. This name will appear in the e-mail programs of people to whom you send e-mail (for example, *Joe User*). You can use the name of your business if you'd like. Click Next.

3. On the Internet E-mail Address page, type the e-mail address provided to you by your ISP. Click Next.

4. On the E-mail Server Names page, select the incoming mail server type from the drop-down list (most often this is POP3). Then type the names of the incoming and outgoing mail servers in the appropriate boxes. Click Next.

5. On the Internet Mail Logon page, type your account name and your password (such as *joeuser* and *apple99*). If you share your Windows 2000 user account with other people and you don't want them to read your e-mail, clear Remember Password. Then you'll have to enter your password each time.

6. If your ISP requires you to log on with Secure Password Authentication, select the Log On Using Secure Password Authentication (SPA) check box.

7. Click Next and then click Finish to close the wizard.

Setting Up Multiple E-Mail Accounts

If more than one person in your business accesses the Internet, you'll probably want multiple e-mail accounts so that each person has a private mailbox. You can use a single ISP connection with multiple e-mail accounts—most ISPs offer extra e-mail addresses as part of their service, sometimes with an additional fee. Even in a small business, this can be a very effective way to send out reminders, memos, or other information to employees—an e-mail service through an ISP can be used for both internal and external communication.

If the employees in your business have separate computers, they can set up connections to the ISP used by your business (preferably through the local area network) and configure their e-mail accounts as described previously in "Setting Up a Single Account." However, even if people share computers, they can still access separate e-mail accounts. You can set up multiple e-mail accounts on one Windows 2000 Professional computer using Outlook Express in two basic ways:

- You can run separate versions of Outlook Express in individual Windows 2000 Professional user accounts. This provides maximum privacy at the price of requiring each user to log on to Windows 2000 Professional to access e-mail (which often means logging someone else off and shutting down running programs). *See "Setting Up Multiple E-Mail Accounts," on page 224, to learn how to set this up.*

- You can run Outlook Express in a single user account and use separate identities. This is handy if you have one computer that is used by several employees and you don't want them logging on and off and connecting and disconnecting from the ISP just to check their e-mail. *See "Creating Identities," on page 226, for more information about this approach.*

Configuring Outlook Express in User Accounts

Configuring Outlook Express in separate user accounts on one computer is mostly a matter of getting the dial-up connection to work in each user's account. Once that works, you just set up your e-mail account as described in "Setting Up a Single Account." Assuming that you've set up an ISP account

What About Using Hotmail?

Another approach to providing separate e-mail accounts for employees is to use a Web-based e-mail program such as Microsoft Hotmail. Employees can then manage their own e-mail through an Internet browser such as Internet Explorer without logging off. One disadvantage to this approach is that Web-based e-mail is sometimes slower to access than ISP-based e-mail, so you may encounter a productivity bottleneck. You can even set up your Hotmail account through Outlook Express and use Outlook Express to manage that e-mail account. (To sign up for a new Hotmail account, on the Tools menu, click New Account Signup, and then click Hotmail.) The advantages of Web-based e-mail are that it's a free service, paid for by advertisements, and it can be accessed from any computer that has an Internet connection (even Internet connections in airports and cyber cafés). This might be ideal if employees typically access several different computers connected to the Internet during the work day and you don't want to set up individual e-mail accounts on each one.

for the primary user of the computer, or the administrator, how do you enable other users to access this ISP connection from their individual accounts? The answer is two basic ways—by enabling the administrator ISP dial-up connection for that user, or by setting up a private dial-up connection to the ISP from the user's account.

The dial-up connection that you created in the Network And Dial-Up Connections folder when you the ran Internet Connection Wizard as a member of the administrators group is automatically available in all user accounts. However, there's one big caveat here: if you haven't enabled it to prompt for a name and password, only members of the administrator's group can use the connection. Otherwise, if a user without administrator privileges clicks the dial-up connection icon, the connection will attempt to log on with the user's Windows 2000 Professional account name and with no password, which will fail.

To enable others to use the administrator's dial-up connection from any user account:

1. Log on as the administrator.

2. Click Start, point to Settings, and double-click Network And Dial-Up Connections.

3. In the Network And Dial-Up Connections folder, right-click your ISP dial-up connection and choose Properties from the shortcut menu.

4. In the Properties dialog box, click the Options tab.

5. Select Prompt For Name And Password, Certificate, Etc.

6. Click OK.

You'll need to provide the user with the correct name and password to enter when connecting to the ISP. Then log on to the user's account and make sure that person can connect to the Internet through your ISP connection. Finally, run Outlook Express, as described earlier in "Setting Up a Single Account," to set up the user's e-mail account.

The other way to get a connection to the Internet from a user's account is just to run the Internet Connection Wizard from that account and set up a private dial-up connection for that user. In this case, log on as that user, run the Internet Connection Wizard, and use all the same ISP account information you used when setting up your administrator dial-up connection. Go ahead and run the e-mail configuration portion of the wizard when you do this and be sure to save the user's dial-up connection with a recognizable name (consider putting a shortcut on the user's desktop).

Creating Identities

Identities are the solution provided by Outlook Express to solve the problem of multiple e-mail accounts. When you create an identity, it's just as if you were setting up an Outlook Express e-mail account. When you run Outlook Express, you're asked to choose the identity with which to log on and to provide a password. Identities work especially well when a single computer is shared by several employees for occasional e-mail duties and when the computer runs software that shouldn't be shut down during business hours.

To create a new identity for any user:

1. On the File menu in Outlook Express, point to Identities, and click Add New Identity.

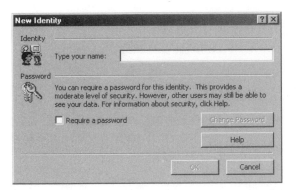

2. You can select the Require A Password check box and then enter and confirm a new password for the identity.

3. Click Yes when a message appears asking if you want to switch to the new identity. If you're currently connected to the Internet, a message appears asking if you want to keep the current connection for this identity. Click Yes unless you have a separate dial-up account for this user (which would not be typical).

4. The Internet Connection Wizard appears. Follow its steps and enter all of the information for the new e-mail account. When you are finished, the new e-mail account opens in Outlook Express as if it were a single account.

Selecting an Identity

With multiple identities in Outlook Express, each user with an identity has the option of logging on and logging off that identity. So when Mary logs on to her identity to check her e-mail and wants to exit Outlook Express, she can either log off by choosing Exit And Log Off Identity from the File menu or simply exit the program by choosing Exit from the File menu. If she chooses Exit rather than Exit And Log Off Identity, the next time Outlook Express runs, her account opens (even if it's password protected).

Note

For several users to work effectively and securely in Outlook Express, each user should click Exit And Log Off Identity when finished using Outlook Express.

Each time a user starts Outlook Express, the Identity Login dialog box appears as shown in Figure 12-1 (assuming the previous user has logged off the identity). This enables that person to select an identity and type in a password if required. To switch identities while running Outlook Express, click Switch Identities on the File menu and the Switch Identities dialog box appears (this looks the same as the Identity Login dialog box), enabling you to select a different identity. Notice that there is a Log Off Identity button here as well to enable users to log off.

Figure 12-1

You can choose your identity in the Identity Login dialog box.

Basic E-Mail Survival Kit

This section describes the essential set of skills you'll need to work with e-mail in Outlook Express. Although Outlook Express offers many options for customizing your e-mail environment, it provides defaults that work quite well for most users, making learning and using Outlook Express straightforward.

Note

For those totally unfamiliar with e-mail or Outlook Express, this section describes the most basic operations such as reading, replying to, and writing e-mail messages . For help in learning about the many features in Outlook Express, an excellent book is *Running Microsoft Internet Explorer 5*, published by Microsoft Press.

Starting Outlook Express

Starting Outlook Express is the same as starting any other program in Windows 2000 Professional, except that it normally requires an Internet connection unless you work offline (*see "Working Offline," on page 235*). Also, if you've configured Outlook Express to use multiple identities, you'll need to log on to your identity.

To start Outlook Express:

1. Click Start, point to Programs, and click Outlook Express, or click the Outlook Express icon on the Quick Launch toolbar. If you have multiple e-mail accounts enabled through identities, an Identity Login dialog box might appear to enable you to select an identity. In this case, select an identity and click OK. Outlook Express will run and attempt to connect to the mail server. If you are currently connected to an ISP, this should be successful, and you're ready to use Outlook Express.

2. If you're not currently connected to your ISP (and you're not using a LAN to connect), you'll be prompted with a Dial-Up Connection dialog box. Click Connect.

Note

If you see a dialog box that informs you that you're not connected and gives you two choices: Work Offline and Try Again, your computer is configured to use autodial, a feature of Windows 2000 Professional. Autodial is part of a service called the Remote Access Connection Manager, which is enabled in some cases, such as when hosting an Internet Connection Sharing connection. With autodial enabled, you'll see a different set of dialog boxes appear before the connection is made. Click Try Again, and then click Dial in the subsequent dialog boxes you encounter, and you'll eventually connect.

When the connection is made, Outlook Express will search for the mail server and download and upload e-mail.

Retrieving and Reading E-Mail

By default, Outlook Express sends and receives all messages when it starts up and then does so again at 30-minute intervals (you can set these options on the General tab of the Options dialog box). You can force Outlook Express to retrieve e-mail from your mail server at any time, however.

To retrieve your e-mail, click the Send/Recv button on the toolbar, or click the Tools menu, point to Send And Receive and click Send And Receive All, or just Receive All.

Tip

You can also press Ctrl+M to send and receive e-mail.

All e-mail goes to your Inbox unless you've set up rules to shuttle it elsewhere (rules are a handy but advanced subject). The Outlook Express Panel (shown in Figure 12-2) appears in the right pane of the Outlook Express window and the Folders list appears in the left pane.

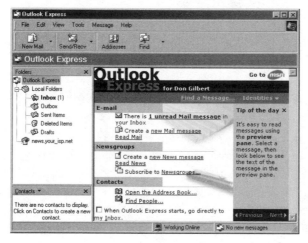

Figure 12-2
The Outlook Express Panel appears in the right pane of the Outlook Express window.

To view messages in the Inbox, click the link at the top of Outlook Express Panel on the right, which reads "1 unread Mail message" in Figure 12-2, or click Inbox under Local Folders in the Folders list.

On the right side of the Outlook Express window, the message list in the upper pane will display message headers and the preview pane beneath it will display the contents of the selected message. Outlook Express displays messages that you haven't yet opened in bold text.

To read any message, click the message header in the message list and read the message in the preview pane, scrolling it if necessary.

Tip

After five seconds, the message header loses its bold font, assuming you've read the message preview. If you want it to remain bold so you'll remember to read it later, right-click the header and choose Mark As Unread from the shortcut menu. You can adjust this five-second timeout on the Read tab of the Options dialog box.

To read a message in a separate window, double-click the message header. After you've read a message, press Esc to close it.

Replying To and Forwarding E-Mail

After reading your e-mail, you can reply to it or forward it on to someone else by clicking the Reply, Reply All, or Forward buttons on the toolbar in Outlook Express or in the message window if it is open.

To reply to or forward a message:

1. Click Reply to respond to the sender of the message, or click Reply All to reply to the sender and everyone on the To: and Cc: lines. Alternatively, click Forward to forward the message to someone else.

2. Type your reply above the original message or any information you want to include if you're forwarding the message.

3. Type the address on the To: line if you're forwarding the message.

4. Click the Send button in the message window to send the message. Alternatively, use the commands on the File menu to save the message in the Drafts folder, save it as a file, send it later, or work offline (*see "Working Offline," on page 235*).

Writing E-Mail

E-mail is easy to compose and send, which is probably one of the reasons for its increasing popularity. You can dash off a message with as much or little formality as you care to use. If you're new to e-mail, you'll need to learn the few steps to composing and sending e-mail messages, and you should also consider some of the e-mail tips provided in the sidebar on page 234.

Composing and Sending a Message

Unless you're forwarding or replying to a message, click the New Mail button on the Outlook Express toolbar to compose a message. The New Message window appears so you can compose the e-mail message, as shown in Figure 12-3.

Figure 12-3

Compose a message in the New Message window.

Tip

To address a message, double-click a contact name in the contacts list.

The following steps outline the process of creating an e-mail message. You don't have to follow most of these in one set order.

To compose a message:

1. On the To: line or Cc: line, type the e-mail addresses of the people you want to send the message to or type the names of those who are contacts in your Address Book.

2. Type a short description of your message on the subject line. This description will appear as a header when the message is received, so it should provide enough information for the person receiving it to identify the contents.

3.   Type the message in the New Message window.

4.   Optionally, use any of the buttons on the toolbar in the New Message window, as described in Table 12-1, to perform other functions. (Only the Check and Spelling buttons appear unless you make the window wider or click the chevron button at the right end of the toolbar to show more buttons.)

5.   When you're ready to send the message, click the Send button on the toolbar. Alternatively, you can save a draft of the message in the Drafts folder (*see "Saving a Message," on page 234*).

Table 12-1. Outlook Express Toolbar Button Actions

Button	Click to...
Check	Check the Address Book and replace names you've typed with e-mail addresses from the Address Book.
Spelling	Check the spelling of the message. This is highly recommended, especially in the business world.
Attach	Attach files to your message.
Priority	Change the priority of your message. By default, the priority is Normal Priority, but you can select Low Priority or High Priority to help recipients determine when they need to read the message.
Sign	Digitally sign a message (an advanced capability).
Encrypt	Encrypt (scramble) the contents of a file. This isn't normally necessary and is an advanced capability.
Offline	Work offline (*see "Working Offline," on page 235*).

Tip

When composing a message, you can format it using any of the buttons on the Formatting toolbar. For example, you can change the font and size of characters, apply bold, italic, underline, and color to characters, format paragraphs as bulleted and numbered lists, apply justification to paragraphs and even insert pictures. Be aware that Outlook Express formats text using HTML, so only e-mail programs that read HTML, such as Outlook Express and Microsoft Outlook, will display this formatting—an HTML-formatted message will be mostly unintelligible in e-mail programs that don't use HTML. For this reason, consider sending messages as plain text unless you know which e-mail program the recipient is using.

E-Mail Tips— Better E-Mail With Fewer Regrets

E-mail is fast to create and easy to forward and can quickly take on a life of its own, so before you click Send, think carefully about what you're sending.

If you're angry, compose your message but don't send it—save it as a draft. In fact don't even address it—that way you'll be writing with the safety on. Composing an e-mail message is a great way to cool off, and nine times out of ten you'll write a more constructive message the next day or not send the message at all.

Be careful using humor in e-mail with people who don't know you well—humor often falls flat in e-mail and can be easily misinterpreted. While humor can be effective in marketing and sales, it's best to leave it out of routine business messages.

Don't send messages that you wouldn't want read by customers (or their lawyer), anyone in your office, or your mother. E-mail isn't private unless it's digitally signed and even then it can be copied and forwarded by anyone it's sent to. Assume it will be forwarded to the one person you think shouldn't see it, and you'll be OK.

When replying to a message, consider removing those on the Cc: line. Most people get far too much e-mail and don't appreciate group replies (e-mail threads can get very long when everyone starts replying to everyone). In fact, Reply All should be a button you click rarely.

Keep your e-mail message short and to the point and keep your paragraphs short. Long paragraphs are hard to read and long messages often don't get read (at least not all the way through).

Saving a Message

If you're composing a message but aren't quite ready to send it, you can save it in the Drafts folder.

To save an e-mail message you're composing as a draft:

- Click Save on the File menu of the message window.

When you want to finish this saved message later, click the Drafts folder in the Folders list and double-click the message header in the message list pane to open the message.

Working Offline

If you want to compose e-mail messages while you aren't connected to an ISP, you can work offline in Outlook Express and then connect later to send your message.

To compose or edit a message while not connected to an ISP:

1. Start Outlook Express. If you aren't connected to the Internet, a dialog box should appear informing you that no connection to the Internet is currently available.

2. Click Work Offline.

3. Continue to work in Outlook Express and compose your message.

4. Click the Send/Recv button on the toolbar and a message box will appear asking if you want to go on line.

Receiving an Attachment

The ability to attach and send files is one of the best things about e-mail. You can attach files of any type to an e-mail message. The recipient of the e-mail can then open or save the attachment. Unfortunately, this capability also presents a huge hole in the security of your computer, because hackers often use e-mail attachments to spread computer viruses.

When an e-mail message in your Inbox has an attachment, a paper-clip icon appears next to it in the list of message headers. When you double-click a message header to open the message, all the files attached appear in the Attach: box in the message.

Caution

Never open an attachment unless you recognize the sender of that message. Even then, viruses sometimes replicate by sending out e-mail to everyone in an Address Book with an attachment of the virus. To be safe, save the file to a floppy disk and run a virus checker on it before opening it; or use a virus checker that scans e-mail attachments.

To save an attachment without opening it:

1. Open the e-mail message, and from the File menu, choose Save Attachments.

2. In the Save Attachments dialog box, click Browse and locate a folder in which to save the file, and then click Save.

Using Contacts and the Address Book

Typing the addresses of people to whom you're sending e-mail can take a long time and it's all too easy to type this information incorrectly. You might end up sending e-mail to a total stranger if it isn't returned by the mail server as undeliverable.

A better way to enter addresses is to build a list of contacts with whom you communicate. Then, instead of typing the entire address on the To: line, you simply type the name of a contact, and Outlook Express will substitute the actual address. With the autocomplete feature, you typically need to type only the first letter or two of the contact name and the rest is filled in for you. Also, all contacts in the Address Book show up in the Contacts list below the Folders list in Outlook Express. To compose a new e-mail message to a contact, you can just double-click the name in the list.

Creating Contacts

Every contact has a Properties dialog box that contains many tabs, including Summary, Name, Home, Business, Personal, Other, NetMeeting, Digital IDs, and Financial. Typically, you fill in only the Name tab, as shown in Figure 12-4, for most contacts.

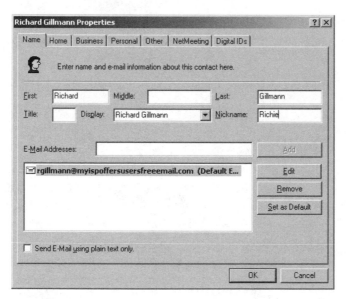

Figure 12-4
The Properties dialog box for a contact lists information about the contact.

By default, all people to whom you reply are added as contacts. In this case, instead of a nickname, the full e-mail address identifies these contacts in the Address Book or Contacts list; however, you can edit the contact properties at any time to add a name. You can also create contacts individually, one at a time.

Tip

You can disable automatic contact generation, so those to whom you reply are no longer added to the Address Book. Click Options on the Tools menu, click the Send tab, and clear Automatically Put People I Reply To In My Address Book.

Creating a Contact Manually

You can create a new contact by entering an e-mail address for someone or by using the address in an e-mail message.

To create a contact manually:

1. Click Contacts at the top of the Contacts list and click New Contact.

2. Enter the information in the Name tab of the Properties dialog box that appears.

3. Type the e-mail address or addresses in the E-Mail Addresses box, and click Add. Click OK.

When you create contacts based on e-mail messages, the Address Book does not produce a name or nickname. Instead, the full e-mail address of that contact appears in the Contacts list and the Address Book. You can edit the Properties dialog box for that contact at any time to add a name, nickname, and other information.

To create a contact based on an e-mail message:

- Right-click the e-mail header and choose Add Sender To Address Book from the shortcut menu.

To selectively add contacts based on e-mail addresses in a message:

1. Open the message.

2. Click the Tools menu in the message, point to Add To Address Book, and click one of the menu items that appears, such as Sender or Everyone On The To List.

Sending a Business Card

If you create a contact for yourself or your business, you can add your own information as a virtual business card (vcard) with every e-mail message you send. Vcard is a standard format supported by many popular e-mail programs, such as Outlook Express, Microsoft Outlook, and Netscape Messenger.

To create and send a business card with each e-mail message:

1. Create a contact (*see "Creating a Contact Manually," on page 237*) that includes all the information about yourself that you want to send. For a business, be sure to fill out the Business tab in the contact's Properties dialog box.

2. From the Tools menu, choose Options, and click the Compose tab.

3. Under Include My Business Card When Creating New Messages, select Mail.

4. Select your contact name from the drop-down list box.

5. Click OK.

When someone receives your e-mail in Outlook Express, an icon resembling a Rolodex file card appears in the upper right of the message, indicating that the message contains a business card. When the recipient clicks the icon, an Open Attachment Warning appears, enabling the person receiving it to save it to a folder or open it. When the recipient opens it, the contact's Properties dialog box appears. You can add to the Address Book any business cards you receive and open in Outlook Express by clicking Add to Address Book in the contact's Properties dialog box.

With your ISP and e-mail connections established, you've finished the basics of getting Internet connectivity to your Windows 2000 Professional computer. However, for computers with fax modems installed, there's one more basic communication hookup you might want to consider making. The next chapter describes configuring and using the Windows 2000 Professional fax service in your computer. If you don't plan on using your computer to send or receive faxes, you can skip to Part 5 for a tour of the user interface features and the Control Panel.

Chapter 13

Step Three: Setting Up the Fax Service

The fax machine is probably one of the most relied-upon communication devices in most small businesses today. Yet the fax modem, residing in just about every computer, tends to be one of the least-used devices in the computer. Computers have yet to take over the role of fax machines partially because fax machines are familiar, easy to operate, and reliable. You'll find, though, that Microsoft has built an excellent fax solution into Microsoft Windows 2000 Professional to help you get the most out of your computer's fax hardware and to help you centralize your communication activities.

The Windows 2000 Professional Fax Service makes computer-based faxing an appealing alternative to the dedicated fax machine, especially for faxing documents or information already in your computer or for dashing off quick memos or notes as faxes. Receiving faxes in your computer is also an improvement over strictly paper-based solutions, because received faxes can be stored on your hard disk as electronic media and then printed at your convenience, archived, routed to other people, and so on.

The Windows 2000 Professional Fax Service provides features that surpass most dedicated fax machines, even though many people don't use the advanced features in their current fax machines. Probably the biggest obstacle to using the advanced features of any office equipment, whether it's a fax machine, copier, or telephone, is the user interface—it's usually just too hard to remember how to use all the features of most office equipment. Windows 2000 Professional makes faxing much easier. For example, by storing fax numbers in the Address Book that's already in your computer, you can consolidate all your contact information in one place and easily recall fax numbers and other information that might be useful when faxing. Also, archiving faxes, generating cover pages, and logging fax events are automatic. Just being familiar with Windows gives you a lot of leverage when it comes to learning and remembering how to use both basic and advanced fax services.

This chapter provides an overview of the Windows 2000 Professional Fax Service to help you decide if it's a solution your small business can use. If you're already using computer-based faxing services on another platform, you'll see what Windows 2000 Professional provides and you might discover you don't need any fax software other than the service that's built in.

Sending a Fax

If you have a fax modem installed in your Windows 2000 Professional computer, your outgoing fax service is enabled by default. The default fax printer, in the Printers folder (click Start, point to Settings, and click Printers), provides faxing capabilities to any program that can print. Sending a fax is as simple as printing from a program. You don't have to create the fax printer; it's created automatically if you have a fax modem installed. When you print to the fax printer, you're presented with the Send Fax Wizard, which collects all of the required information from you (including the fax recipients' names and numbers), helps you attach a cover page if you want one, and then sends the fax immediately or schedules it for later.

Faxing a Document

You can fax anything that you can print in Windows 2000 Professional, such as word processor documents, text files, web pages and graphics, and scanned pages.

To fax a document or file:

1. Start a program that has printing capabilities for the document or file that you want to fax. For example, if you want to fax any type of file you can open in Microsoft Word, start Word and open the document.

2. Choose Print in the program, select the fax printer as the print device, and click OK. The Send Fax Wizard appears.

3. Click Next. If you've run this wizard before, continue at step 5. If this is the first time you've run the wizard, you're asked if you want to edit your user information. User information is used on the cover page, and your full name should already be in the user information (you can fill in other user information at any time). Click Edit The User Information Now or Keep The Current User Information, depending on when you want to fill in user information, and click OK to continue. If you decline to edit user information, continue at step 5.

4. If you chose to edit the user information, the User Information page appears. Enter your information and click OK.

5. On the Recipient And Dialing Information page, type the name and fax number of each person to whom you want the document faxed, and then click Add. Select Use Dialing Rules if you want to use dialing rules. Otherwise, type the entire fax number in the editable space next to Fax Number. Click Next.

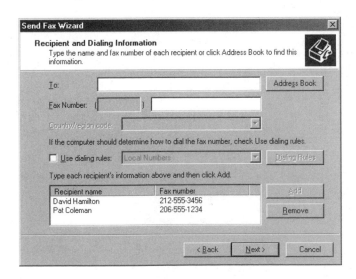

Tip

You can click the Address Book button to open and choose contacts from the Address Book. The Send Fax Wizard will accept only contacts that include a fax number in their properties. You can add a fax number to the properties of any contact in the Address Book to include a fax number by selecting the contact, clicking the Properties button, clicking either the Home or Business tab, and entering a fax number. If you've set up multiple identities in Outlook Express, each identity will have its own Address Book. If you don't see any contacts listed, be sure to click the drop-down list that displays Shared Contacts and choose your identity's Contacts.

6. If you want to include a cover page, click Include A Cover Page, select one of the cover page templates from the drop-down list, type a subject line, and include any optional notes you want to add to the cover page. Click Next.

7. On the Scheduling Transmission page, specify when you want to send the fax. You can send the fax immediately, pick a specific time to send it, or send it when discount rates apply. (The discounted time defaults to between 8:00 p.m. and 7:00 a.m. but it can be changed. *See "Setting Fax Service Properties," on page 250.*) You can also enter any billing code for your internal reference that you want at this point.

8. Click Next and review the information on the Completing The Send Fax Wizard page, and then click Finish. The fax is placed in the fax queue (see Figure 13-1).

Sending Multiple Faxes

All faxes that you create are placed in the fax queue, so you can create multiple faxes to different recipients using different billing codes if you want, and scheduled for different times of the day. Windows 2000 Professional handles all the scheduling for you.

• To view the fax queue, click Start, point to Programs, point to Accessories, point to Communications, point to Fax, and click Fax Queue.

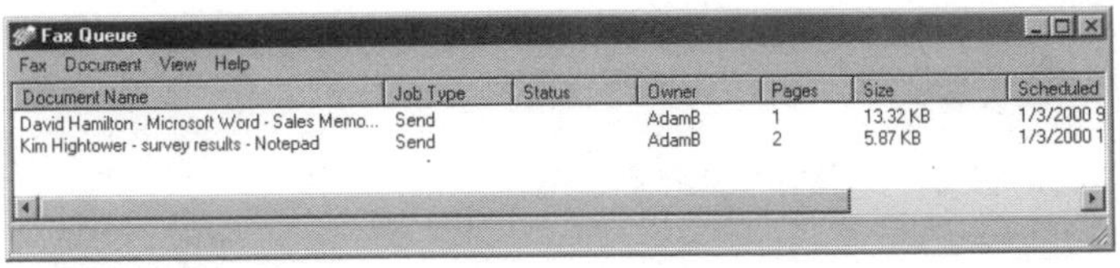

Figure 13-1

Your fax is placed in the fax queue.

You can also create multiple fax printers, although faxes you send to them all enter the same queue. The advantage of having multiple fax printers is that you can set properties for each one, such as the default time to print and a billing code. When you choose to print to a fax printer, the default print time and billing code information appear in the Send Fax Wizard, but you can overwrite them.

To create multiple fax printers:

1. Click Start, point to Settings, and double-click Control Panel.

2. Double-click the Fax icon.

3. Click the Advanced Options tab in the Fax Properties dialog box.

4. Click Add A Fax Printer. A message box tells you that the fax printer was created successfully. Click OK. Repeat this step for as many fax printers as you want to create.

5. Click OK to close the Fax Properties dialog box.

You can open the Printers folder from the Start menu and rename the new fax printers, from "Fax (Copy 2)" to "Delayed Fax," for example.

Sending a Quick Memo

Often you can communicate by just faxing a short note. You accomplish this in Windows 2000 Professional by sending a cover page as a fax.

To send a cover page:

1. Click Start, point to Programs, point to Accessories, point to Communications, point to Fax, and click Send Cover Page Fax.

2. If you have multiple fax printers, the Select Fax Printer dialog box appears. Select a fax printer from the list and click OK.

3. The Send Fax Wizard appears. Follow the wizard and enter the fax recipient or recipients, prepare the cover page by selecting a cover page template, entering a subject line and entering a note, and determining when you want the fax sent.

Working With User Information and Cover Pages

When you run the Send Fax Wizard and choose to use a cover page, you can either select one of the cover pages provided or a custom cover page that you've created. You can create custom cover pages either from scratch or by modifying one of the cover pages provided using the Fax Cover Page Editor, which runs automatically whenever you double-click an existing cover page file. The information in the coversheets comes from user information you provide the first time you run the Send Fax Wizard (or any time after that) and from information you provide about the fax recipients.

Editing User Information

Each cover page that you fax contains information from the User Information tab in the Fax Properties dialog box. Figure 13-2 shows this tab.

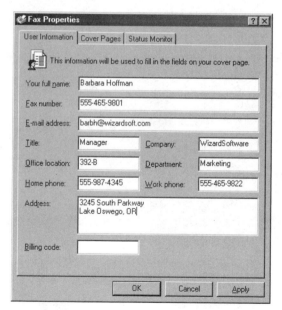

Figure 13-2

The User Information tab holds all your information.

You can open the Fax Properties dialog box to change information by following these steps:

1. Click Start, point to Settings, and double-click Control Panel.

2. Double-click Fax. The User Information tab of the Fax Properties dialog box appears.

3. Enter or change information in any of the boxes.

4. Click OK to close the dialog box and save the information.

Creating a Cover Page

You can create your own cover pages for faxes. The easiest way to do this is to start with an existing cover page.

Tip

You can also create a cover page by double-clicking Fax in the Control Panel, clicking the Cover Pages tab, and clicking New. However, this method doesn't provide an existing template to work from.

To create a cover page:

1. Click Start, point to Programs, point to Accessories, point to Communications, point to Fax, and click My Faxes.

2. Double-click the Common Coverpages folder. You'll see four cover pages: CONFDENT.COV, FYI.COV, GENERIC.COV, and URGENT.COV. You can double-click these cover pages to open them in the Fax Cover Page Editor.

3. Double-click a cover page that is close to what you want your cover page to look like (for example, GENERIC.COV). The Fax Cover Page Editor opens and the Cover Page Editor Tips dialog box opens on top of it. Click the OK button to dismiss the tip dialog box.

4. From the File menu, choose Save As. Save the file with a different name (for example, GENERIC_LOGO.COV). To make it accessible by everyone using the computer, save it in the Common Coverpages folder.

5. Now use the Fax Cover Page Editor to modify the original cover page. Try dragging information fields around, adding or deleting them and so on. Figure 13-3 shows the Fax Cover Page Editor.

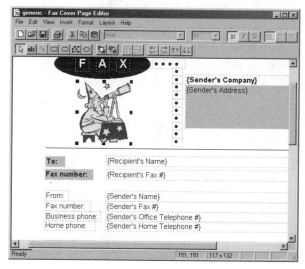

Figure 13-3

You can change the look and layout of a cover page in the Fax Cover Page Editor.

Receiving Faxes and Managing Fax Services

By default, your computer isn't set up to receive faxes. You can enable fax reception by opening the Fax Service Management Console and setting the properties for your fax modem. Enabling fax reception might be the only thing you'll want to do in the Fax Service Management Console, but you can check out other options while you're there.

The Fax Service Management Console, as shown in Figure 13-4, is a Microsoft Management Console (MMC) that provides access to all facets of the Fax Service. You can perform the following activities in this console:

- Set Fax Device properties. Click Devices in the console tree in the left pane and the right pane will display all fax devices. You can then double-click any fax device to enable or disable sending and receiving faxes or to set properties for receiving faxes.

- Set the level of detail for logged events. Click Logging in the console tree in the left pane and the right pane will display logging settings for faxes, which specify how much information is logged about various fax events that occur.

- Set Fax Service properties. Right-click on Fax Service On Local Computer in the left pane and click Properties, and you can set general properties for sending faxes, such as when discount rates apply or the number of retries to allow, and security properties (permissions) for the Fax Service.

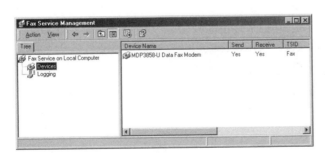

Figure 13-4

Set properties for the Fax Service in the Fax Service Management Console.

Note

By default, you must be logged on as a member of the Administrators or Power Users group to make changes in the Fax Service Management Console.

Setting Fax Receive Properties

You use the Fax Service Management Console to enable or disable sending and receiving faxes for any fax device you've installed. The console also enables you to set some preferences for receiving faxes.

To enable fax receiving and set preferences for receiving faxes:

1. Click Start, point to Programs, point to Accessories, point to Communications, point to Fax, and click Fax Service Management. The Fax Service Management Console opens.

Tip

You can also open the Fax Service Management Console by clicking the Fax Properties icon in the Control Panel, clicking the Advanced Options tab and then clicking the Open Fax Service Management Console button.

---

2. Right-click the fax device located in the right pane, and then choose Properties from the shortcut menu. The Properties page for your fax device opens.

3. To enable faxes to be received, select Enable Receive. To set the number of rings before answering the call as a fax, set the number in the Rings Before Answer option.

You can also click the Received Faxes tab to set other properties that apply when receiving faxes. By default, printing to a default printer is selected if you have a printer installed, and saving faxes to the My Faxes/ Received Faxes folder that is common to all accounts is also enabled. You can disable either option by clearing Print On or Save In Folder and you can change the printer name or select a different folder in which to save faxes. Faxes are saved as .TIF files.

Note

If you have a MAPI-enabled mail program, such as Microsoft Outlook, you might be able to select Send To Local E-Mail Inbox, which lets you route the fax as e-mail. Enabling this option entails some advanced system administration tasks that enable the Fax Service to log on to the mail client. For that reason, it's beyond the scope of this book and best left to a system administrator or advanced user.

Setting Fax Log Detail and Viewing Fax Logs

Windows 2000 Professional maintains a log of all fax activity and you can set the degree of detail that is written to the log for fax events, for the categories of Inbound, Outbound, Initialization/Termination, and Unknown events. For each of those categories, you can choose a level of detail setting.

To set a log level for any category of fax event:

1. In the Fax Service Management Control Tree, click Logging.

2. Right-click a category in the right column, such as Inbound.

3. Point to Level Of Detail on the shortcut menu and click one of the options. The None option logs no events, the Minimum option logs only severe events such as those that occur when a fax is not transmitted, the Medium option adds informational events such as attempts that were made and successful transmissions, and Maximum adds everything else.

Fax events are logged with all other application events. Application events are generated by various programs at specific times such as the start or end of an operation and when warnings and errors occur.

To view fax and other application events, open the Computer Management Console (in the Administrative Tools folder of the Control Panel). In the Console Tree on the left, expand Event Viewer (under System Tools), and then click Application. All application events appear in the right pane. Look for those with Fax Service in the Source column (you can click Source at the top to sort by Source and bring all Fax Service events together). Figure 13-5 shows the Fax Service events grouped together. *See Chapter 19, "Using the Computer Management Console," for more information on working with event logs.*

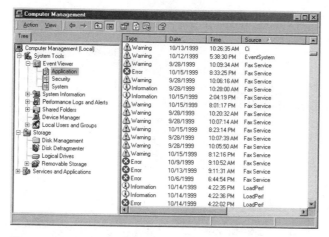

Figure 13-5

The Computer Management Console shows the Fax Service events.

Setting Fax Service Properties

You can set overall Fax Service properties by opening the Fax Service On Local Computer Properties dialog box. The controls on the General tab are mostly related to sending faxes, and they enable you to configure these options:

- The number of times to retry sending a fax
- The time interval between retries
- The number of days to keep any unsent faxes
- Whether to print a banner on each page sent
- Whether to print your Transmitting Station Identifier (TSID) on each page sent
- Where to archive outgoing faxes
- When discount rates apply

You can also disable the use of personal cover pages and allow only default cover pages. If you click the Security tab, you can set permissions for the Fax Service.

To change Fax Service properties:

1. Click Start, point to Programs, point to Accessories, point to Communications, point to Fax, and click Fax Service Management. The Fax Service Management Console opens.

2. Right-click Fax Service On Local Computer in the Tree pane, and click Properties to open the Fax Service On Local Computer Properties dialog box.

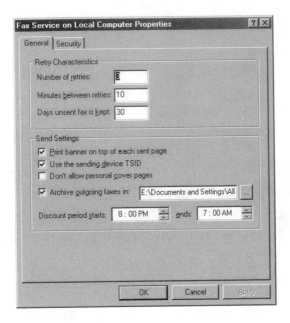

3. When you're done making changes, click OK to close and update the Fax Service properties.

More Fax Properties

In addition to the Fax Service properties and the Devices properties described above, you can use two other Properties dialog boxes that are associated with faxes. Both are called Fax Properties, but you open one from the Control Panel and the other from the Printers Folder.

Control Panel Fax Properties

When you double-click the Fax icon in the Control Panel, the Fax Properties dialog box that appears has four tabs:

- User Information—contains information used on cover pages.

- Cover Pages—provides a way to open the Fax Cover Page Editor program to create or edit a cover page that is stored in your Personal Coverpages folder.

- Status Monitor—provides options for the Fax Monitor and a window that displays the current status of a fax, and it allows you to have the next call answered by the fax machine or to interrupt a fax call. By default, this window appears whenever you send or receive a fax.

- Advanced Options—provides three buttons that enable you to open the Fax Service Management Console or the Fax Service Management Console Help, or to add a fax printer.

Fax Printer Properties

When you right-click a fax printer in the Printers folder and choose Properties from the shortcut menu, the Fax Properties dialog box that appears has the following four tabs:

- General—contains the fax name, location and comment fields. It also contains a button for printing preferences, which let you set properties such as when to fax, paper size, image quality, orientation, e-mail notification alias, and billing code.

- Sharing—not enabled, because fax printers can't be shared on a network.

- Security—enables permissions to be changed on the fax printer.

- User Information—contains information used by cover pages.

That pretty much wraps up the description of the Windows 2000 Professional communication services that you'll want to hook up right away. Next, you can move on to getting a better understanding of the user interface and Control Panel features and differences in Windows 2000 Professional by reading the chapters in Part 5.

Chapter 14

A Quick Tour of the New Windows

If you've been reading the chapters in this book in sequence, you've already had quite a lot of experience with Microsoft Windows 2000 Professional. You got a glimpse of the Windows environment in Chapter 4 and you've undoubtedly already noticed a few other things that are different from the Microsoft Windows 95 or Microsoft Windows NT 4.0 user interfaces you're used to. This chapter connects the rest of the dots to give you a more complete picture of how Windows 2000 Professional has changed and how you can use some of its new features to your advantage.

Starting with the Start Menu and Taskbar

The Start menu will be a familiar and welcome sight for anyone coming from a version of Windows released in the last five years. Windows 2000 Professional has focused on making the Start menu simpler and less cluttered and it has also made getting at anything in a folder considerably faster. Windows 2000 Professional has improved the Start menu in several ways.

- It monitors your usage of programs and automatically puts those you use most often on the main menu and those you use less often on an extended menu. This feature is called Personalized Menus.

- It makes some items optional on the Start menu and not present on the Start menu by default.

- It enables direct browsing of folders and items in folders from the Start menu.

- It includes several other more subtle changes.

  Each of these areas of improvements is discussed below.

Personalizing the Start Menu

To change any of the settings for the Start Menu, open the Taskbar And Start Menu Properties dialog box (see Figure 14-1). To do this, right-click an empty area on the taskbar and choose Properties from the shortcut menu. You can also open this dialog box by clicking Start, pointing to Settings, and clicking Taskbar & Start Menu.

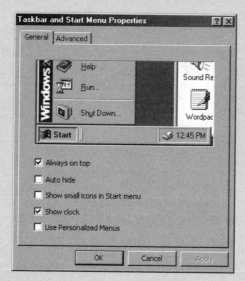

Figure 14-1

You can change Start menu settings in the Taskbar And Start Menu Properties dialog box.

Personalized Menus

The most obvious change—in fact, one that can be almost startling at first sight—is the feature called Personalized Menus. Perhaps it should have been called the Hidden Menus feature, because that's what actually happens. Two weeks after you've installed Windows 2000 Professional, you'll click the Start menu and see an information balloon titled "Where are my programs?" This balloon tells you that the programs you haven't used for a while are no longer visible on the menu but that you can easily get to them by clicking the down arrow at the bottom of the Programs menu.

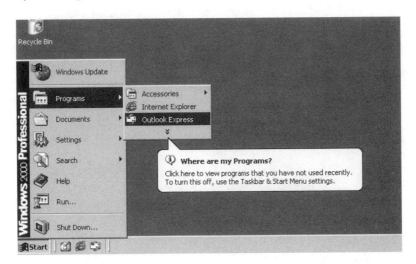

Not all users like this feature and you can easily disable it in the Taskbar and Start Menu Properties dialog box by clearing Use Personalized Menus. Before you rush to disable this feature, however, try living with it for a while; you might find you don't really miss seeing the programs you don't use all that much.

Optional Start Menu Items

By default, the Start menu doesn't display three optional menu items: Favorites, Log Off, and Administrative Tools. To add them, just open the Taskbar and Start Menu dialog box (right-click the taskbar and choose Properties), click the Advanced tab, select the appropriate check box in the Start Menu Settings area, and click OK. Figure 14-2, on the next page, shows this tab.

The check boxes to enable or disable the three optional menu items are:

- Display Favorites—Selecting this option displays the Favorites folder on the Start menu. Favorites is a list of bookmarks that originated in Internet Explorer and has migrated to Windows. While Favorites is usually associated with Internet links, you can create folders as favorites as well.

- Display Log Off—Selecting this option displays the Start menu item Log Off *username*, where *username* is the name of the current user logged on. Clicking the Log Off item then opens the Log Off dialog box so you can exit your current session (log off) or shut down.

- Display Administrative Tools—Selecting this option displays an Administrative Tools submenu on the Programs menu containing tools for advanced system administration. Because this submenu contains advanced tools, most people leave it off the Start menu and just go to the Control Panel to access the Administrative Tools folder if they need it.

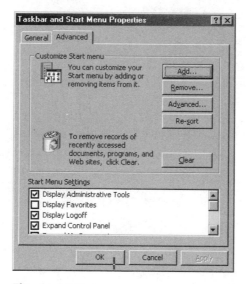

Figure 14-2
You can add options to the Start menu on the Advanced tab of the Taskbar And Start Menu Properties dialog box.

Direct Browsing from the Start Menu

In previous versions of Windows, most of us opened files by using Windows Explorer or My Computer to browse to the folder containing the file and then double-clicking the file to run the program associated with it. Of course, the other common way to open a file is to run the program from the Start menu and then click Open on the Program's File menu. Wouldn't it be great if you could combine these activities, and just open the document directly from the Start menu?

Windows 95 started down this path by placing a Documents folder on the Start menu, which gave you single-click access to the fifteen most-recently accessed files. Windows 2000 Professional has taken this one step further by letting you expand the contents of folders on the Start menu so that the folder's contents (files or other folders) appear as menu items. Once you try this, you'll probably love it—simply opening menus under your My Documents folder and then clicking on the document is definitely more convenient than opening the My Documents folder, finding the document in it, double-clicking the document, and then closing the My Documents folder.

You can apply this behavior to the My Documents folder under Documents, as well as other folders under Settings on the Start menu, which include the Control Panel, Printers, and Network And Dial-Up Connections folders. Figure 14-3, on the next page, shows opening Control Panel items directly from the Start menu.

You can make each of these folders expandable by selecting or clearing the following check boxes in the Start Menu Settings area of the Advanced tab of the Taskbar And Start Menu Properties dialog box:

- Expand Control Panel
- Expand My Documents
- Expand Printers
- Expand Network and Dial-up Connections

Enabling these folders from the Start menu can considerably speed up the time it takes to open things. A good example is the Control Panel—by expanding all Control Panel items on the Start menu, you can very quickly open any item with a single click. Also, if you keep your documents in folders within the My Documents folder, those folders will appear on the Start menu and your documents will appear listed there as well, so you can open any document with a single click.

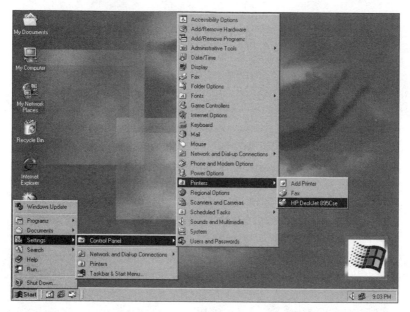

Figure 14-3

You can open items in folders from the Start menu.

Other Additions to the Start Menu

If you look closely, you'll see a few other changes to the Start menu in Windows 2000 Professional.

The most obvious one is the addition of a new folder under Settings called Network And Dial-Up Connections. You might recall a folder called Dial-Up Networking in Windows 95, buried under Start/Programs/ Accessories/Communications, which you used for creating and establishing Internet connections. In Windows 2000 Professional, this feature has been renamed and expanded in scope to handle many other types of network connections as well. Not only is this folder under Communications, it's also under Settings, where you can get to it much faster.

On the Programs menu, you'll see that the Accessories menu has an expanded set of applications under Accessibility. Table 14-1 gives a brief summary of all of the Accessibility applications available in Windows 2000 Professional.

Here's a very small change, but one worth noting: the Taskbar And Start Menu Properties dialog box provides a way to sort the Start menu by simply clicking the Re-sort button in the Advanced tab. By default, the Start menu is sorted in alphabetical order. However, you can rearrange it by dragging items around on it, just as you can in Windows 95. Unlike in Windows 95, though, you can now have the menu sorted again, if you want.

Table 14-1 The Accessibility Applications

Accessibility Application	Description
Accessibility Wizard	Helps you optimize Windows 2000 Professional to make it more accessible based on your specific needs.
Magnifier	Designed for sight-impaired users, this utility presents an enlarged view of the area close to the mouse pointer. It also offers a Properties dialog box so you can adjust the magnifier or close it.
Narrator	Reads the contents of the current window aloud to help sight-impaired users.
OnScreen Keyboard	Displays a virtual keyboard to enable users with mobility impairments to type using a joystick or pointing device.
Utility Manager	Provides a single window from which you can start and stop Accessibility tools.

Belly Up to the Taskbar

The taskbar, shown in Figure 14-4, is the area that lives at the bottom of the screen and contains the Start button. (Technically, you can make the taskbar appear on any other screen edge by dragging it there, but most people leave it at the bottom.)

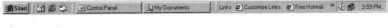

Figure 14-4

The Windows 2000 Professional taskbar contains the Start button and buttons for windows.

The Start menu pops up from a button at one end of the taskbar while the status area, which contains the clock as well as various other icons, such as Volume, sits at the other end. These two items are not optional, but several other toolbars in between them are, most of which are the same as in Windows 95. These include

- The Quick Launch toolbar, which shows icons for Internet Explorer, Outlook Express, and Show Desktop. This is the only optional toolbar that appears by default.

- The Desktop toolbar, which includes all of the icons on the Desktop.

- The Address toolbar, which provides an Internet Explorer address bar and a Go button to locate Web pages (by the WWW address) or even local files or folders (if the complete file or folder pathname is typed in).

- The Links toolbar, which provides a toolbar with the Links items from Internet Explorer for shortcuts to your favorite Web sites.

Tip

A cool and often-overlooked feature of the taskbar is that you can add your own personal toolbar, which can be any folder you select. The contents of that folder will then appear on the taskbar. To add a personal toolbar, right-click the taskbar, point to Toolbars, click New Toolbar, select a folder in the New Toolbar dialog box, and click OK. This feature is also available in Windows 95 and Windows 98.

To make changes to the taskbar, such as adding or removing toolbars, right-click any blank space on the taskbar—that is, anywhere not on a button—and select an option from the menu that appears. You'll get a slightly different menu, depending on where on the taskbar you right-click. Figure 14-5 shows the menu that appears when you right-click in any area that represents a folder, such as the Desktop toolbar. In other areas the menu doesn't contain the top five menu items.

Figure 14-5
Choose options from the taskbar shortcut menu.

The taskbar shortcut menu is identical to the equivalent menu in Windows 95 with one slight difference: In Windows 2000 Professional, you can click Adjust Date/Time on any taskbar menu to quickly open the Date/Time Properties dialog box and set the clock on your computer. In Windows 95, this is only available when you right-click in the status area of the taskbar, near the clock.

Opening, Saving, and Browsing Files

The dialog boxes that appear in most applications when you click Save As or Open on the File menu, or when you click a Browse button in some other place (such as in a wizard, for instance), are actually part of the Windows 2000 Professional user interface. When writing applications, programmers have the option of using these built-in system dialog boxes for letting users choose files and folders, or providing their own; most programs written for Windows 95, Windows NT, or Windows 2000 Professional use these system dialog boxes (although there's no guarantee that they will).

The new dialog boxes, such as the Open dialog box shown in Figure 14-6, on the next page, contain five buttons on the left side, which take you immediately to that folder or location. At the top of the dialog box, the Look In drop-down list shows the current location displayed in the dialog box. Double-click any disk drive or folder in the dialog box to open it. Click the arrow next to Look In and the drop-down list shows you the hierarchy of folders above the current location. A back arrow, to the right of the drop-down list, lets you quickly return to previous screen, and an Up One Level button lets you go up one level in the folder hierarchy.

Here are the buttons that appear in the Open, Save As, and Browse dialog boxes and a description of what they do:

- History—Click this button to see a list of all folders containing documents recently saved or opened. When you change the Files Of Type setting at the bottom of the dialog box, the list changes to include the history for those files. This defaults to your program file type, which is usually the most appropriate choice.

- Desktop—Click this button to see all the folders and shortcuts to folders on your desktop; again, the files and file shortcuts on your desktop that appear depend on what you've selected in Files Of Type.

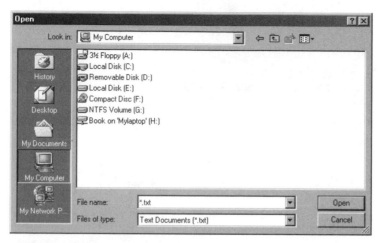

Figure 14-6

The common Open dialog box is provided by Windows 2000.

- My Documents—Click this button to see all of the files and shortcuts that apply to your file type in the My Documents folder—subfolders and links to folders are also listed.

- My Computer—Click this button to see all disk drives in My Computer. You can navigate to any of them by double-clicking the disk drive.

- My Network Places—Click this button to see all of the items in the My Network Places folder, which includes Entire Network and Computers Near Me but can also include any other network connections you've made.

What's New with Windows Explorer

Windows Explorer has adopted the Explorer bar buttons from Internet Explorer. These three buttons—Search, Folders, and History—change what's in the Explorer bar at the left side of the Explorer window. Folders is the default Explorer bar that appears when you open Windows Explorer, and History shows a daily and weekly list of the files and folders you've opened and the Web sites you've visited.

Tip

If you're used to opening Windows Explorer from the Programs menu in Windows 95 or Windows 98, you'll find it moved one menu over to the Accessories menu in Windows 2000 Professional.

History is probably the most interesting Explorer bar because, like the History button in the system Open, Save As, and Browse dialog boxes, it shows files as well as Web sites you've visited (in Internet Explorer, you need to click My Computer in the History list to view files). This further integration of the Internet with your desktop is one of the hallmarks of Windows 2000. If you can't remember where you put a file, you might be able to remember when you last used it and find it that way.

Customizing Folder Appearances

Speaking of Internet integration, the ability to view folders as Web pages came about a few years ago in Windows. However, Windows 2000 Professional has definitely made this easier to use with the new features in the Customize This Folder Wizard.

To customize any folder in Windows Explorer, open the folder, click Customize This Folder on the View menu, and then walk through the wizard that appears. The wizard provides three check boxes to tailor your customization—you can select as many as you want:

- Choose Or Edit An HTML Template For This Folder—Figure 14-7, on the next page, shows the choices you get when you select this check box and click Next. One of the cooler options, Image Preview, provides an image viewer—it's applied by default to the Pictures folder in My Documents. If you're up on your HTML, you can choose any of the options and tweak it the way you want, by selecting I Want To Edit This Template.

- Modify Background Picture And Filename Appearance—Select this option and you'll be able to select a picture for the background of the folder and colors for the text and background of the objects in the folder.

- Add Folder Comment—Select this option and you can enter any comment you'd like. The comment you enter appears as a tool tip (pop-up description) when you let the mouse hover over the folder in the Explorer and it also appears on the left when you view the folder.

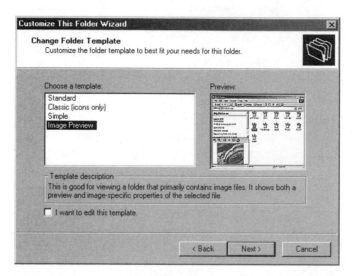

Figure 14-7

Change the appearance of folders in the Customize This Folder Wizard.

This ends the tour of the new or different user interface features found in Windows 2000 Professional. There are many more, less obvious, changes to uncover if you start examining the operating system controls more closely, and Chapter 15 does just that by describing what's new or different in the Control Panel in Windows 2000 Professional.

What's New in the Control Panel

The Control Panel in Microsoft Windows 2000 Professional provides the same types of services that it has in previous versions of Microsoft Windows. As before, it provides a central area in which you can change settings affecting most areas of the operating system. Each icon in the Control Panel represents a Properties dialog box or a folder. Sometimes you'll run a wizard from a Properties dialog box, but more often you just set properties. Folders in the Control Panel contain objects created for that folder and usually a wizard that creates the objects. The Printers folder, for example, contains printers added to your computer and an Add Printer Wizard to create them.

Coming from Microsoft Windows 95 or Microsoft Windows NT 4.0, you'll already be familiar with many of the icons in the Control Panel, so this chapter covers the new and different features, omitting features that are identical to those in both Windows 95 and Windows NT 4.0.

What's Covered Where

Because the Control Panel is central to many operations in Windows 2000 Professional, this book discusses specific Control Panel items in other chapters, while covering topics that relate to them. Table 15-1 lists the features that are described in other chapters.

Tip

To get a description of any control not covered here, click the question mark arrow in the upper-right-hand corner of the Properties dialog box and then click the control—a popup description will appear.

The Accessibility Options Control

As in Windows 95 and Windows NT 4.0, Accessibility Options in Windows 2000 Professional enables people with physical impairments to use Windows. The Keyboard, Mouse, and Display tabs of the Accessibility Options dialog box are exactly the same as their Windows 95 and Windows NT counterparts (except that the dialog box in Windows NT has no Display tab) and the Sound tab and General tabs have a few changes.

Sound Tab Changes

The Sound tab enables hearing-impaired users to request visual cues from the system when sounds are emitted. In the settings for SoundSentry, Windows 95 has an extra control not available in Windows 2000 Professional called Warning For Full Screen Text Programs, which lets you choose what part of the screen flashes in a full screen text program when a sound is emitted.

General Tab Changes

The General tab provides miscellaneous accessibility controls. Figure 15-1, on page 270, shows the General tab, which now contains an extra section named Administrative Options, with two check boxes:

- Apply All Settings To Logon Desktop—Causes the accessibility options to automatically apply to the current user at logon.

Table 15-1 Control Panel Features

Control Panel Feature	Described in	Differences
Add/Remove Hardware	Chapter 6	Similar to Add Hardware in Windows 95 and Windows NT
Add/Remove Programs	Chapter 7	
Administrative Tools	Chapter 19	New to Windows 2000 Professional, but contains advanced tools so it's covered in Part 7, "Advanced Administration Tasks."
Date/Time	No description	
Display	Chapter 4 and this chapter	
Folder Options	Chapter 18 and this chapter	Similar to Folder Options on the Start menu of Windows 95, Windows 98, and Windows NT 4.0. Offline Files is a new feature described more fully in Chapter 18.
Fonts	No description	
Internet Options	Chapter 11	
Network And Dial-Up Connections	Chapter 11	Similar to the Dial-up Networking folder in Windows 95 on the Communications menu under Start/Programs/Accessories.
Phone And Modem Options	Chapter 11	Combines Modems and Telephony from Windows 95.
Printers	Chapter 5	Similar to Windows 95 and Windows NT 4.0.
Regional Settings	No description	Similar to Windows NT 4.0 with the addition of Input Locales to the Windows 95 version. See Keyboard Properties for information on Input Locales.
System	Chapter 6, Part 6, and this chapter	Same name as in Windows 95 but quite different in layout and functionality. More similar to Windows NT 4.0 functionality.
Users And Passwords	Chapter 9	Extends capabilities of the Users Properties dialog box in Windows 95.

- Apply All Settings To Default For New Users—Causes all new user accounts to have the accessibility options applied.

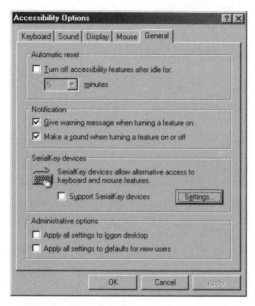

Figure 15-1

You can set miscellaneous accessibility options on the General tab.

Tip

Windows NT 4.0 users might notice a new check box under Notification named Give Warning Message When Turning A Feature On.

The Display Properties Control

The Display Properties dialog box, in which you configure how your computer screen looks and operates, is similar in most ways to previous Windows versions.

Background Tab Changes

The Background tab enables you to set a background image or pattern for your desktop. This is virtually the same dialog box as in previous versions, with slight renaming and button placement compared to Windows 95 and a different layout compared to Windows NT 4.0.

Screen Saver Tab Changes

Using the Screen Saver tab, you can enable, or set the properties of, the screen saver that appears when you're not using your computer. This tab is similar to the Windows 95 version, but the Settings button under Energy Savings Features Of Monitor is now named Power. If you're migrating from Windows NT 4.0, you'll notice that this whole Energy Saving Features area is new. Also, when you click Power, you get the new Power Options Properties dialog box, which is different from Windows 95 or Windows NT and is described in more detail in "The Power Options Controls," on page 281.

Appearance Tab Changes

The Appearance tab, on which you choose styles, fonts, and colors for Windows components, has changed the least of any Control Panel dialog box. There's one small change that might interest you, however: Windows 2000 Professional has altered its Windows Standard scheme colors slightly and created a Windows Classic scheme that contains the old Windows Standard colors.

Web Tab Changes

The Web tab, which contains the Active Desktop parameters, is virtually the same as it is in Windows 95 and Windows NT 4.0, except that the Internet Explorer Channel Bar is gone from the list of items that you can place on the Active Desktop. Also, the New Active Desktop Item dialog box that opens when you click New is much friendlier in Windows 2000 Professional and gives you the option of adding any Web page or picture from the Internet to your Desktop (that's right, visiting Microsoft's Active Desktop Gallery is optional in Windows 2000 Professional). This tab is new to Windows NT 4.0 users.

Finally, previous versions of this tab had a Folder Options button at the bottom so you could jump directly to that Properties dialog box to set options for viewing folders as Web pages. This is no longer available in Windows 2000 Professional, presumably because Folder Options is now in the Control Panel.

Effects Tab Changes

The Effects tab enables you to customize overall visual effects of items in the display, such as how menus and tool tips appear. This tab is similar to the Effects tab in Microsoft Windows 98 and the Plus! tab in Windows NT 4.0, with some changes. The new options:

- Use Transition Effects For Menus And Tooltips—Enables you to use the new fade-in effect or the old scroll effect when menu and tool tips appear.

- Hide Keyboard Navigation Indicators Until I Use The Alt Key— Keeps the underlined letters from appearing in programs, menus, and dialog boxes unless you press Alt. This feature helps to make the user interface less cluttered looking.

The following options, found in other versions of Windows, are absent in Windows 2000 Professional:

- Hide Icons On The Desktop When The Desktop Is Viewed As A Web Page (Windows 98)

- Animate Windows, Menus, And Lists (Windows 98)

- Stretch Desktop Wallpaper To Fit The Screen (Windows NT)

Settings Tab Changes

You set the screen size, color depth, font size, and advanced options of the display card on the Settings tab. The functionality on this tab is basically the same, but the layout has changed among various versions of Windows. The Windows 2000 Professional Settings tab (shown in Figure 15-2) is most similar to the Windows 98 version, providing one extra button called Troubleshoot, which opens the Display Troubleshooter in Help. Also, the Windows 98 check box Extend My Windows Desktop Onto This Monitor is missing (multiple monitors are supported in Windows 2000, but in a different way).

When you click Advanced, you get a dialog box with options that pertain to your monitor and display card, and on the General tab, you see the same controls as you do in Windows 98 (this is where you can choose the font size for the display). The Show Settings Icon On Taskbar option, found in Windows 98, is gone. In Windows 95, the Font Size controls are on the Settings tab, and a Change Display Type button is the only advanced option.

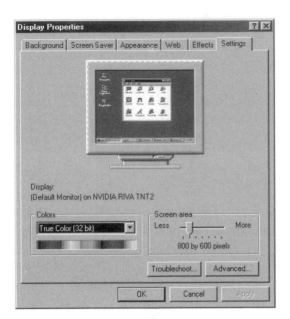

Figure 15-2

You can change size, color, font, and advanced settings on the Settings tab of the Display Properties dialog box.

If you're coming from Windows NT 4.0, several controls on the Settings tab have moved to the dialog box that opens when you click Advanced. The Font Size option is on the General tab, the List All Modes button is on the Adapter tab, and the Refresh Frequency drop-down list box has moved to the Monitor tab. Also, the Display Type button is gone; you can click Advanced and then click the Adapter tab to view or change your adapter. You'll also find that you no longer need to click a Test button to test out new display modes. Instead, after you set a new display mode, Windows 2000 Professional automatically reverts to the previous display mode within 15 seconds unless you choose to accept the new display mode.

What's Different About Folder Options

Folder Options lets you configure the way you work with files and folders in Windows 2000 Professional. The Folder Options Properties dialog box is a descendant of the Folder Options dialog box in previous versions of Windows, which you opened either from the Windows Explorer View menu or directly from the Settings menu on the Start menu. In Windows 2000

Professional, you open Folder Options in the Control Panel or from the Tools menu in Windows Explorer.

General Tab Changes

On the General tab, you can customize the way folders appear. At first look, the General tab appears totally different from previous versions, until you see that things are just moved around a bit. Formerly, the General tab had options for viewing a folder as a Web page (called Web style), or as a normal Windows folder (called Classic style), or in a Custom style when you clicked the Settings button to open a Custom Settings dialog box. Windows 2000 Professional has simply placed the contents of the Custom Settings dialog box on the General tab (see Figure 15-3) so you always change custom settings on this tab. The Web View option, which covers the two options previously on the General tab—that is, viewing folders as a Web style or as Classic style— is just one of many options on the page now.

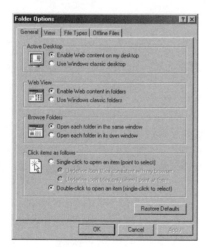

Figure 15-3

The General tab of the Folder Options dialog box contains custom settings.

The other custom settings are the same as in the Custom Settings dialog box that existed in older versions of Windows—you can enable or disable Active Desktop, determine whether folders open in their own window or not, and set whether you single-click or double-click items to open them. The General tab is missing one feature from older versions: you can no longer set one folder to Classic style and another to Web style—all folders are the same. However, if you choose the Web style, you can customize the way individual folders look by clicking Customize This Folder on the View menu in Windows Explorer or My Computer. (*See "A Tour of the New Windows," Chapter 14, for more information about customizing folders.*)

View Tab Changes

On the View tab, you can customize various attributes of the way files and folders appear. You'll see the following new options in Windows 2000 Professional:

- Display Compressed Files And Folders With Alternate Color—Helps to distinguish compressed files and folders on NTFS partitions.

- Display The Full Path In The Address Bar—Puts the path (such as C:\Program Files) in the Address bar in the Explorer.

- Hide Protected Operating System Files (Recommended)—Does not display operating system files (in the WINNT directory, by default).

- Launch Folder Windows In A Separate Process—Increases the stability of Windows at a slight cost to performance.

- Show My Documents On The Desktop—Enables you to add the My Documents icon to the desktop.

A few options found in Windows 95 and Windows NT 4.0 are not in Windows 2000 Professional, including all of the options under Visual Settings and these options:

- Allow All Uppercase Names

- Show File Attributes In Detail View

- Show Map Network Drive Button In Toolbar

File Types Tab Changes

On the File Types tab, you can associate an application with documents or files that have a particular filename extension—you do this so you can double-click the file and automatically run the program it's associated with. Applications usually install their own file type associations so most people never need to get into this kind of detail. You might need to, however, if a file type (extension) can be opened by different applications and you want to change the default association to your favorite program (for example, to change text files with the .TXT extension to always open in Word rather than in Notepad). This tab displays all the file types registered on your computer. You can select a file type and then change various properties connected with the file type, including its associated program, the icon displayed in a browser, or menu commands that appear when you right-click the file, such as Open, Print, and so on.

File Types in Windows 2000 Professional has a considerably changed user interface, but the underlying functionality is the same. The good news is that now, in order to change the program that opens the document by default, you can simply select the file type from the list (for example, a file type with the extension .TXT), click the Change button, select a new program from the list of registered programs (for example, Word), and click OK. In previous versions, the way to change associations was much less obvious.

Other changes include the layout of buttons in the tab and changes to the button names (New instead of New Type, Delete instead of Remove, and Advanced instead of Edit). The Edit File Type dialog box, which opens when you click Advanced, is virtually the same as in older versions of Windows but it also has a better layout. The Edit File Type dialog box enables you to change the icon associated with the file type and add commands to the menu that pops up when you right-click the file.

The Offline Files Tab

Offline Files is a new feature of Windows 2000 Professional that enables you to view and edit files and folders on a network when you're not connected to it. Sounds a little too much like magic? Not really. When you enable Offline Files, you can use Windows Explorer to select which network files and folders you want to have available when you're not connected to the network. Before disconnecting, you perform a synchronize operation and the files and folders you selected as offline files are copied to a cache on your computer. When you are disconnected from the network, these files appear in Windows Explorer exactly as they did when you were connected. You can work on any of these files and then synchronize when you reconnect your computer to copy any changes you made back to the original location.

This tab provides most of the controls for using Offline Files. *You can find a complete description of how to use Offline Files, including the options on this tab, in Chapter 18.*

The Game Controllers Control

You configure and test devices like joysticks and other controllers used primarily for games in the Game Controllers dialog box (shown in Figure 15-4). If your small business involves developing or selling games, or if you have a home office and use your computer to play games when you're not working, you might have occasion to visit this dialog box. I've spent more than a few hours testing game controllers myself, totally in a business capacity, of course.

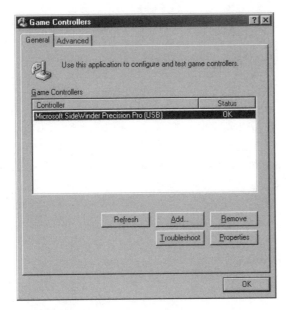

Figure 15-4

You can configure game controllers in the Game Controllers dialog box.

The Game Controllers dialog box is very close to its counterpart in Windows 95. The only differences on the surface are the added Refresh and Troubleshoot buttons. When you click Add to add a controller, you'll see the Add Game Controller dialog box and a Rudder/Pedals check box. You might also notice slightly fewer supported controllers in the list. If you click the Custom button in this Properties dialog box, you'll see that the Custom Game Controller dialog box is rearranged for easier use, but it has most of the same features as in Windows 95.

Of course, you can't compare the Game Controllers dialog box in Windows 2000 to the one in Windows NT 4.0 because Windows NT doesn't have one. Whether these advances in games technology directly help your business is anybody's guess, but it's nice to know that your computer can serve other purposes in addition to business applications, especially if you're using a Windows 2000 Professional computer in your home as part of a home office.

The Keyboard Properties Control

The Keyboard Properties dialog box, shown in Figure 15-5, provides options you can use to set various characteristics of your keyboard. Adjustments include how long to delay before characters start repeating when you hold down a key (Repeat Delay), how fast to repeat the characters (Repeat Rate), the cursor blink rate, and, on the Input Locales tab, which language you are using. In Windows 2000 Professional, the Speed tab is identical to that of Windows 95, and the Input Locales tab takes the place of the Languages tab in Windows 95. A third tab, Hardware, shows you what keyboard is detected and provides all the hardware details of the keyboard.

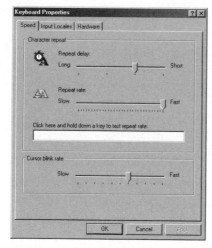

Figure 15-5

You can change how the keyboard works in the Keyboard Properties dialog box.

Input Locales Tab Changes

The Input Locales tab is very much like the Windows 95 Languages tab and the Windows NT 4.0 Input Locales tab; it enables you to add languages, which appear in the Installed Input Locales list, and configure the key sequence (keyboard shortcuts) to switch between languages. The Windows 2000 Professional version also adds the abilities to create a key sequence to switch to each of the languages in the Installed Input Locales list and to define how to turn off the Caps Lock key (by pressing the key again or pressing Shift).

The Hardware Tab

In many Control Panel dialog boxes, the Hardware tab takes the place of the General tab in previous Windows versions and provides a standardized way to access the device driver parameters. To change a driver in the old model, you clicked the Change button on the General tab. For all Control Panel items that represent hardware devices in Windows 2000 Professional, you click the Properties button on the Hardware tab to access all of the device properties. You can then click the Driver tab and click Update Driver if that's what you want.

Mouse Properties

The Mouse Properties dialog box for the standard mouse will be familiar to both Windows 95 and Windows NT 4.0 users (see Figure 15-6, on the next page).

Note

If you've installed a mouse such as the Microsoft IntelliPoint mouse, which adds its own tabs in the Mouse Properties dialog box, all bets are off for this comparison.

The Mouse Properties dialog box in Windows 2000 Professional has the same three tabs as older versions, with only slight changes on the tabs, plus the new Hardware tab.

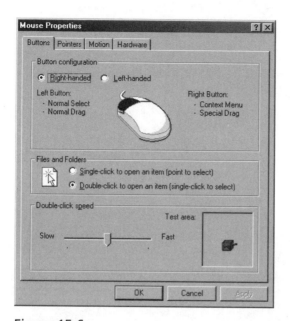

Figure 15-6

Controls for the mouse are in the Mouse Properties dialog box.

Buttons Tab Changes

The Buttons tab, where you configure how the mouse buttons function, has an additional Files And Folders option for either single- or double-clicking items to open them (you can also change this setting in Folder Options).

Pointers Tab Changes

The Enable Pointer Shadow check box on the Pointers tab, where you change the way the mouse pointer appears, enables or disables the new shadow under the mouse pointer. As in previous versions, you can change each of the pointer shapes that appears while you work in Windows, such as when you move around and select items, when you resize windows, and so on. You can save your own settings as a scheme or select from a large variety of built-in pointer schemes—unlike Windows 95, which only has a few pointer schemes.

Motion Tab Changes

As in previous versions, a control on the Motion tab changes the speed of the pointer. The Motion tab also has a new Acceleration section with None, Low, Medium, and High options. Selecting the Move Pointer To The Default Button In Dialog Boxes check box in the new Snap To Default section makes it faster to click through dialog boxes as they appear. For example, when the OK button in a dialog box is the default button, the mouse pointer is already on the OK button, so you can simply click the mouse button without repositioning the mouse pointer.

The Show Pointer Trails check box from Windows 95 is absent here. Also, Windows NT users will notice that the General tab is gone, the Snap-To Default check box has been incorporated into the Motion tab, and all other Mouse Manager controls on that tab are gone.

The Power Options Controls

Power Options is the Windows 2000 Professional name for its Power Management controls; Windows NT 4.0 does not support power management. Windows 95 users will see several differences here—namely a new Hibernate tab, a new APM tab (if your computer supports APM rather than ACPM—more about these later), and missing Power Meter and Alarms tabs.

Power Schemes Tab Changes

On the Power Schemes tab of the Power Options Properties dialog box, shown in Figure 15-7, on the next page, you can select a power scheme that applies to your computer setup. Each scheme conserves power when the computer is unattended. Three parameters specify how long to wait before turning off the monitor, turning off hard disk drives, and putting the system in a standby state. For example, a power scheme for a desktop computer usually will turn off only the display to conserve power, so only the Turn Off Monitor parameter is set. A power scheme for a portable or laptop computer typically will need to turn off the display and hard disk drive and go into standby mode to conserve power, so all of these parameters are set.

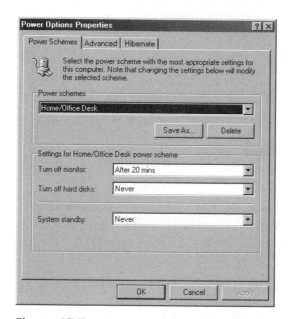

Figure 15-7

You can choose and control power schemes in the Power Options Properties dialog box.

You can alter any of the built-in power schemes just by choosing a different value in the drop-down list box next to a parameter and clicking OK. You can also create custom power schemes by altering an existing scheme and clicking Save As, and then saving it with a new name. All of this works the same as it does in Windows 95, although Windows 95 enables you to indicate separate values for a scheme depending on whether the computer is plugged in or running on batteries, and Windows 2000 Professional uses one set of values whether you're running on batteries.

Advanced Tab Changes

The Advanced tab has a new control for determining whether your computer powers off or goes into standby when you press the power button, and a check box for determining whether your computer prompts for a password when it comes out of standby. These options are available only when your computer supports the ACPM power management system, however.

Another check box on the Advanced tab enables you to put a power icon on the status area of the taskbar. You can right-click this icon to choose a scheme from a shortcut menu. You can also double-click this icon any time to open the Power Options Properties dialog box directly without the need to open the Control Panel first.

Hibernate Tab

The hibernate feature is new for Windows 2000 Professional. To enable it, you select the Enable Hibernate Support check box.

When a computer hibernates, it stores the contents of memory to the hard drive before shutting down so that it can immediately recall the previous state when it comes out of hibernation. This makes booting much faster, since the computer doesn't need to initialize. It achieves this benefit at the relatively small expense of requiring enough hard disk drive space to store your computer's memory (if you have 64 MB of memory, it allocates 64 MB of disk space to store the contents).

Hibernation is a feature that might not be built into the BIOS on your computer. If it's built in, Windows 2000 Professional takes over control of this feature from the BIOS; if not, it provides its own support. Because desktop computers derive as much benefit from this feature as laptop computers, hibernation is one area of power management worth taking a look at, regardless of the portability of your computer.

APM Tab

APM stands for Advanced Power Management, the power management scheme that is supported by Windows 95 and Windows 98. Portable computer manufacturers created software in the computer's BIOS (which is read before Windows starts) that enabled APM features. On those computers, you could press F2 before Windows loaded and make changes to the APM BIOS settings. Windows then took over this functionality when it started.

Windows 2000 Professional supports ACPM, a more advanced power management scheme based on the OnNow initiative. If your computer supports APM rather than ACPM, Windows 2000 Professional still provides partial support for some APM-BIOS features and you'll see an APM tab in the Power Options Properties dialog box. Select the check box on this tab, Enable Advanced Power Management support, to turn this feature on. If your computer doesn't have an APM BIOS, this tab won't be present.

Scanners and Cameras Properties

Scanners And Cameras Properties is a simple dialog box with one tab that shows which scanners and digital cameras are installed. It provides buttons you can click to add, delete, or review the properties of installed scanners and cameras (see Figure 15-8). Clicking Add opens the Scanner And Camera Installation Wizard, which helps you install imaging devices that Plug and Play doesn't recognize.

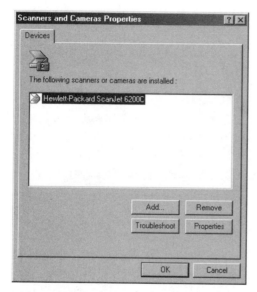

Figure 15-8

The Scanners And Cameras dialog box lets you add or remove scanners and digital cameras.

The Windows 98 version of this dialog box has an extra tab for logging scanner activities. Because this feature probably wasn't used much, it's gone in Windows 2000 Professional. Windows NT 4.0 doesn't have this icon in the Control Panel.

The Scheduled Tasks Folder

The Scheduled Tasks folder is a new feature in Windows 2000 Professional. It contains an Add Scheduled Task button which opens the Schedule Task Wizard. This wizard walks you through setting up a program to run at a specified time. It also contains entries for all the scheduled tasks you've created, either through the Schedule Task Wizard or the Windows Backup program. A clock on the icon for the scheduled task in the Scheduled Tasks folder indicates the task is enabled; an x icon indicates it's disabled.

When you run the Schedule Task Wizard, you select a program to run, determine how often you want to run it (daily, weekly, monthly, one time only, and so on), decide what time and date to start running it, give it a logon password in case you're logged off, and that's about it. You can click any scheduled task in the Scheduled Tasks folder to open a dialog box in which you can enable or disable the task, change the schedule, change the program that runs, or change other settings. You can delete a scheduled task by deleting its icon.

Scheduling Messages or Documents to Appear

The Schedule Task Wizard makes scheduling a program fairly easy, but how do you schedule something like a reminder to go to the dentist? The easiest way to do this is as follows:

1. Create a text file containing the message you want, for example "Time to go to the dentist!" and save it with a name that includes a .TXT extension such as My Documents\Reminders\dentist.txt.

2. Run the Schedule Task Wizard and, when it asks you to select a program to run, click Browse, click the History button, and click the file you just created—or browse to any other document you want opened at a specific time.

3. Set the time and account information as requested in the wizard and finish the wizard. You should see your job in the Scheduled Tasks folder.

   Even though your DENTIST.TXT file isn't a program, it's automatically associated with Notepad, so the Notepad application will appear at the time you specified and display the message you entered. At any time, you can click the job in the Scheduled Tasks folder and change its properties, such as disabling it or changing its schedule.

Chapter 11 provides details about running the Windows Backup program, which uses a different wizard to schedule backups, but uses many of the same concepts in scheduling tasks.

The Sounds and Multimedia Controls

The Sounds And Multimedia Properties dialog box combines in a single, unified set of controls two items from earlier Windows Control Panels: the Sounds icon and the Multimedia icon.

Sounds Tab Changes

The Sounds tab represents the Sounds Properties dialog box in previous versions of the Control Panel. Here you can set the sounds associated with activities in Windows and many of its programs, such as Windows Explorer. The Windows 2000 Professional version is little different from older versions in Windows, apart from some rearrangement of the controls and the Sound Volume section, which has a slider control you can use to set the general level of all sounds. It also has a Show Volume Control On The Taskbar check box (which is in Multimedia Properties in Windows 95 and Windows NT 4.0).

> ### *Tip*
>
> You can also set the volume on any audio components using the Play Control accessory. Click Start, point to Programs, point to Accessories, point to Entertainment, and then click Volume Control. This accessory has volume sliders for six different audio components. The Sound Volume control on the Sounds tab is the same as the slider labeled Play Control in the Play Control accessory. When you select Show Volume Control On The Taskbar, you can right-click the Volume icon on the taskbar and click Open Volume Controls to open this same accessory.

Audio Tab Changes

This tab provides most of the controls found in the Multimedia Properties dialog box in earlier versions of Windows. Because the older Multimedia Properties dialog box had several tabs and there is only one Audio tab, you'll find several differences. Figure 15-9 shows the Audio tab of the Sounds And Multimedia Properties dialog box.

The Audio tab has three Preferred Device sections instead of two. A new Volume button in each section opens the Play Control accessory. The Sound Playback and Sound Recording sections enable you to select a preferred device—for example, when you have more than one sound card

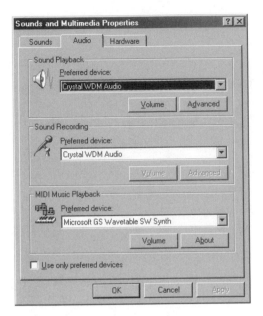

Figure 15-9

You can change audio devices on the Audio tab in the Sounds And Multimedia Properties dialog box.

installed and want to force programs to use only one of them. Each of these has an Advanced button (called Advanced Properties as in the older versions of Windows), where you can adjust performance or select other available properties.

The MIDI Music Playback section, which enables you to select the preferred MIDI playback device, is new. This takes the place of the MIDI tab in the old Multimedia Properties dialog box. The only things missing are the Windows 95 advanced MIDI features that enabled you to add a new instrument or select or create a custom MIDI configuration.

The Hardware tab replaces the Devices tab. Also, the Video and CD Music tabs in Windows 95 Multimedia Properties dialog box are gone.

System Properties: Lots of Switches, Lots of Changes

The System Properties dialog box provides a central location for many operating system controls. This dialog box is packed full of switches and dials (figuratively speaking), some of which are covered in other chapters in this book.

What's MIDI Again?

MIDI (Musical Instrument Digital Interface) is the standard that enables your computer to play music without requiring huge digitized audio files—the difference is like using a player piano roll to play music on your piano as opposed to putting on a CD of recorded piano music. A CD contains up to 600 MB of data, whereas the digital code for a piano roll would be only a few kilobytes of data—a significant difference when you're downloading files! MIDI was originally invented for synthesizer-based music, but these days even inexpensive audio cards feature MIDI-compatible sounds that are quite realistic.

Windows NT 4.0 users will notice that four tabs from their familiar System Properties are missing: Performance, Environment, Startup/Shutdown, and Hardware Profiles. The first three are now options on the Advanced tab, and the Hardware Profiles tab is now a button on the Hardware tab. That leaves just the General tab and User Profiles tabs, which are basically unchanged from Windows NT.

Windows 95 users will look for the Device Manager tab and find it missing—look for the Device Manager button on the Hardware tab instead. Also, the Performance tab is now a Performance button on the Advanced tab and Hardware Profiles is a button on the Hardware tab.

The Network Identification Tab

On the Network Identification tab, you can view the name of the computer and the workgroup or domain name of the network. You can also rename the computer and join a domain, or run a wizard to join a network. (*See Chapter 16 for more information on joining an existing network or creating your own.*) This tab is similar to the Identification tab in the Network Properties dialog box of prior versions of Windows.

The Hardware Tab

The Hardware tab combines three hardware functions under one roof and it's where the Device Manager lives, previously a tab in Windows 95 System Properties. Figure 15-10 shows this tab. Here's a description of each of the three sections.

- The Hardware Wizard button runs the Add/Remove Hardware Wizard, which is described in Chapter 6. The wizard also runs when you click the Add/Remove Hardware icon in the Control Panel.

- The Device Manager section has two buttons: The Driver Signing button opens a dialog box you can use to ignore drivers that are not digitally signed, send a warning when unsigned drivers are encountered, or prevent unsigned drivers from installing. The Device Manager button implements what occupied the Device Manager tab in the Windows 95 version of System Properties— a complete list of every device on your computer. You can double-click any device to see and change its properties. (Be careful when poking around here so you don't make unintended changes to devices on your computer.)

- The Hardware Profiles button opens a dialog box that's virtually identical to the Hardware Profiles tab in the Windows NT 4.0 version, and it adds support for multiple hardware profiles to the Windows 95 version. Hardware profiles are needed mostly for computers that dock and undock and you'll learn more about them in Chapter 18, "Connecting Your Portable Computer."

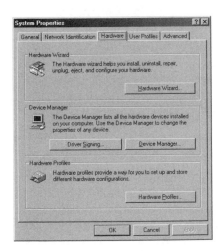

Figure 15-10

The Hardware tab in the Systems Properties dialog box shows information about the devices in your system.

The User Profiles Tab

User profiles contain the settings that stay with a user's account. Unless you're administering a domain network, you probably won't care about this tab, which involves roaming profiles associated with network administration and other advanced administration duties, such as copying an existing profile for a new user. (Roaming profiles provide the ability to store your profile on the domain server so you can log on from any computer on a domain network and obtain your desktop preferences.) This is exactly the same tab as the Windows NT 4.0 User Profiles tab. If you've implemented a domain (client/server) network in your office, your network administrator or contractor providing this service will be able to help set up user profiles if you want.

The Advanced Tab

One of the rules Microsoft engineers followed when designing Windows 2000 Professional must have been "Put the important controls up front and put everything else on an Advanced tab or button." So here's where to find everything else, namely three buttons that represent tabs previously found in Windows NT 4.0:

- Performance Options button—Opens a dialog box in which you can change whether foreground programs or background services are optimized. You can also change the paging file size (the amount of disk space that's used to extend the memory in your computer). These controls are very close to their Windows NT equivalents but fairly different from those in Windows 95, which enable optimization for hardware such as graphics adapters and disk drives, but not for background and foreground programs.

- Environment Variables button—Opens a dialog box that looks almost identical to the Windows NT Environment tab. Environment variables are not typically used by average users, however, so they won't be covered here.

- Startup And Recovery button—Opens a dialog box of the same name, providing the same controls as the Startup/Shutdown tab in Windows NT 4.0. In this dialog box, you can choose which operating system you want to start by default when you reboot in a dual-boot configuration, and how long to wait before booting to the default system from the list that's presented at startup. You can also determine what you want the system to do when it receives a fatal system error (called a STOP error). Possible options include writing an event to the system log, sending an administrative alert, writing debugging information to a selected location, and automatically rebooting.

Note

As the name of the tab indicates, the options on the Advanced tab are advanced system properties. There's probably little reason for average users to reset any of these properties.

Wireless Link

This Control Panel icon is present when your computer has an infrared communications port, which is usual only on portable computers. In Windows 98, the Control Panel item that monitors the infrared port is named Infrared, but it bears little resemblance to Wireless Link in the Windows 2000 Professional Control Panel. Figure 15-11 shows the Wireless Link dialog box.

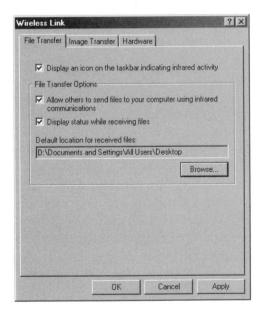

Figure 15-11
You can change how your infrared port works in the Wireless Link dialog box.

The Image Transfer Tab

On this tab, you can enable the transfer of pictures from a digital camera to your infrared port by selecting Use Wireless Link To Transfer Images From A Digital Camera To Your Computer. You can also select the folder that the pictures will be saved to after being transferred and you have the option to enable Windows Explorer to open that folder automatically after receiving pictures.

The File Transfer Tab

Transferring files between two computers with infrared links is straight-forward:

1. On the File Transfer Tab, select Display An Icon On The Taskbar Indicating Infrared Activity.

2. Position the infrared transceivers on the two computers so they're facing each other until a wireless icon appears on the taskbar and a Wireless Link icon appears on the desktop.

3. To transfer a file, select it in Windows Explorer, My Computer, or on the desktop, and drag it onto the Wireless Link desktop icon. Alternatively, right-click a file, point to Send To on the shortcut menu, and then click Infrared Recipient.

The File Transfer controls on this tab enable you to accept files sent by other computers (and set where they will go) and display the status of the transfer. When you select Display Status When Receiving Files, a dialog box opens while the files are being transferred.

The Hardware Tab

Use this tab to select an infrared device, in the rare event you have more than one, and to set hardware properties by clicking the Properties tab.

This wraps up the tour of the Windows 2000 Professional Control Panel. Few of us will memorize this vast area of controls, but you can refer to this chapter in the future whenever you need to find a particular control. For those who aren't interested in networking or advanced administration (the final two parts in this book) this is the final stop—you're ready to put Windows 2000 Professional to work in your business! The chapters in the next part of this book describe connecting Windows 2000 Professional computers in your office using a network, a direct connection, or a dial-up connection.

Chapter 16

Creating or Connecting to a Network

This chapter shows you the shortest route to setting up a simple network for your small business or connecting your new computer to an existing network in your office. While the topic of creating a network might bring to mind horrific complexities and high costs, it really doesn't need to. If your small business has light networking needs with fewer than a dozen or so computers to connect together, you can create a simple workgroup (peer-to-peer) network by buying the hardware you need from an office supply retailer and installing and configuring everything yourself. This type of network will allow computers to share files, printers, and even a connection to the Internet.

Note

If you have a network in your office, you might already be familiar with many of the basics of networking. Or maybe you've already bought a kit containing all the essential networking hardware and really just want to get it up and running. In either case, you can skip the sections of this chapter that introduce network architectures and hardware and jump right to "Configuring the Computer," on page 304, to get directly to hooking up your Windows 2000 Professional computer to an existing network.

Networks gained their reputation as a technical nightmare because they were invented for large corporate use and originally designed to serve hundreds of connected computers and terminals. Out of this necessity grew different types of networks, such as Ethernet and Token Ring, different cabling specifications and cable types, and different ways to physically connect computers together. Ethernet is by far the most common type of network, so it's the topic of this chapter.

Rather than describe corporate network solutions you don't need, this chapter focuses on the simplest and least expensive solution for creating a network for a small office whose computers are running Microsoft Windows 2000 Professional. While you'll find tips for setting up other versions of Windows to work on your network, only a Windows 2000 Professional configuration is described in detail. Using this scenario as a starting place, you'll have only a few options to worry about and you'll have your own network up and running with surprisingly little work. Windows 2000 Professional makes this solution work effortlessly and most of the network hardware available today has become affordable and easy to use.

Along the way, the chapter will cover some basic terminology that'll help you understand what you're working with and make it easier to buy network components. It also helps you keep an eye on the future—when your business outgrows a workgroup network, you won't have to ditch everything you've installed to step from a workgroup solution to a larger domain (client/server) solution.

Note

If you find that your business requires a more sophisticated network than the one presented here, you'll probably do best by contracting or hiring someone to install and manage your network. In that case, you can read this chapter as a basic introduction to networks.

An Introduction to Network Designs

While you might not want to become a network guru, you'll need a little theory up front to understand the basic technology and to make the best decisions about what's right for your business. This section describes what's good and bad about workgroup networks, discusses the basic designs available for networks, and provides enough background on hardware, speed, and bandwidth for you to put together the pieces of a workgroup network in your office.

Workgroup Versus Domain Networks

Before you jump into how to set up a workgroup network in your office, it's good to get an idea of just exactly what a workgroup network is and what it isn't.

Workgroup (or peer-to-peer) networks have been in use for many years. As opposed to a domain network, in which a central server manages resources (such as files or printers) for its many client computers to use, a workgroup network has a number of computers, each of which can act as a server of its resources to every other computer on the network.

A domain network is designed to handle many client computers in an efficient manner but at the expense of requiring someone to act as a network administrator. An advantage of workgroup networks is that they have many of the same capabilities as domain networks without requiring a network administrator. On the other hand, a workgroup network disadvantage is that it can become overloaded with network traffic when too many computers are added to the network.

You should also compare the ease of administering user accounts on both network types. On a domain network, a single server validates all user accounts and passwords so users on client computers can use resources on the network. A network administrator sets up each user account once on the server, and then each user can set up a connection from any client computer on the network by running the Network Identification Wizard. However, on a workgroup network, every computer acts as its own server and therefore must validate the user account and password of any client that tries to access its resources on the network. To do this, each workgroup computer checks its local user accounts—if the user trying to access its resources over the network has a local user account on that computer, it validates the connection. This works beautifully but requires each user to have an account on every computer to access its resources over the network.

Comparing Physical Topologies

The physical topology of a network represents the actual layout of cables, computers, and any other hardware components in the network. Two physical topologies are in common use these days: star and bus. A star topology incorporates a central hub, and the computers in the network connect directly to the hub and radiate out in a star pattern. Figure 16-1 shows a star network configuration.

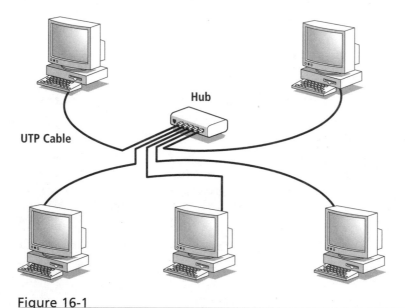

Figure 16-1

A star topology connects all computers to a central hub.

If you're using a star network and hub, you'll likely be using unshielded twisted pair (UTP) cabling, which has a limit of 100 meters (328 feet) from NIC (network interface card) to hub. This means that the absolute distance between any two computers is 200 meters (656 feet) without using a device called a repeater. An advantage with star topologies is that they are easy to troubleshoot because each computer has a connection only to the hub, so you can easily isolate a connection that's not working. A disadvantage with star topologies is that they require more cable and have limited range without repeaters.

In a bus physical topology, computers are linked together in a chain. Figure 16-2 shows a bus network configuration.

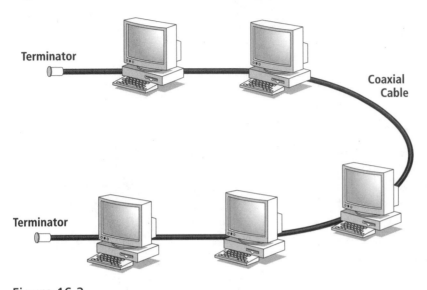

Figure 16-2

A bus topology connects one computer to the next in a chain.

Bus topologies typically employ coaxial cable (they can also use fiber-optic cable, but this is still very expensive). A bus topology can use a single thick "backbone" cable, typically installed between walls or under the floor, to which all computers (or subnetworks of computers) are attached by intermediate cables, or it can use a thin cable that links from one computer to the next, with each computer connecting to it using a T-connector. Thick coaxial cable offers greater distance but it's less flexible so it's more difficult to install. Regardless of whether it's thick or thin, each end of a bus cable is capped with a terminator.

The advantages of bus topologies are that they often require less cabling per computer, you can run the cable farther, and you don't need the hub required by the star topology. A disadvantage with bus topologies is that they're harder to troubleshoot than star topologies because it can be difficult to isolate the connection that has the problem.

More About Cable Types

Twisted pair cable is similar in appearance to telephone cable and comes as shielded twisted pair (STP) and the more common unshielded twisted pair (UTP). Five categories are UL certified as meeting EIA/TIA-586 standards, but only two of those categories are typically used in Ethernet LANs: Category 3 and Category 5. Category 3 cable (also called 10Base-T cable) can transmit up to 10 Mbps. The term 10Base-T means that it transmits at *10* Mbps *Base*band and uses *T*wisted pair wire. Category 5 cables can transmit up to 100 Mbps (referred to as 100Base-T in twisted-pair configurations) and are the best solution because they provide ten times the bandwidth for a small price difference and provide upward compatibility if you need more network bandwidth in the future.

Coaxial cable looks just like television cable. It's shielded and is therefore a good candidate for environments that contain radio frequency interference, which can slow down data transmission. (Twisted pair also rejects radio interference quite well, however.) Coaxial cable comes in two basic diameters, referred to as thick and thin. Each is used in a different type of LAN specification.

Thick coaxial cable (also called 10Base5 or thicknet) is used as a backbone on large Ethernet LANs for very long distances of up to 2500 feet. Cable rated as 10Base5 transmits at *10* Mbps *Base*band for *500* meters and is typically a corporate solution for large offices and buildings. Thick coaxial cable, difficult to work with because of its diameter and stiffness, is about 1 cm in diameter.

RG-58A/U coaxial cable (also called 10Base2 or thinnet) is used on coaxial Ethernet networks where any two computers can be up to 185 meters (607 feet) apart. The 10Base2 term here means it will transmit at *10* Mbps *Base*band for 200 meters (in this case, the actual rating doesn't quite match the specification). While the maximum distance between any two computers is 185 meters, the total distance on the bus is 925 meters (3035 feet), or five times 185 meters. Thinnet cables use BNC barrel connectors to connect cables together, BNC T- connectors to connect to each NIC, and BNC terminators at each end of the network. While some NIC cards have both thinnet connectors (BNC) and twisted pair connectors, many support only one or the other, so choose carefully now. You might find yourself replacing your NICs if you end up wanting to go from a bus topology now to a star topology later for greater bandwidth.

Fiber optic cables are used in a bus topology but they're still quite expensive and they're therefore typically used only by businesses that require extremely high-bandwidth or ultra-secure connections, such as digital video feeds or military installations, or for long runs between repeaters in different buildings.

Understanding Speed and Bandwidth

The speed of a network is simply how fast data is transferred, and bandwidth describes how much traffic a network can handle—like a freeway, wider is better and too much traffic slows everything down. Many factors affect the speed of the network, and cabling is only one of them (but at least it's one that's fairly easy to quantify and understand). Other factors that affect network speed are how many computers are connected and the distance between computers. The distance factor causes problems because whenever one computer tries to communicate with another and fails because they're too far apart, the data is retransmitted, which clogs the network with more traffic. However, if you don't try to overload your workgroup network with too many computers and you don't exceed the specifications for cable lengths, you'll probably be happy with the speed and bandwidth of your network.

What about Phoneline Networks?

A solution that's recently appeared in the market is the phoneline network. Aimed at home computer users with more than one computer, but potentially useful for home offices or some small offices, this technology enables data transmission over the regular telephone wires that are already installed, using frequencies not employed by voice communication (so you can use the phone at the same time). The speed of this networking solution has been a limiting factor for serious small business use, because it has been mainly limited to about 1 Mbps. However, at least one company now advertises phone network interface cards with up to 10 Mbps speed. If you're interested in exploring this approach to the hardware requirements of a workgroup network, check out the Home Phoneline Networking Alliance (HomePNA) site for more information at *www.phonelan.org*.

Purchasing the Hardware

You can obtain the hardware you'll need to implement a workgroup network from most office supply outlets these days. Before you start, you'll need to decide which physical topology you'll be using. The solution provided in this chapter assumes you will set up the most commonly used small business network, an Ethernet LAN in a star topology.

Hardware for a Star Network

For an Ethernet network using a star topology, you'll need network cards, at least one hub, and cabling. Each of these is described next.

Network Interface Cards

You'll need a NIC (network interface card) for every computer that you connect to the network. NICs are available as internal cards for desktops, PC Cards for portables, and USB devices. Be sure to check the HCL (hardware compatibility list) or the manufacturer for Windows 2000 Professional compatibility, and buy NICs that support plug and play—NICs are notoriously difficult to configure manually.

For a star topology, you'll use twisted pair cables with RJ-45 connectors (which look like chunky telephone connectors), so be sure the 10Base-T Ethernet NICs you buy have RJ-45 jacks rather than, or in addition to, BNC connectors. If you want maximum speed (and you soon will even if you don't now), you can buy Category 5 cables and NICs rated for 100Base-T. If you do go for higher bandwidth, make sure all the components in your network support this (all cards, hubs, and cables).

Tip

With today's network component prices, it's probably more cost effective to start with the 100Base-T solution now than to realize you need it later and have to replace your network components.

Hubs

A hub is the device into which all of your cables connect. Hubs are sometimes combined with other devices such as switches or routers. If you're just setting up a single network, you can get by with a simple hub—that is, one that's just a hub. (Switches are used to segment a network into subnets and routers are used to connect to remote networks—both of which are outside the modest requirements of the network described here.) Hubs are widely available and vary in the number of ports they provide. Because a workgroup network is really best with fewer computers, you can get by with one that has eight or ten ports. Hubs often come with lights that indicate activity on individual ports and it's worth buying one that has those indicators, which you'll appreciate if you have to troubleshoot at some point. Hubs are rated as 10Base-T or 100Base-T, like cables. 100Base-T hubs are often rated for dual speed (10/100) and are the best bet for upward compatibility.

Tip

It's usually easier to upgrade a hub from 10Base-T to 100Base-T than to replace all of your cabling, so consider installing Category 5 cabling now even if you plan on using a 10Base-T hub.

Cables

Before you buy any cables, first decide where you'll put the hub and then measure the distance to each computer that you'll want to connect. Write these measurements down and be generous with your estimations—there's nothing more aggravating than coming up two feet short after crawling under desks and behind furniture!

Buy a single twisted pair cable with RJ-45 connections for each computer according to the distances you've estimated. You'll find unshielded twisted pair (UTP) cables, such as Category 3 or Category 5 cables, most common and they'll do the job just fine. You can use shielded twisted pair (STP) cables to guarantee the rejection of radio frequencies but UTP cables have many twists per inch, which typically provides good noise rejection.

Hardware for a Bus Network

If you decide to use a bus topology and coaxial cabling, you'll probably want to go with thinnet cabling, since it's easier to install in a typical small business office. Installing a thicknet Ethernet backbone is definitely a job for a professional, who should specify and supply the cabling. Here's the basic list of parts you'd need for installing a thinnet Ethernet network:

- NIC cards that accept BNC connectors and support 10Base2 Ethernet.

- A length of BNC cable that reaches from one computer to the next for each computer you're connecting.

- A T-connector for every computer.

- A BNC terminator for each end of the cable. Usually a 50 ohm terminator—be sure that both terminators are the same rating.

Installing the Hardware

You install a NIC the same way you install any hardware device. If it's an internal plug and play card, you should be able to just turn off the computer, remove the cover, install the card, replace the cover, and power up the computer. If the driver is native (provided by Windows 2000 Professional), that's about all there is to it. PC Card and USB network interface devices are even easier because you don't even have to power down to install them. Once the NIC is installed, a Local Area Connection representing that NIC appears in the Network And Dial-Up Connections folder.

> ### *Tip*
>
> Chapter 6 describes installing hardware, so revisit that chapter if you need any help.

When you set up a network for the first time, you should start by connecting the network cables to just two computers. If you have two computers in your office running Windows 2000 Professional, use those first. When you verify that those two computers are working on the network, move on to connect and very additional computers.

Configuring the Computer

Whether you're setting up a new workgroup network or adding a computer to an existing network, you're ready to configure your computers on the network once you've installed NICs and connected the computers.

The first step in network configuration (and often the only one in the case of workgroup networks) is to identify your computer on the network. This is the same process whether you're creating a new workgroup network or connecting to an existing workgroup network.

Note

During the Windows 2000 Professional setup, you're given the opportunity to enter networking information in the Network Identification Wizard. If you have an existing network and you've already entered this information correctly during setup, you can skip to "Configuring Network Components," on page 310, or "Testing Your Connection," on page 313.

When you're connecting to an existing network, you need to know whether your network is a domain or workgroup network and you need the exact name of that domain or workgroup. If you didn't set the network up yourself, contact the person who set up the network and ask for this information.

You also need to know whether the existing network uses Microsoft Networks or Novell NetWare as the network operating system, and if it uses any special TCP/IP protocol settings. You'll probably need to add network components only if you're using a Novell network or have some advanced network requirements. The network components installed by default are Client for Microsoft Networks, File and Printer Sharing for Microsoft Networks, and Internet Protocol (TCP/IP). Of these, the Internet Protocol (TCP/IP) is often the only component that requires specific configuration.

Note

If you're connecting to a domain network, you'll find instructions in "Connecting to a Domain Network." on page 309.

In Windows 2000, you configure the network in two dialog boxes:

*   The System Properties dialog box in the Control Panel
*   The Local Area Connection Properties dialog box in the Network And Dial-Up Connections folder

In the System Properties dialog box (double-click System in the Control Panel), you can click the Network Identification tab and specify whether you're using a workgroup or domain network, assign a name to your computer, and enter the workgroup or domain it will use. See "Setting

Up a Workgroup Network Identification," on page 307, for the steps to follow. Alternatively, you can set up network identification for your computer using the Network Identification Wizard, which you run by clicking Network ID on the Network Identification tab in the System Properties dialog box. While you can use this wizard for workgroup network identification, it's more beneficial when setting up connections to domain networks, where it also creates a user account on the local computer to match the domain account.

You use the Local Area Connection Properties dialog box when you need to make additional configuration changes, such as when you connect to an existing network using network components or protocols other than the default (Microsoft Networking and TCP/IP). More specifically, you use this dialog box if you need to do any of the following:

- Configure or troubleshoot your NIC

- Add or remove network components

- Configure a network component, such as TCP/IP protocol settings

Note

TCP/IP settings are often the part of any network that requires the most configuration, but this can be avoided in Windows 2000 Professional, which uses a service called Automatic IP Addressing when no DHCP server is available to automatically generate an IP address. This eliminates the need for a static IP address or a DHCP server. However, if you enable Internet Connection Sharing on a computer on the network, as described in Chapter 17, DHCP services will be provided by that computer, and any older computers on your network can be set to receive their IP address automatically. In this case Windows 2000 Professional will use the DHCP service instead of Automatic IP addressing.

If you're connecting to an existing network that requires that you add or remove network components or configure protocols, read "Configuring Network Components," on page 310. To troubleshoot your NIC, read "Troubleshooting Your Connection," on page 315.

Don't Remember Creating a Local Area Connection?

In Windows 2000 Professional, you use the Network And Dial-Up Connections folder both for local area network connections and dial-up connections. Unlike setting up another connection, which requires you to double-click Make A New Connection to create a connection icon, you don't have to do anything special to create a Local Area Connection icon—one icon appears for every NIC that's installed in your computer. Double-clicking this icon opens a Connection Status dialog box for the LAN connection, in which you can click the Properties button to view the connection properties (if the connection's unplugged, double-clicking the icon opens the Properties dialog box directly).

Setting Up a Workgroup Network Identification

For a computer to recognize the workgroup and be recognized on it, you must inform Windows 2000 that it's on a workgroup network and supply the name of the workgroup. You should also take the opportunity at this time to rename your computer to something that makes more sense and is easier to remember than the name cooked up by the setup application.

Note

You must be logged on to the computer as a member of the Administrators group to make changes to a computer's network identification.

All computers that you want to have communicate on a workgroup network must use the same workgroup name. If you're setting up a new workgroup network, you can provide a workgroup name that makes sense to you or just use the name WORKGROUP, which is the default in every Windows computer. If you're connecting to an existing workgroup network, use that workgroup's name. Also, the name of each computer in the workgroup must be unique, and you should use a name that makes sense to other users on the network. If each computer belongs to a different user, you can identify the computer by the user's name, for example.

You can enter the workgroup name in the Network Identification Wizard, but you still need to set the computer name manually. For workgroup networks, it's easiest to do both by following the steps here.

To set up a computer's network identification:

1. Click Start, point to Settings, and click Control Panel.

2. Double-click System to open the System Properties dialog box.

3. Click the Network Identification tab and click Properties to open the Identification Changes dialog box.

4. In the Member Of area, enter the name of the workgroup in the Workgroup box.

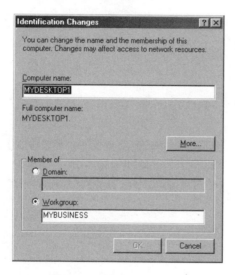

5. In the Computer Name box at that the top of dialog box, enter the name of your computer. This name will identify the computer on the network to other computers.

Tip

If you're connecting to a workgroup network, you can choose any name that isn't already being used on the network and is different from the workgroup name. The limit is 15 uppercase characters if the TCP/IP protocol isn't installed or 63 characters (uppercase and lowercase plus the numbers 0-9), if it is (you'll probably be using TCP/IP but it's a good idea to keep it short anyway). Choose a name that will be descriptive so that others will recognize the computer if you're sharing resources.

6. Click OK to close the Identification Changes dialog box, and then click OK to close the System Properties dialog box.

Connecting to a Domain Network

If you didn't have the network information when you ran Setup or if you are just now installing your network hardware, you'll need to start by identifying the computer on the network, which you can do most easily for domain networks by running the Network Identification Wizard.

Running the Network Identification Wizard

Identifying your computer involves configuring it to work with an existing domain and providing a name to identify your computer on the network. A computer name was provided by default when you ran Setup, and you can run the Network Identification Wizard to do the rest. The Network Identification Wizard enables you to choose between domain and workgroup networks and provide information to set up a logon to both the computer and domain for domain networks. You might recognize this wizard from Setup. You can change the computer name to something that makes more sense, but you must do it manually, not in the Network Identification Wizard.

The wizard has one extra benefit for connecting to domain networks—it automatically creates a local user account on the computer that matches the domain account provided by your administrator, so you can log on to both the network and the computer at the same time. The wizard also verifies the domain account name and password. Therefore, using the wizard is the preferred way to go if you have a domain network.

Before running the Network Identification Wizard to configure a domain network account, make sure you have the following information from your network administrator:

• A valid user name and password.

• The user account domain.

• The computer name and domain (these are needed in the wizard only if it can't find the user name and password in the domain you've entered). You can click the Properties button on the Network Identification tab in the System Properties dialog box to find this.

With this information in hand, go ahead and run the Network Identification wizard as follows.

To run the Network Identification Wizard:

1. Click Start, point to settings, and click Control Panel.

2. Double-click System to open the System Properties dialog box.

3. Click the Network ID button and follow the steps in the Network Identification Wizard.

4. On the Connecting To The Network page, select This Computer Is Part Of A Business Network, And I Use It To Connect To Other Computers At Work, and then click Next.

5. When asked what kind of network you use, select My Company Uses A Network With A Domain.

6. Click Next on the Network Information page.

7. On the User Account And Domain Information page, you will be prompted for the user name, password, and account domain that you've been given. If your name and password aren't found, you'll be prompted to enter the name of the computer and the computer domain. Continue to enter the information and follow the wizard. If you run into problems, contact your administrator to make sure you have the correct name and password.

8. Click OK to close the Identification Changes dialog box and click OK again to close the System Properties dialog box.

Note

After you're finished, be sure to reboot for the changes to take place.

Configuring Network Components

Configuring components can mean either adding or removing client, service, and protocol network components, or changing settings in any of those components.

Adding and Removing Components

You connect to other computers on the network through a connection called the Local Area Connection, which has an icon in the Network And Dial-Up Connections folder. The network connection uses three component types to actually perform and manage the connection: Clients, Services, and Protocols. By default, Windows 2000 Professional provides these basic components to connect to a Microsoft domain or workgroup network:

- Client for Microsoft Networks—Provides the client component for connecting to a LAN running Microsoft Networks.

- File and Printer Sharing for Microsoft Networks—Provides a file and printer server to other computers on the network.

- Internet Protocol (TCP/IP)—Provides the low-level mechanism for exchanging information. TCP/IP is the most popular protocol in use today because it's the protocol used by the Internet.

You can install other components in addition to those installed by default in Windows 2000 Professional, such as the Client Service for NetWare, which is provided by Windows 2000 Professional to connect to a Novell network. You can also install the following protocols in Windows 2000 Professional to connect to different networks: AppleTalk protocol, DLC protocol, Network Monitor Driver, and NetBIOS.

To install any other supported protocol:

1. Click Start, point to Settings, and click Network And Dial-Up Connections.

2. Double-click the Local Area Connection icon, and then click Properties.

3. In the Local Area Connection Properties dialog box, click Install.

4. Select Client, Service, or Protocol and click Add.

5. Select the component you want to add and click OK (or click Have Disk if you have one that's more current than the Windows 2000 Professional version).

Making Changes in Components

The components you're most likely to reconfigure are the protocols. As an example, here's how you'd reconfigure TCP/IP.

To change the TCP/IP protocol configuration:

1. Click Start, point to Settings, and click Network And Dial-Up Connections.

2. Double-click the Local Area Connection icon, and then click Properties.

3. Select Internet Protocol (TCP/IP) and click Properties.

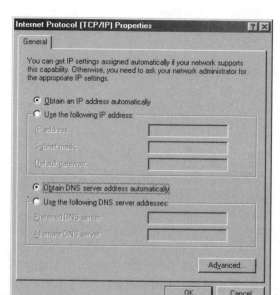

4. In the Internet Protocol (TCP/IP) Properties dialog box, you can set the IP address and the DNS (Domain Name System) server addresses or choose to have the computer obtain these settings automatically. (The IP address uniquely identifies your computer on the network and it can be dynamically allocated by the network using a DHCP service. DNS is used to match names with the numbers used in the TCP/IP protocol by maintaining lookup tables on a server.) Again, your network administrator should give you this information. If you're in doubt, choose to obtain the IP address and DNS server address automatically.

5. If you need to make more configuration changes, click Advanced. Here you can add and configure gateways (routers to connections beyond your LAN), make various DNS settings, make WINS changes (WINS is an older service for resolving names with numbers), and much more. As the button indicates, this is even more technically challenging than TCP/IP settings, so get clear instructions on what to set if you do anything here.

Testing Your Connection

The best way to test your connection is to view another computer on the network. If you're using a workgroup network, you'll need to have a user account with the same name and password on both computers that are communicating on the network. If you have shared a folder on the other computer, you should be able to view files in that folder (*you'll learn about shared folders in "Sharing Folders and Drives," on page 317*). But you can at least see if the other computer is recognized on the LAN before trying to use shared resources on the network.

Understanding User Accounts

A network relies on user names in exactly the same way as Windows 2000 Professional does when you set up separate user accounts on your computer. When you log on to a Windows 2000 Professional computer that's connected to the network, you're also logging on to the network. On a domain network, the domain server authenticates everyone logging on to the network. However, because every computer on a workgroup network runs its own server, each computer must validate the user name and password of any computer trying to access it. It does this by requiring a user accessing the computer over the network to have a user account on that computer.

On a workgroup network, you must have a user account on every computer that you want to access. This account must be set up with the same user name and password that you use to log on to the network (by logging on to another computer on the network). If you're not recognized by another computer when you try to access its printer or folder, you'll be prompted to provide a user name and password that are recognized by that computer. You can get around setting up accounts for everyone on every computer by just establishing a guest name and password that are installed on every computer. That way, when users want to access a printer or folder, they can enter the guest name and password at the prompt.

To test your network connection with another computer on a network:

1. If you're connected to a workgroup network, make sure you have a user account that is the same on both computers and you're logged on to one of the computers using that account. If you're

313

testing a connection to a domain network, make sure you're logged on to the domain.

2. On the desktop of a Windows 2000 Professional computer, double-click My Network Places.

3. Double-click Computers Near Me. You should now see your own computer listed, along with all of the other connected computers on the workgroup or domain that you've specified for your computer. Figure 16-3 shows the local desktop computer (Mydesktop1) along with a portable, named Mylaptop, and another desktop computer, called Mydesktop2, in a local workgroup.

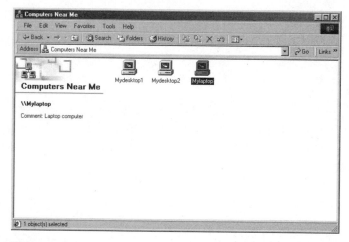

Figure 16-3

Computers Near Me shows all computers on your workgroup or domain.

4. Double-click one of the other computer icons in the Computers Near Me folder to see any shared folders or drives that exist.

5. If you've shared any folders on the other computer, double-click the icon for a folder in the Computers Near Me folder and the content of the folder should be visible on your computer. If you haven't shared any folders on the computer you are viewing, do that now (*read "Sharing Folders and Drives," on page 317, to learn how*) and then press F5 on the computer you're using to refresh the folder. The shared folders or drives should appear.

Other Ways to Access Computers on the Network

While you can always navigate to any computer on the network from My Network Places by navigating through Computers Near Me, you can also connect directly to a computer's shared folder using the Add Network Place Wizard. Just double-click the Add Network Place icon in My Network Places, enter the name of the computer and folder in the format \\server\share (the "share" portion represents the shared resource) and click Next. For example, to access a shared folder called MyDocs on the computer named MyDesktop1 enter *MyDesktop1\ MyDocs*. Then enter a name for the icon that will be created in My Network Places and click Next. This is a good way to make shared folders that you use often easy to access. It's also a good way to test (and use) a connection that isn't showing up under Computers Near Me for some reason. You can also use this wizard to put icons for Web folders or FTP sites in the My Network Places folder.

By the way, you can also use the \\server\share address format to access shared folders from many other places—in fact, anywhere you can enter an address in Windows 2000 Professional, including Windows Explorer, Internet Explorer, the Run command, any Save As or Open dialog box, and so on.

Troubleshooting Your Connection

If you find that your network is not responding, you'll want to view the status of the connection and the properties of the NIC.

To view the status of the Local Area Connection:

1. Click Start, point to Settings, and then click Network and Dial-Up Connections.

2. Double-click the Local Area Connection icon. If your connection is enabled, the Local Area Connection Status dialog box appears, as shown in Figure 16-4, and it displays the speed of the connection and how long the connection has been up.

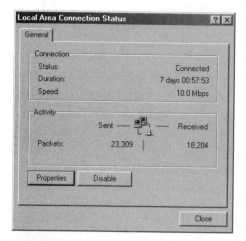

Figure 16-4

You can view the connection in the Local Area Connections Status dialog box.

Tip

You can open the Local Area Connection Status dialog box from the status area on the taskbar in the future by clicking the Properties button, selecting Show Icon In Taskbar When Connected, and clicking OK.

Note

If no connection has been established (for example, your NIC is unplugged), you should see a red X on the Local Area Connection icon in Network And Dial-Up Connections. In this case, double-clicking the Local Area Connection icon opens the Local Area Connection Properties dialog box.

To open the Local Area Connection Properties dialog box, shown in Figure 16-5, double-click a Local Area Connection icon and click the Properties button. Alternatively, right-click the Local Area Connection icon and click Properties.

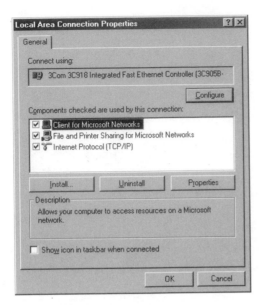

Figure 16-5

Troubleshoot the connection in the Local Area Connections Properties dialog box.

Sharing Resources

The whole point of a workgroup network is to share resources. File and printer sharing, available on many Windows platforms including Windows 2000 Professional, is the oldest service provided by Microsoft. *For a description of the new Internet Connection Sharing service provided with Windows 2000 Professional, see Chapter 17, "Sharing an Internet Connection."*

Sharing Folders and Drives

You can make files available to other computers on your network by sharing the folder or drive in which the file resides. The shared resource is then called a *share*. To users of other Windows 2000 Professional computers in your workgroup, the shared folder or drive then appears in your computer's folder. They can locate this folder in Computers Near Me (under My Network Places) on their computers. (Older versions of Windows display network computers in Network Neighborhood.) File sharing has been around for many years in Microsoft Windows operating systems and it works similarly in all versions of Windows. Windows 2000 Professional has a few extras, however, not found in the consumer versions of Windows.

• Only Windows 2000 enables you to specify a limit to the number of users who can access a share.

• Windows 2000 uses permissions for determining who can access the share. This enables you to specify different access rights for different users or block specific users. Microsoft Windows 95 only has the ability to grant everyone Read-Only access, Full access, or access dependent on a password.

• Windows 2000 enables caching for other computers that connect to a disk or folder and use the Offline Files feature. (*See Chapter 18 for more information about using Offline Files.*)

• Only Windows 2000 allows you to create more than one share for the same folder or drive (for example you might have a share called public but also want to share it with your name, say Fred, if the name of your computer doesn't uniquely identify you on the network.

To enable file sharing in Windows 2000 Professional:

1. In Windows Explorer, select a folder or drive that you want to share.

2. Right-click the folder or drive and choose Sharing. The Properties dialog box for that file or folder appears with the Sharing tab selected.

3. Click Share This Folder.

4. In the Share Name box, enter a share name that you want to have appear on the network. In the Comment box, enter any comment you want to have appear next to the folder.

5. If you want to limit the number of users who can access the share at the same time, click Allow and adjust the number of users in the Users box. With only a few computers on your network, you can typically leave this option at Maximum Allowed. However, if performance suffers because too many users are accessing the share, try adjusting this value.

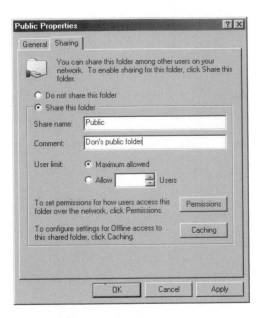

6. If you want to determine how users can access the share, click Permissions. By default, everyone is granted Full Control of the shared resource. See "Changing Share Permissions," next, to learn how to change permissions.

    If you have a Windows 95 computer on the network, you can use the same steps to open the Properties dialog box and share folders or drives, but the Sharing tab looks a little different.

Changing Share Permissions

Windows 2000 Professional enables you to control who accesses your shared folders and drives. Figure 16-6, on the next page, shows the Permissions dialog box that appears when you click the Permissions button in the Sharing tab of a folder's Properties dialog box.

By default, everyone is allowed full control, which means that they can both read and make changes to files in the folder or drive. You can limit the access to individuals or groups and then further decide who is allowed or denied specific access levels.

To limit permissions on a folder or drive:

1. In the Permissions dialog box for the folder, click Add.

2. In the Select Users, Computers, or Groups dialog box, select a user or group in the dialog box and click Add. Repeat this for all users or groups you want to add and then click OK.

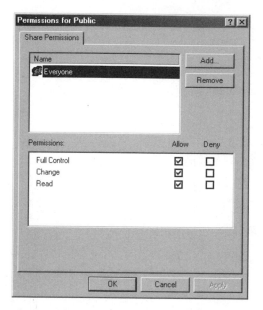

Figure 16-6

Set permissions for the level of access to a folder or drive.

3. Select the Everyone group and click Remove.

By default, all users and groups you've added are given only Read permissions, but you can change the permissions for any user or group listed under Name. Although there are three categories (Full Control, Change, and Read), you can do one of two things: enable read-only access, so users can only view the files, or enable full control, so users can change folder contents or add to the folder. To enable read-only access, clear the Allow check box next to Change, and to enable full control, select the Allow checkbox next to Full Control.

If you want to deny access to some user or group, first add the user or group's account name under Name (for example, add *BobB*), select that name, and then select the appropriate Deny check box (for example, deny Change). Here again, it makes logical sense to either deny all access by selecting the Deny check box next to Full Control, or deny the ability to make changes by selecting the Deny check box next to Change. The example here denies BobB the ability to make changes.

Permissions can get complicated when a user or group you set permissions for belongs to another group that also has permissions set. In that case, be aware that Deny permissions take precedence over Allow permissions. So, for example, if BobB is allowed full access, but Everyone is denied full access, BobB will be denied full access because he is a member of the Everyone group (which includes, not surprisingly, everyone). But if Everyone is allowed full access and BobB is denied full access, only BobB will not be given full access.

Note

Any drive or folder that you share automatically causes all subfolders to be shared and accessible with the same set of permissions. So if you share your C: drive, for instance, all files in all folders on that drive are shared.

Some Ways to Use Shared Disk Space

The more you work with sharing drives and folders, the more you'll appreciate this capability. Here are just a few ways organizations can use shared disk space to improve efficiency, communication, and the safety of data.

- Place common files you want others to be able to access in a shared folder. Consider making it read-only if you don't want the files changed. If you expect the files to be edited by more than one person, selectively enable full control to only one person at a time to avoid collisions that are caused when different users save their edited versions. A better way is to use software, such as Microsoft Office 2000, that locks the file when it's being edited.

- Share the important folders or the entire hard drive of older computers and back up those files over the network to the newer tape or removable storage devices connected to your Windows 2000 Professional computer. Or consider backing up important files to another computer nightly to guard against data loss.

- Use a shared folder to display Web pages and create a simple Intranet. If you don't want to take up the disk space and incur the overhead of using a Web server to create an Intranet—such as the Microsoft Internet Information Service that comes with Windows 2000 Professional, just post the Web pages and graphics on a shared folder and instruct users how to access them. For example, if you placed a Web file named INDEX.HTM on a shared folder named Benefits on a computer named MyDesktop, users could simply enter the address *MyDesktop1\Benefits\ index.htm* in Internet Explorer or Windows Explorer to open the INDEX.HTM Web page. Or users could just browse to that folder on the network and double-click INDEX.HTM to open it.

Sharing Printers

Printer sharing is one of the best things about a workgroup network because it provides good use of printers by making them more accessible to everyone. Like file sharing, printer sharing has been around for many years in Windows computers and it's easily enabled on older Windows computers as well as those using Windows 2000 Professional.

To share a printer in Windows 2000 Professional:

1. On the Start menu, point to Settings and click Printers.

2. Right-click the printer you want to share, and click Sharing.

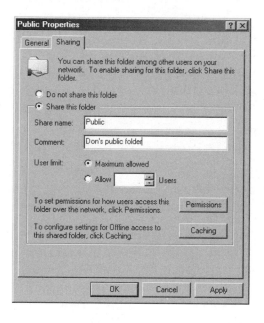

3. Click Shared As and enter the name for the printer that you want to have appear on the network.

Sharing printers and files, as described in this chapter, is a network technology that's been around for many years. Windows 2000 Professional adds another dimension to network sharing by enabling one computer with an Internet connection to share that connection with other computers on the local area network. Internet Connection Sharing (ICS) is described next, in Chapter 17.

Sharing an Internet Connection

Until very recently, peer-to-peer networks were limited to sharing files and printers. Microsoft Windows 2000 Professional adds another technology to your networking arsenal by providing a means to share an Internet connection on one computer with every computer on the network. By simply enabling this feature on the computer with the connection to the Internet, you can share a single ISP account with all the computers on your network. The only requirement is that every other computer on the network be configured to use the network rather than a dial-up connection for applications that use the Internet.

This chapter shows you how to enable Internet Connection Sharing (ICS) on a computer connected to the Internet. It also describes how to enable the applications on other computers on the network, such as Internet browsers and e-mail clients, to use the shared connection.

Enabling Internet Connection Sharing

The actual steps to enabling Internet Connection Sharing on the computer that will act as a gateway to the Internet are simple. But first, you might want to understand a little about how this service actually works. If not, skip ahead to "Sharing the Connection," on page 326, and get on with setting up ICS.

Note

You must be logged on as a member of the Administrators group to enable Internet Connection Sharing.

What Internet Connection Sharing Does

What's the big deal about sharing a connection to the Internet and how does it work? While the ICS service in Windows 2000 Professional connects the local area network to the Internet, it also protects individual computers on the LAN that are running TCP/IP from being accessed by computers on the Internet. In effect, this creates a *firewall*, which keeps outsiders from accessing data inside your office computers. Firewalls are necessary because when a LAN that runs TCP/IP is connected directly to the Internet (which also runs TCP/IP), all resources shared by computers on the LAN are exposed to the greater network that is the Internet—not something most businesses want.

If you've encountered the word "firewall" before, you might also have heard about proxy software, which allows an Internet connection to be shared by computers on a local area network. Unlike proxy software, which also maintains a firewall, ICS is based on NAT (network address translation) technology. Whereas proxies require all computers on the LAN to be configured to use a proxy address for Internet access, ICS does not require that you specially configure computers or devices sharing the Internet connection. While this is a nice time saver for network administrators of large corporate networks, it can make your life easier even if you have only a handful of computers in your office.

So how does ICS work? Each packet of TCP/IP data that is sent across the Internet or your network is encoded with an IP address, much the way a letter has address information on its envelope. Also, every computer has a unique IP address, so packets can find their way from sender to recipient.

ICS works by actually modifying the IP address in every data packet that crosses the bridge between your network and the Internet in either direction. That's the "translation" part of the NAT acronym. When packets go out to the Internet, ICS replaces the return address (originally to a computer on the LAN) with a pseudo-address. When servers send information back to the pseudo-address, ICS replaces that address with the real IP address. This keeps any computer outside your LAN from having any real address information for any computer in your office. It's sort of like having an unlisted number on the Internet.

NAT Versus Proxy Solutions

Which solution provides better security, NAT or proxy, is controversial. Is the firewall in ICS as good as a proxy firewall? The firewall protection provided by a NAT gateway is based solely on the fact that the IP addresses on the private network are hidden. This works quite well in most cases and ICS should be all that you'll need. Of course, ensuring security on the Internet is an ever-changing goal, as hackers perpetually look for holes to slip through, so if you're especially concerned about security, consider using a proxy solution in place of NAT or use proxy software that works in conjunction with ICS to hedge your bets.

You should consider other points besides security as well. Proxy software runs as an application, so it is a little slower than a built-in NAT solution, and it also requires configuring all applications that use the Internet connection. On the other hand, proxy solutions with dedicated firewalls often allow more flexibility for enabling or disabling access to individual users, and proxies usually cache downloaded data so that access to often-viewed Web sites can be faster. As always, the tradeoff is how much time you want to spend configuring your Internet connection solution. ICS requires very little, if any, configuration.

In order for this to work, ICS must know the addresses of all computers on the LAN. It does this by implementing DHCP (Dynamic Host Configuration Protocol), which allocates IP addresses to computers on the network that are configured to obtain them automatically. (Note that ICS should not be used if you already have DHCP service running on your network—for example, if your LAN is connected to a domain server.) So it's important to make sure all the computers on your LAN, except the one sharing the connection, are set up to obtain their IP addresses automatically (the procedure for this is described later in this chapter). The connection-sharing computer (or gateway) is given a static IP address on the internal network.

While the Internet protocol works with IP addresses, humans tend to prefer names (like the ones that usually end in .com), so the translation between names and IP address numbers comes from a huge database called DNS (Domain Name System) that's out on the Internet. Computers connected directly to the Internet use the DNS to translate familiar names like microsoft.com to IP addresses (although most people don't realize this). But because ICS stands between the office network and the Internet, it provides a "proxy" DNS server, which connects to the real DNS on behalf of all the computers on the network to translate Internet names to IP addresses.

Tip

Because ICS implements DHCP, you might find that enabling ICS clears up problems you are having getting Microsoft Windows 95 or Microsoft Windows 98 computers to show up in Computers Near Me. Make sure you configure other computers to obtain their IP addresses automatically, however, or DHCP will not work properly.

Sharing the Connection

Enabling Internet connection sharing requires just a few clicks in the Network And Dial-Up Connections folder.

To enable connection sharing on your Internet connection, follow these steps:

1. On the Start menu, point to Settings and click Network And Dial-Up Connections. Right-click the Internet connection and click Properties. If the Internet connection is through a DSL or cable modem connected to a NIC in your computer, you'll need to right-click the Local Area Connection icon that represents the modem.

2. Click the Sharing tab in your connection's Properties dialog box.

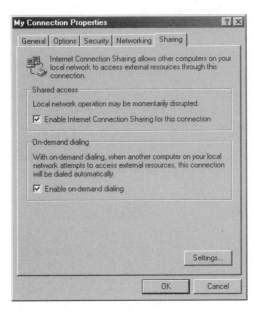

3. Select Enable Internet Connection Sharing for this connection.

4. If this is a dial-up connection, and you want other computers on the network to automatically dial when they require a connection, select Enable On-Demand Dialing.

Note

On-demand dialing is available only when a user who is a member of the Administrators group is logged on to the gateway computer.

5. Click OK. A message dialog box will appear indicating that the IP address on the gateway computer is changing to 192.168.0.1 and to set other computers to obtain their IP addresses automatically. Click Yes.

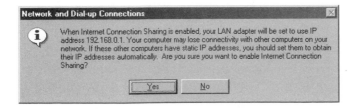

For most small office uses, this is all you'll need to configure for sharing your connection. The Settings button opens a dialog box in which you can configure applications and services to work over the Internet.

Using the Shared Connection

Now you'll need to visit every other computer on the network that you want to enable to use the shared Internet connection. Typically, you'll want to set up your browser and e-mail clients, but you might also have other applications that access the Internet. First, however, you need to make sure that each computer uses dynamic IP address allocation.

To enable dynamic IP address allocation on Windows 2000 Professional computers:

1. Double-click the Local Area Connection icon in the Network And Dial-Up Connections folder and, in the Local Area Connection Status dialog box, click the Properties button.

2. Select the Internet Protocol (TCP/IP) component and click Properties.

3. Make sure Obtain An IP Address Automatically is selected.

4. Click OK and then click Close to close the Local Area Connection Status dialog box.

On Windows 95 and Windows 98 computers, click the Network icon in the Control Panel, select the network component labeled TCP/IP —> followed by the name of your network adapter card, and click Properties. Then click Obtain An IP Address Automatically.

Now you're ready to change the Internet Connections settings. The following procedure works when you use Microsoft Internet Explorer as your browser and Microsoft Outlook Express as your e-mail client.

1. In the Control Panel on each computer on the network, double-click Internet Options.

2. Click the Connections tab.

3. If you've already made a connection to the Internet on this computer, the connection name appears in the Dial-Up Settings area. Select the connection and then, if you always want to use the

shared connection, click Never Dial A Connection or Dial When-ever A Network Connection Is Not Present, to use the shared Internet connection when it's available or your modem when your computer is not connected to the network (for example, on a portable computer away from the office).

If you haven't yet made an Internet connection on this computer, click the Setup button to run the Internet Connection Wizard, and then click the last option, I Want To Set Up My Internet Connection Manually, Or I Want To Connect Through A Local Area Network (LAN), and then follow the wizard steps.

Using an Unattended Shared Modem

ICS doesn't work if the gateway computer is logged off, which is fine if you want the connection to be unavailable when the gateway computer is unattended. However, if you do want to share the connection when the gate-way computer is unattended, then you can either enable password protec-tion on the computer's screen saver, or lock the computer before leaving. This leaves the computer on but makes it unavailable to other users.

If your Internet connection is a dial-up connection and you leave the gateway computer available with on-demand dialing enabled, there is nothing in Windows 2000 Professional that lets someone else on the network disconnect the Internet connection. If you want the phone line to be free when everyone leaves for the night (perhaps if you use that phone line for faxing at discount rates or pay charges for Internet connection time), you can set it to disconnect after a certain period of inactivity or you can provide an account password for others to unlock your computer and disconnect the dial-up connection.

Note

There's one caveat here to watch for, regardless of how you disconnect the connection: when you enable on-demand dialing, any program running on a network computer that periodically requests an Internet connection (such as an e-mail program that checks for e-mail) will continue to dial up to the Internet. So, if you really need to keep the connection unavailable, you should disable on-demand dialing before you leave.

Windows 2000 Professional provides the ability to automatically disconnect a dial-up connection after a specified period of inactivity. To set disconnect properties, double-click Internet Options icon in the Control Panel, click Connections, select the connection name, click Settings, and then click Advanced. You can then select the Disconnect If Idle option and set the amount of time to wait before disconnecting.

If you've created or connected to a LAN in your office and shared Internet connections, folders, or printers, you've covered most of the networking features in Windows 2000 Professional, but definitely not all of them. For businesses that use portable computers, a new feature in Windows 2000 Professional, called Offline Files, is making accessing networked files while away from the office about as easy as it could possibly be. The next chapter covers Offline Files and also shows alternate methods of connecting any two computers together through direct or dial-up connections, so you don't even need a LAN to use Offline Files.

Chapter 18

Connecting Your Portable Computer

Mobility is key to many small business computer users, whether they spend time traveling, selling or marketing their product, or just end up taking their work home a lot. Answering this need, portable computers have become more and more popular as tools for professionals in all sizes of businesses. And with computing power, displays, and hard disk drives rivaling all but the very latest desktop computers, a portable has even become the primary computer for many users.

If you have a portable in your business, it's more than likely that you also have one or more desktop computers with files that you sometimes need to take away from the office. In the last chapter, you learned how to put together a simple network that includes your portable. If you have that network going, you've already found how quickly you get used to accessing files on other computers.

If you're a mobile computer user, the biggest problem you might face is making sure you have the files you need when you're not at work. The solution to this problem comes in three parts:

- Connecting to your office desktop computer or network

- Making sure you have the current versions of the files you need on the portable

- Updating files on the office desktop computer or network with changes made on the portable while away from the office

This chapter describes the various ways you can connect a portable computer to a desktop computer, assuming they're both running Microsoft Windows 2000 Professional. While you can still communicate between portables and desktops running different operating systems, describing the solution using Windows 2000 Professional on both sides of the connection makes the model easier to understand.

One of the biggest benefits to running Windows 2000 Professional on your portable computer is the new Offline Files feature, the best Windows feature for mobile users since Briefcase appeared in Microsoft Windows 95. (Briefcase still works the same way in Windows 2000, incidentally.) Offline Files is Microsoft's solution for transferring files back and forth between desktop and portable computers and for keeping track of what's where and what's most current. The Offline Files feature is also useful for working at home on a desktop computer because it enables you to mirror your office files at home and keep synchronized by dialing in to your office computer.

Getting Connected

You can take advantage of three solutions for connecting your desktop and portable computer in a typical small office environment while keeping administrative overhead at a minimum:

- Using a local area network connection. This is the solution when you are at the office and your office has a network.

- Using a direct connection. This is the approach to take when you don't have a network in your office (or don't have a network connection for your portable) and you want to access files on your desktop.

- Using a dial-up connection. This is the solution when you're away from your office and need to retrieve or send in files.

Note

Connecting to your office network through a virtual private network (VPN) by point-to-point tunneling through an Internet connection is not covered in this chapter. VPN connections are an excellent solution when your office has many mobile users and maintains a public IP address or DNS name. This chapter focuses on Windows 2000 Professional connection solutions that require the least amount of administration.

When you connect two computers together using any of these methods, one computer always acts as a host (or server) and the other acts as a client. When you connect your portable, it acts as the client. When you dial up to your office computer from home, the home computer is the client.

For LAN connections and dial-up connections, the host performs user authentication. On a LAN connection, you're authenticated when you log on to your computer or try to use a shared resource, depending on the network type. When you start a dial-up connection from a client computer, you're authenticated by the host when it accepts the incoming connection; you must use a valid user account name and password to log on over a dial-up connection—an account that exists on the host computer—and you must use an account that has incoming dial-up connections enabled. For direct connections, you can require a user account name, but that account name is not authenticated by default (not requiring authentication enables simple devices such as palmtop computers to make direct connections).

When you set up your host computer to accept incoming connections, you're actually setting up a remote access service. The remote access server can handle connections from multiple devices, such as a regular modem and an ISDN line, and after you've set up an incoming connection, it's represented on the host computer by the Incoming Connections icon in the Network And Dial-Up Connections folder (see Figure 18-1, on the next page).

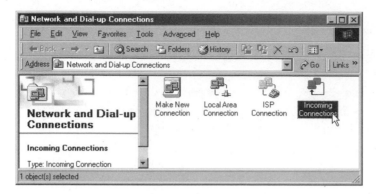

Figure 18-1

Incoming Connections provides remote access service for direct and dial-up connections.

You can set up Incoming Connections to accept connections from a number of sources by running the Network Connection Wizard. You can also modify the properties of any incoming connection (such as restricting who is accepted or what security is required) by double-clicking the Incoming Connections icon. When an incoming connection is established, this icon disappears and a new icon appears that represents the active incoming connection. The new icon displays either the authenticated user name that has logged on (see Figure 18-2), or it indicates an unauthenticated direct connection.

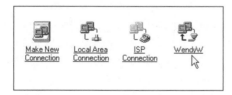

Figure 18-2

The Incoming Connections icon changes to the user name while a connection is active.

Because Incoming Connections supports many incoming connection types, you might see more than one connection icon at a time; for example, you could have a dial-up connection from a home computer and a direct connection from a portable. Or, if you have more than one modem and phone line, incoming connections can support multiple dial-up connections. (For large-scale dial-up support, you should use the more robust remote access server (RAS) feature available in Windows 2000 Server or look into its VPN capabilities.)

Connecting Through a Local Area Network

If you have a network in your office and you use your laptop at work, it makes the most sense to get a network interface card for the portable computer. Chapter 16 describes how to connect to an existing LAN and create a peer-to-peer network using Windows 2000 Professional computers. Using a LAN connection offers several advantages:

- LAN connections are typically faster than either dial-up or direct connections.

- When you log on to your computer, you also log on to the network. This is especially useful when you use the Offline Files feature, which can be set to update shared files between your portable and the network at logon and logoff times.

- If you use Internet Connection Sharing on your network, you can browse the Internet from your portable over the office network and use offline Web pages to view Web pages while you're away from the office.

Connecting Through a Direct Connection

If you don't have a network set up in your office, you can still hook up a direct connection between your portable and the host computer, or between any two computers, using a parallel cable, a null modem cable, or a pair of infrared ports. This enables you to transfer files between computers and use the Offline Files feature. Unlike the direct connection feature in Windows 95 and Microsoft Windows 98, which provides a shortcut to an application that manages the connection, Windows 2000 Professional uses the Network Connection Wizard to create a Direct Connection icon in the client computer's Network And Dial-Up Connections folder and an Incoming Connections icon on the host computer. Then, by connecting the computers and double-clicking the Direct Connection icon on the client computer, you establish a connection.

Direct Cables and Infrared Connections

You can use two cable types for direct connections, based on the two oldest computer ports: serial and parallel. The RS-232 null modem cable (a serial cable) is the most commonly used direct connection cable and connects the COM ports on two computers. Off-the-shelf null modem cables should work, but if you want to check the pin connections, open Windows 2000 Help and search for the topic "null modem cabling." The overview topic provides tables with the correct wiring for 9-pin, 25-pin, and 9-pin to 25-pin null modem cables.

The other type of cable is a parallel port cable. A company called Parallel Technologies (*www.lpt.com*) is Microsoft's recommended vendor for parallel cables and it produces a cable called DirectParallel that has been tested with Windows 2000 Professional. You can contact them for more information on the products they offer, to obtain a list of distributors, or to purchase a DirectParallel cable directly. Many other parallel cables designed for laptop-to-desktop data transfer should also work—cables that worked with Windows 95 should work with Windows 2000 Professional.

If both client and host computers have infrared ports, you can also make a direct infrared network connection. To do this, position the two computers with their infrared ports facing each other until the wireless link icon appears on the taskbar, indicating you have a link. An infrared connection works just like a cable connection, but at a slower transmission speed.

Setting Up a Direct Connection on the Host Computer

As with every other incoming connection type, you use the Network Connection Wizard to enable direct connections, and you must be logged on as a member of the Administrators group to do this.

To configure the host computer to accept direct connections:

1. On the Start menu, point to Settings, and click Network And Dial-Up Connections.

2. Double-click Make New Connection to run the Network Connection Wizard and click Next on the Welcome page.

3. On the Network Connection Type page, select Connect Directly To Another Computer, and click Next.

4. On the Host Or Guest page, select Host, and click Next.

5. On the Connection Device page, select the device from the list of devices for the connection (typically ports) and click Next.

Note

You can select only one port at a time but you can run this wizard many times to select multiple devices. As you add ports, modems, and other devices to the incoming connections, the list of available devices in this wizard becomes smaller.

6. If you want to enforce user account verification, on the Allow Users page, select the users to whom you want to give access to your computer using the direct connection, and click Next.

7. The Completing The Network Connection Wizard page shows the name Incoming Connections (you can't change this). Click Finish to end the wizard. If an Incoming Connections icon isn't already available in the Network And Dial-Up Connections folder, one will be created. If one exists, you've just added direct connections to its list of capabilities.

Should I Password-Protect a Direct Connection?

While unprotected access to your computer is not normally a good idea, a direct connection, which is usually within a few feet of the host computer, probably won't create a security hole. For this reason, direct connection access is unauthenticated by default and you'll see <Unauthenticated User> appear as the name on the icon that represents the direct connection on the host computer when the connection is active.

If, however, you want to enforce password verification for direct connections, right-click the Incoming Connections icon in the Network And Dial-Up Connections folder, click Properties, click the Users tab, clear the lower option (Always Allow Directly Connected Devices Such As Palmtop Computers To Connect Without Providing A Password), and then click OK.

Setting Up and Using a Direct Connection on the Client Computer

You can use the Network Connection Wizard on the client side of the connection too, although you don't need to be logged on as a member of the Administrators group to establish a direct connection from the client computer.

To set up a direct connection from a client computer to the host computer:

1. Hook up the cables between the two computers or, if you're using infrared ports, place the infrared ports facing each other and look for the wireless connection icon to appear on the status bar.

2. On the Start menu, point to Settings, and click Network And Dial-Up Connections.

3. Double-click Make New Connection to run the Network Connection Wizard and click Next on the Welcome page.

4. On the Network Connection Type page, select Connect Directly To Another Computer, and click Next.

5. On the Host Or Guest page, select Guest, and click Next.

6. On the Select A Device page, select the port you want to use. For example, choose a Communications port if you're using a null modem cable, or Direct Parallel port if you're using the parallel port. Click Next.

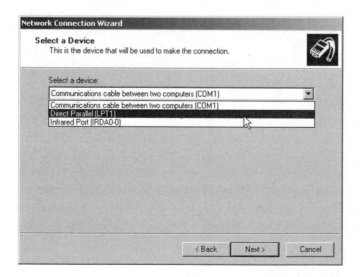

7. Choose whether you want to enable the connection only for yourself or for all users and click Next. (If you select Only For Myself, other users won't see the Direct Connection icon in their Network And Dial-Up Connections folders.)

8. If you want, you can type a name for the connection. Click Finish to exit the wizard. A direct connection icon with this name will appear in the Network And Dial-Up Connections folder and you'll immediately be prompted with a dialog box to attempt the connection.

8. If you've set up the host to require a password, enter your password. Otherwise, just click OK to connect to the host computer. You'll see messages indicating that you're connecting and being registered on the network. If your connection is successful, a Connection Complete dialog box will appear.

10. Click OK. You can click the network icon in the status area of the taskbar at any time to check the connection status.

You can disconnect a direct connection from the Network And Dial-Up Connections folder of either the client or host computer. To disconnect from the client computer, double-click the direct connection icon and click the Disconnect button. To disconnect from the host computer, double-click the direct incoming connection icon (which will be titled your logon name or <Unauthenticated User>, depending on whether your connection requires password verification or not) and click the Disconnect button.

Connecting Through a Dial-Up Connection

If both client and host computers have a modem, you can dial up your host computer from a client computer, such as a portable computer or your home desktop computer. For portables, establishing a dial-up connection for remote access provides a good addition to using a LAN or direct connection at work. You can transfer larger collections of files using the faster speeds of LAN or direct cable office connections, and then use a slower connection for files you need to transfer while away from the office. Dial-up connections also work well for connecting a home computer with an office computer or network. Unlike direct connections, dial-up connections always require account authentication.

Setting Up an Incoming Dial-Up Connection on the Host

You use the Network Connection Wizard to establish incoming dial-up connections and you must be logged on as a member of the administrators group.

Note

If your office computer is connected to a domain network, check with your network administrator, who will likely want to set up the host dial-up connection on the server rather than on your Windows 2000 Professional workstation.

To configure the dial-up connection on the host computer:

1. On the Start menu, point to Settings, and click Network And Dial-Up Connections.

2. Double-click Make New Connection to run the Network Connection Wizard and click Next on the Welcome page.

3. On the Network Connection Type page, select Accept Incoming Connections, and click Next. You will now see the devices that are available for incoming connections, such as modems and ports.

4. On the Devices For Incoming Connections page, select the modem on which you want to enable incoming connections, and click Next.

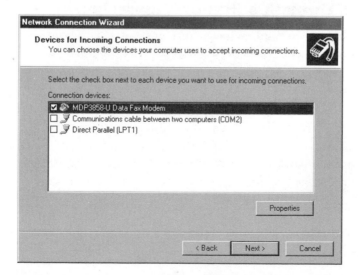

5. On the Incoming Virtual Private Connection page, make sure Do Not Allow Virtual Private Connections is selected and click Next.

6. Select all the users that you want to be able to log on to your computer using the dial-up connection, and click Next.

7. On the Networking Components page, select an installed protocol, such as Internet Protocol (TCP/IP), and make sure that File And Printer Sharing For Microsoft Networks and Client For Microsoft Networks are both selected. You can optionally set the properties for the protocol.

Note

TCP/IP has many options so it isn't always easy to use. For a simpler protocol, consider installing and enabling the NetBEUI protocol on the host, client, and any network computers you want to access. *See "Configuring Network Components," on page 310 in Chapter 16, for more on this subject.*

8. Click Next. The Completing The Network Connection Wizard page appears with the name Incoming Connections (you can't change this). Click Next to finish the wizard.

Setting Up and Using a Dial-Up Connection on a Client Computer

You use the Network Connection Wizard to set up the client side of a dial-up connection as well. You don't need to be logged on as a member of the Administrators group to establish a direct connection from the client computer, but you'll need to be logged on with administrator privileges to enable any other users on your portable to access the dial-up connection. Remember that you'll need an account on the host computer in order to dial up and log on to that computer.

To set up a dial-up connection to the host computer:

1. On the Start menu, point to Settings, and click Network And Dial-Up Connections.

2. Double-click Make New Connection to start the Network Connection Wizard, and click Next on the Welcome page.

3. Select Dial-Up To Private Network, and click Next.

4. Enter the telephone number of the host, and click Next.

Tip

You can use dialing rules at this point if you want. If you typically dial up your office desktop from several different places (like home, a client's office, or your cell phone's data connection), dialing rules will make your life easier.

---

5. If you're logged on as a member of the Administrators group, the Connection Availability page appears so you can select whether to create the connection for all users or only for yourself. This determines if other users who log on to your computer will see this dial-up connection in their Network And Dial-Up Connections folder. Select an option and click Next.

6. On the final page of the wizard, you can change the name of the dial-up connection and select Add A Shortcut To My Desktop if you want one. Click Finish to exit the wizard. A dial-up connection is created in the Network And Dial-Up Connections folder.

7. You will immediately be prompted with a dialog box to attempt the connection. If you've already set up the incoming connection on the host computer to accept your dial-up, enter your password and click OK to connect to the host computer. Alternatively, click Cancel if you want to postpone connecting.

To establish a connection with the host computer at any time, connect your client computer's modem to a phone line, open the Network And Dial-Up Connections folder, and double-click the dial-up connection icon you just created. Then enter your password and click OK.

Tip

Once you've established a dial-up connection, you can choose to automatically connect to your office network when you log on to your client computer. First log off Windows. Then, at the Log On To Windows prompt, select Log On Using Dial-Up Connection, enter your password, and click OK. The Network And Dial-up Connections dialog box appears. Select the name of the dial-up connection to use and click Dial. When your connection dial-up box appears, select (or type) your user name and password and click Dial. After dialing the number and being authenticated by the host computer, you'll be connected. You'll be reconnected each time you log on to your computer.

Viewing Shared Folders on the Desktop

When you connect to the desktop, you should be able to view any shared folders on the desktop by clicking My Network Places, double-clicking Computers Near Me, and then double-clicking the name of the desktop computer. *To learn how to share folders on your desktop, read "Sharing Folders and Drives," on page 317 of Chapter 16.* Once you can view shared folders on your desktop, you can open them and navigate to files and folders you want from your portable computer. You can then copy the files between your client and host computers, or even better, use Offline Files, covered next, to manage the whole process of replicating and synchronizing files.

If You Don't See Any Computers Nearby

When you double-click Computers Near Me, do you get a message telling you that the list of servers for your workgroup is currently not available? If so, there's a problem with the browser service on the host computer (the service that finds and displays the names of computers on the network). There's an easy workaround for this, fortunately.

To view the host computer (or any computer on the network), click Search in My Network Places, and then type the name of the computer you're looking for under Computer Name (for example *mydesktop1*), and click Search Now. After a few minutes, the computer you're looking for should appear in the Search Results pane. You can open the computer directly from here or drag it as a shortcut to some other place, such as the desktop. If the computer can't be found using Search Now, there's probably a more serious problem with the connection. Note that you can also search for a computer from just about anywhere you can view files, such as Windows Explorer or My Computer, by clicking Search, clicking the Computer hyperlink in the left pane, and continuing the search as described above.

Using Offline Files

Offline Files is a feature that comes to Windows 2000 from Microsoft Internet Explorer; Offline Web pages, a similar feature, was introduced as a feature of Internet Explorer 5.0 (the version that's included with Windows 2000 Professional).

Offline Files works by enabling you to view and work with network files on your portable computer when you leave work. The files you select to work with offline appear as if they're still on the network even when you're no longer connected, so you can find files more easily and understand the context of the files by their original location. (Have you ever copied a file to your portable and forgotten where it came from?) Even better, files are transferred back and forth between your portable and their original location in an organized and automated way called synchronization, which is flexible enough to match the way that you work.

Of course Offline Files isn't magic—the offline files are really kept in a folder maintained by the system in a cache (that is, you won't see it in Windows Explorer). By default, 10 percent of your hard drive is set aside for this storage, but you can vary this setting (*see "Setting Up Offline Files," on page 345*). You access these files from the network location, which appears even when you're not connected to the network. Once you've enabled Offline Files, you'll notice an Offline Files icon in the status area of the taskbar and you'll also see informational balloons pointing to this icon periodically, telling you the current status, such as whether you're currently working online or offline (see Figure 18-3). This is also configurable for those who don't like reminders.

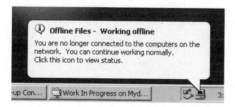

Figure 18-3

Informational balloons indicate the status of Offline Files.

Offline Files is designed to be used on any Microsoft network (it doesn't work on Novell NetWare networks), but if you don't have a network in your office and are using it over a connection between just two computers, it works the same—your connection is essentially a network and the desktop computer you're connected to can be viewed as a computer on that network. Even on a network, Offline Files works between two computers, enabling one computer to mark files shared by another computer as offline and then take copies of those files away for offline work. Also, only the computer marking the files as offline (for example, the portable) needs to be running Windows 2000 Professional.

While this chapter mostly describes using Offline Files with mobile computers, Offline Files is also quite useful when you connect to your office computer or network using a dial-up connection—from computer on your desk at home, for example. You can mirror your work files at home and dial up and synchronize files with very little effort.

Setting Up Offline Files

To set up Offline Files, you first need to connect to another computer that's sharing files you want to work on. Then you need to visit two places—one is the Folder Options dialog box on your computer so you can enable Offline Files, and the other is the shared folder on the other computer so you can mark the folder or files in the folder as offline.

First, here's how to enable Offline Files on your client computer:

1. In the Control Panel, click Folder Options.

2. Click the Offline Files tab.

3. Select the Enable Offline Files check box.

4. Click OK to close.

The Offline Files tab of the Folder Options dialog box is also where you set several other properties, including whether to enable reminders that pop up to inform you that you're offline, whether to place a shortcut to the Offline Files folder on the desktop, how much disk space to use for the cache, and whether to automatically synchronize when you log off. You can view or delete offline files from here, as well. You can also open Folder Options from the Tools menu of Windows Explorer and other file browsers in Windows 2000.

Now that Offline Files is enabled, you can visit the files and folders that you want to make offline. It's usually a good idea to work at the folder level, since all files within a folder marked offline will also be available offline. That way, you don't have to remember to mark individual files—you can just put them in an offline folder and know that they'll be synchronized. You'll also find it handy to use Add Network Place to create icons for your Offline Files in My Network Places or create shortcuts to these folders on the desktop.

The first time you mark a file or folder as offline, you'll encounter a wizard that will help you set up your initial Offline Files configuration. After that, it's just a matter of marking folders and files you want to work on. You'll also want to decide when to synchronize files.

To make a file or folder available offline:

1. Locate the computer on the network containing the files you want to work with offline.

2. Find a shared folder containing files or other folders that you want to work on when you disconnect.

Tip

It's a good idea to independently share folders that you work on often, even if they're within shared folders, so you don't have to browse too deeply to find them.

---

3. Right-click the shared folder or an individual file, and then click Make Available Offline. If this is the first time you've tried making a file or folder available offline, the Offline Files Wizard appears. If you've done this before, go to step 6.

4. Click Next on the Welcome page. Now you have the option of enabling the automatic synchronization of files whenever you log on or log off the computer. Enabling this option makes synchronizing offline files almost transparent. If your portable is connected to the office LAN and you're in the habit of logging off and on regularly, you won't have a large amount of data to synchronize at the last minute before disconnecting. If you don't log off and on regularly, you might want to perform manual synchronization periodically in addition to, or instead of, using the automatic synchronization feature. Click Next.

5. If you want an informational balloon to pop up periodically and remind you that you're working offline, leave the Enable Reminders check box selected. If you want to create a shortcut on your desktop to access the Offline Files folder, select Create A Shortcut To The Offline Files Folder On My Desktop (you can also set or change these options in the Folder Options dialog box later). Click Finish to exit the wizard. If you've marked a folder that has a set of subfolders, a dialog box lets you confirm or reject making those subfolders available offline as well. Otherwise, the file or folder is marked as offline (you'll see an icon with a pair of arrows attached, as shown in Figure 18-4).

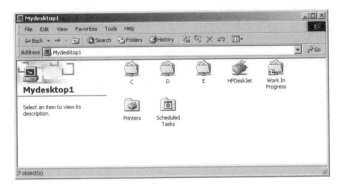

Figure 18-4
A pair of circular arrows on the icon indicates the Work In Progress folder is offline.

The first time you mark a file or folder offline, synchronization occurs automatically, copying the folders you just selected to the Offline Files cache on your computer. While this happens, a dialog box appears showing the progress. Any errors the program encounters will be shown in the Results tab of the Synchronization Complete dialog box. A common cause for errors is open files. If you've mistakenly left files open when you synchronize, just close those files and synchronize again. If someone else has a file open, you can either wait, ask that person to close the file, or just live with the fact that you couldn't synchronize that file. (*See "Understanding Synchronization Conflicts," on the next page, for more about working with other users on the network.*)

Note

You can disable the Offline Files feature at any time, either globally or on individual files or folders. To disable the feature globally, open Folder Options in the Control Panel, click the Offline Files tab, and clear the Enable Offline Files check box. To remove the offline files mark on an individual file or folder, right-click the file or folder and click Make Available Offline to clear it.

Synchronizing Offline Files

You can synchronize files between shared folders and your client computer either manually or automatically. Each method has its own strengths and best uses.

Understanding Synchronization Conflicts

Regardless of how you synchronize, the process is the same: files marked as offline that have changed on the client computer are copied from the Offline Files cache to their original location on the host computer, and those files marked as offline that have changed on the host computer are copied to the client computer. When a file marked as offline has been modified on both computers, a conflict occurs. In this case, the file is renamed and both versions of the file are replicated on the host and the client computer. You can then compare files and decide how to resolve the conflict. (Offline Files doesn't provide version management.)

Synchronizing Automatically

Windows 2000 Professional offers several options for making the synchronization process transparent, or at least easy to use. These options make the most sense for synchronizing a portable computer connected to an office network, but they can also work for synchronizing over a dial-up connection. For example, you can synchronize offline files automatically:

- When you log on or off your computer (or both), preparing your portable for offline work when you log off and updating files when you reconnect and log back on to the network.

- When your computer has been idle for a specified length of time and, optionally, at specified intervals after that.

- At a specific scheduled time.

You can change all of these settings using the Synchronization Settings dialog box (see Figure 18-5), which configures the Synchronization Manager service.

To open the Synchronization Settings dialog box:

1. On the Tools menu of any file browser such as Windows Explorer, click Synchronize. The Items To Synchronize dialog box opens.

2. Click Setup. The Synchronization Settings dialog box appears.

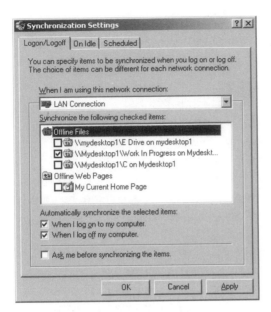

Figure 18-5

You can configure options for synchronizing offline files and offline Web pages in the Synchronization Settings dialog box.

Setting Up Logon/Logoff Synchronization

If you want to enable synchronization when you log on or off, click the Logon/Logoff tab of the Synchronization Settings dialog box, select the connection (more than likely a LAN connection in this case), and then select the offline files to synchronize by selecting the check boxes. You can then choose whether to synchronize when logging on, logging off, or both by selecting the corresponding check boxes. You can also set whether you want to be prompted before synchronization occurs, which is a good idea if you want to want to temporarily bypass the automatic synchronization you've set up for some reason. (You might do this, for example, if you know that someone else in the office has a file open that you've marked as offline on your computer and you want to wait to synchronize until that person has closed the file.)

Setting Up On Idle Synchronization

If you want to synchronize when the computer has been idle for a while, click the On Idle tab, select the connection and files to synchronize, and then select Synchronize The Selected Items While My Computer Is Idle. Click the Advanced button if you want to set or view how long the computer will be idle before synchronization starts or how often synchronization will be repeated thereafter.

Setting Up Scheduled Synchronization

To schedule synchronization, click the Scheduled tab and click Add, which opens the Schedule Synchronization Wizard. Follow the wizard, in which you'll select the connection, the offline files, the start time and date, and the frequency (such as daily, weekly, or some other period). When you finish the wizard, a scheduled synchronization job will be entered in this tab. You can edit this job by selecting it and clicking Edit (which, incidently, gives you more scheduling options than the wizard).

Tip

One useful feature in scheduling for dial-up users is that you can specify that you want to be connected automatically at a given time. This can be quite useful for synchronizing a home computer with an office network over a dial-up connection during off-peak hours or when you're sleeping. You'll find this option on the wizard screen that shows the connection and the offline files. Before you can schedule a connection, you'll need to run the dial-up connection manually and select Save Password so there's an automatic password entered when the scheduled dial-up occurs. Then, your connection will be dialed at the scheduled time, synchronization will occur, and the connection will be closed!

Synchronizing Manually

When you'd rather just pick your own time to run the synchronization rather than use the automatic options (or perhaps in addition to automatic options), you can run a manual synchronization. For example, when using a dial-up connection, you might want to synchronize only after you're sure you've established a fast connection. Or, on a direct or LAN connection, you might not want to wait to synchronize an entire folder if you only need to grab one file for the night. You can use any of the following methods to synchronize at any time while your computer is connected.

- To synchronize a specific folder or a file marked as offline, right-click the file or folder, and click Synchronize. You can do this from any browser window where you can see the file or folder on the network connection. You can also do this from the Offline

Files folder on your computer (*see "Viewing the Offline Files Folder," on page 351*).

- To synchronize all files, right-click the Offline Files icon in the taskbar, and click Synchronize.

- To synchronize all files and folders as well as Internet Explorer 5.0 offline Web pages, from the Tools menu of any file browser, click Synchronize to open the Items To Synchronize dialog box (see Figure 18-6). Select the folders or Web pages you want synchronized and click the Synchronize button.

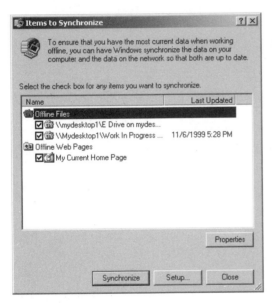

Figure 18-6

Click Synchronize on the Tools menu to synchronize offline files and Web pages.

Viewing the Offline Files Folder

All offline files appear in two places: in their original location on the network and also in the Offline Files folder. The Offline Files folder, shown in Figure 18-7 on the next page, holds all offline files for both Offline Files and Offline Web pages in one place. The files don't appear in their original folder hierarchy, but you can see information for each file, including its synchronization status, availability, access rights, and whether it's currently online or offline. You can also open the file from this folder to edit it.

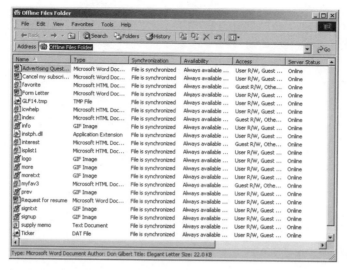

Figure 18-7

The Offline Files folder lets you open or view the status of all offline files.

You can access the Offline Files folder in several ways:

- Click the desktop shortcut if you created one.

- Click the Offline Files icon in the taskbar and click View Files.

- Double-click Folder Options in the Control Panel, click the Offline Files tab, and click View Files.

Now that you've seen how you can use Windows 2000 Professional and your portable computer together to make your connections and file management easier, maybe taking work home or on the road will seem a little easier. This wraps up the networking part of this book, but read on to find out how to use some administration features that will help you maintain your computer.

Part 7

Advanced Administration Tasks

Chapter 19

Using the Computer Management Console

The Computer Management Console is a multipurpose application based on the Microsoft Management Console (MMC) that contains a broad variety of tools covering most advanced administration tasks. Many of the MMC snap-ins in other consoles in the Administrative Tools folder appear in the Computer Management Console as well, including Event Viewer, Performance Logs And Alerts, and Services. And most of the other consoles in the Administrative Tools folder, including Component Services, Data Sources, and Local Security, are beyond the interest of all but the heartiest of technical appetites.

As with any pre-packaged collection of tools, you'll find some to be very useful, some occasionally handy, and others that apply to jobs you'd never want to do. This chapter concentrates only on the tools in the Computer Management Console that are most likely to be useful for those who aren't full-time administrators. This includes tasks such as managing disk volumes, defragmenting disk drives, examining system information and events, and starting or stopping services on your computer.

355

Note

You must be a member of the Administrators group to perform some activities in the Computer Management Console.

Opening the Computer Management Console

The Computer Management Console uses the console tree (in the left pane) to divide its capabilities into three categories: System Tools, Storage, and Services And Applications. Each of these appears as a node on the console tree and contains snap-ins that appear when you expand the node. (Technically speaking, these are snap-in *extensions* in the Computer Management Console, but they function in exactly the same way as independent snap-ins of the same name.)

To open the Computer Management Console:

1. Click Start, point to Settings, and click Control Panel.

2. Double-click the Administrative Tools folder.

3. Double-click the Computer Management icon. The Computer Management Console opens as shown in Figure 19-1.

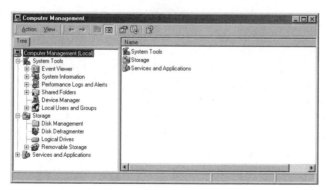

Figure 19-1

The Computer Management Console provides a collection of administrative tools.

The Computer Management Console manages your own computer by default. However, if you're using a network in your office, you can use the

Computer Management Console to administer any Windows computer on the network from your Microsoft Windows 2000 Professional computer. You must have administrator privileges on any computer you want to access remotely and be logged on as an administrator when you run the Computer Management Console.

To connect the Computer Management Console to another computer:

1. In the Administrative Tools folder in Control Panel, double-click the Computer Management icon.

2. Right-click Computer Management at the top (root) of the console tree and click Connect To Another Computer. A dialog box will appear searching for other computers on the network.

3. Select a computer from the list of computers on your network. The Computer Management Console is now managing the remote computer.

Note

Not all Computer Management Console capabilities are provided for remote computers. For example, the Device Manager can only display device information—you can't change any remote device parameters or load device drivers remotely. Also, the Disk Fragmenter doesn't support remote operation.

If you need to configure many computers in your office, you'll find remote management to be a very useful capability. It's particularly helpful when it comes to adding accounts to remote computers, changing passwords, sharing volumes or folders, and accomplishing many other tasks that would otherwise require a visit to the computer and a logon to accomplish.

Working with System Tools

The System Tools node provides several snap-ins you can use to view and modify a system's configuration, to view events generated by a system or applications, and to create performance logs that will enable you to fine-tune the system.

Viewing Events

Events are messages sent by applications, devices, or the system to notify you of error or warning conditions or of occurrences that might be of interest. Events are collected in log files and time-stamped, so you can browse them whenever you want and organize them as you like, for example, listing their entries in order by the time or date on which they occurred, the application, service, or device that sent them, or the type of event.

The Event Viewer can display three event logs, as shown in Figure 19-2: the application log, the security log, and the system log. Application and system logs contain, as you might guess, events generated by applications and the operating system, respectively. Three types of events appear in application and system logs:

- Error events indicate that some component isn't functioning or a failure has occurred that could result in the loss of data.

- Warning events indicate the potential for failure or data loss because of some glitch in normal operation.

- Information events are events other than warnings or errors that mostly serve as notifications.

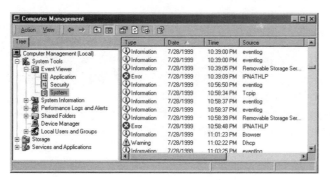

Figure 19-2

The Event Viewer displays logs where events are stored.

Tip

An example of an application event is the Fax Service event, described in "Setting Fax Log Detail and Viewing Fax Logs," on page 249.

The security log contains audit events, which are notifications of the success or failure of specific occurrences related to the security of your computer, such as logging on or off or accessing NTFS folders. *See "Setting Permissions and Auditing on NTFS Volumes," on page 373, to learn more about setting up auditing.*

When would you want to view event logs? You might want to look at them if you're encountering any problem on your computer that you can't seem to track down. The system or application could be generating events that give you an indication of the problem. Or, if you want to monitor the security of your system, you can set up auditing and view the Security log to see who is accessing or attempting to access disks or folders or attempting to log on.

To open any event in any log, double-click the event and the Event Properties dialog box opens (see Figure 19-3). The Description field contains the text of the event message. You can click the two arrow buttons in the upper-right corner to open the next or previous event in the log.

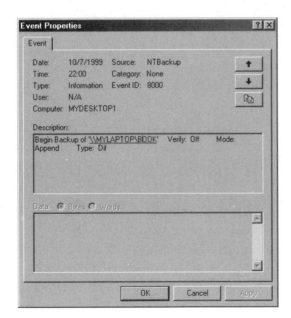

Figure 19-3

The Event Properties dialog box displays the text of the event message.

You can work in event logs in many ways. Right-click any log in the console tree, such as System, and you'll see that you can save the current log as an Event Log (.EVT) file and open it later from this same menu (this creates a snapshot of the log). You can also click Export List and create a text file, or a comma- or tab-delimited list, which you can then import into a spreadsheet program. You can even view the same log in different ways by clicking New Log View, which creates a separate window of the log file, and then sort it or filter it as you want.

Filtering an event log is one of the things you can do from an event log's Properties dialog box, which you open by right-clicking the log in the console tree and clicking Properties (or selecting the log and clicking Filter on the View menu). The Filter tab defaults to displaying all categories of all event types from all sources, but you can clear the event types you don't care to view or choose to view only events from specific sources; you can even limit this further to specific categories for those sources. As shown in Figure 19-4, you could filter the application log to show only errors or warnings from the Inbound category of Fax Services.

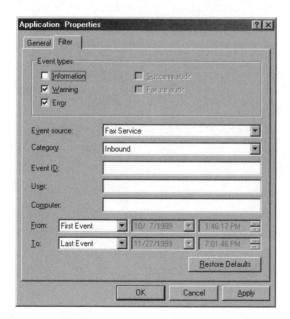

Figure 19-4

Filtering events lets you view only the events you care about.

The General tab of the Properties dialog box is where you can set the size of the log files and determine what will happen when the log file becomes full. For example, you can select Overwrite Events As Needed, so the oldest events will always be overwritten by the newest events. By default, only the oldest events over seven days old (a number you can set) are overwritten by the newest events, ensuring that a history is maintained in case some source starts spewing events and filling up the log.

Viewing System Information

The System Information snap-in provides a single vantage point from which you can view all aspects of the computer's operation. You do this by navigating the nodes and dozens of subnodes organized in the console tree under System Information and viewing the information in the right pane (see Figure 19-5). In most cases, the information is displayed in columns and you can click a column header to sort by that column.

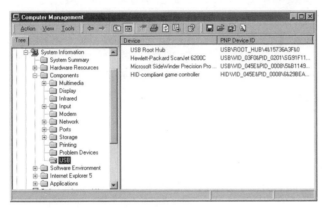

Figure 19-5
Use System Information to view all aspects of the computer you're managing.

As the name implies, the System Information snap-in provides information only and doesn't let you change anything. This snap-in is convenient whenever you have any questions regarding system configuration, such as what's installed, what drivers are used, and what's working or not. It's dynamic, which means it looks up the information as you request it, so you'll always see the latest information. By default, basic information is displayed; to view more information in some areas, select Advanced on the View menu. Here's a summary of each of the main categories in this snap-in:

- System Summary—Provides a list of basic information about the computer and operating system such as the operating system name and version, the system name, manufacturer, model, processor, and total physical and virtual memory.

- Hardware Resources—Includes subcategories for viewing the computer's hardware resources such as Direct Memory Addressing (DMA), Input Output (I/O), Interrupt Requests (IRQs), and memory addresses. If you use plug and play hardware, you won't care about hardware resources, but if you need to manually configure a device you can look here to see what's already assigned. Most of this information is also available in the Device Manager, where you can manually modify resources for devices if you need to, but it's displayed here in a more accessible manner.

- Components—Provides information about hardware details, plug and play device IDs, and the current configuration of a long list of system hardware components. The components displayed include multimedia, display adapters, infrared devices, modems and direct connections, network components, serial and parallel ports, storage devices and adapters, printers and faxes, and USB devices. Under Problem Devices, this snap-in also shows devices that aren't working.

- Software Environment—Provides information about all of the software components of Windows 2000, such as installed drivers and whether they're running or stopped, environment variables, and loaded modules (DLLs that are required by the system). You can view available services here but to stop, start, or configure services, you should use the Services snap-in under the main node Services And Applications (*see "Working With Services," on page 378*).

- Internet Explorer 5—Contains probably more information than you ever wanted to know about Microsoft Internet Explorer, but for those who need this information, it's here.

In addition to the main categories, other applications might add categories under System Information. For example, when Microsoft Office 2000 is installed, an Applications node appears showing information about all the Office 2000 applications that are currently running.

About Performance Logs And Alerts

Performance Logs And Alerts is a snap-in for creating log files with information about your system's performance. Performance is presented as a list of performance objects associated with major hardware components such as memory or processors. Performance objects might also be installed by applications or services to allow their performance to be monitored. You can also use the Performance Console, accessed from the Administrative Tools folder, to monitor current performance statistics in a real-time display, using its System Monitor snap-in.

While this is a powerful tool to fine-tune your system, it isn't one that you can quickly understand or casually use, and it typically isn't worth the learning curve required for most small businesses users.

Managing Shared Folders

The Shared Folders snap-in, shown in Figure 19-6, provides a convenient place for viewing and managing all folders that your local system or a remote system has shared on a network.

Figure 19-6

Use Shared Folders to view and manage all folders the computer shares on the network.

To view all shares, click the Shares node in the console tree. You can then stop sharing any folder by right-clicking the share in the right panel and choosing Stop Sharing from the shortcut menu. You can also set share permissions by right-clicking the share and choosing Properties. *See "Sharing Folders and Drives," on page 317 in Chapter 16, to learn about sharing folders and setting permissions.*

To view all users currently using shared folders on the computer, click the Sessions node in the console tree. The user account name and information appear in the right pane. This can be handy for seeing who's connected when you want to shut down your computer or reboot. You can end the session by right-clicking the user name and clicking Close Session. If users accessing a folder have open files, they can lose information when you do this, so be sure to warn them in advance.

To see exactly what files are currently open in your shared folders, click the Open Files node in the console tree. The open files are listed in the right pane and you can right-click any file and click Close Open File to close it. You should be aware that the user who has this file open will likely lose information if you do this.

Using the Device Manager

Like the Device Manager in Microsoft Windows 95 or Microsoft Windows 98, the Device Manager snap-in in Windows 2000 Professional is the one place where you can view and change properties of hardware devices on the computer. This snap-in is also available as a separate console from the System Properties dialog box in the Control Panel.

Tip

See "Resolving Problems Using the Device Manager," on page 123 of Chapter 6, to see how to access the Device Manager from the System Properties dialog box in the Control Panel to change resources.

You'd want to view devices using the Device Manager if you suspect that a device might not be working and you want to check. You also might want to use the Device Manager to update a driver for a hardware device. Another use for the Device Manager is to set resources for a device manually (that is, if it isn't plug and play).

As shown in Figure 19-7, when you click the Device Manager in the console tree, all devices appear by default in the right pane sorted by the type of device, such as disk drives, modems, and so on.

Figure 19-7

With the Device Manager you can update drivers or view the status of devices.

To open a device's Properties dialog box, expand the type of device (for example, modems) and double-click the device name. The tabs for devices are different, but you'll find these two tabs for most devices:

- General—Provides the device status (whether it's working or not) and enables you to disable the device. You can quickly determine if a device is not installed properly from this tab.

- Driver—Lets you uninstall or update a driver. To update a driver, click Update Driver and follow the Update Device Driver Wizard—for example, if an update becomes available from the manufacturer or from Microsoft.

You might also see a Resources tab, which shows you the computer resources assigned to the device. These are automatically assigned for plug and play devices and can't be changed. Devices that aren't plug and play will need their resources set, which you can do in this tab, if you've had experience with setting resources in other Windows operating systems.

Note

When you run the Computer Management Console on a remote computer, you can view devices in the Device Manager but you can't use the Device Manager to make changes.

Managing Local Users and Groups

With the Local Users And Groups snap-in (see Figure 19-8) in the Computer Management Console, you can perform all account management tasks that you would in the Users And Passwords dialog box. This includes creating a new user account, adding an account to a group, setting or changing passwords, and so on. Try right-clicking the Users and Groups nodes of the console tree and right-clicking the users and groups in the right pane to see what choices you have. With a little experimenting, you might find this snap-in useful for managing users and groups. If not, Chapter 9 provides all the procedures you'll need to manage accounts.

Figure 19-8

Local Users And Groups provides management access to all accounts.

Working with Storage Tools

The Computer Management Console provides four snap-ins for working with storage devices on your computer. This section describes how to use three of these snap-ins. The fourth, Removable Storage, is a useful feature for maintaining libraries of storage media and managing robotic changers, but unfortunately the topic is too large and specialized to be covered by this book. If you use a robotic changer for backup tapes or are otherwise interested in this feature, Windows 2000 Professional Help provides the documentation you'll need.

This section also describes some disk management topics beyond those provided by the Disk Management snap-in. These are primarily NTFS features that can be accessed from the Disk Management snap-in or from any NTFS volume's Properties dialog box, accessed from a file browser such as Windows Explorer.

Basic Concepts of Basic Volumes

If the vernacular of disk drives—volumes, partitions, logical drives, and so on—sounds like coffee break conversation at the local computer repair shop, here's the condensed version of what you need to know to understand the terminology used in Disk Management (or by those guys behind the repair counter).

A *volume* is another name for the drive letters that you see in Windows Explorer. A *basic volume* is the term now used to define volumes supported by MS-DOS and all Windows operating systems. A disk drive needs to contain at least one *partition*. Partitions divide a physical disk into what appear to be separate disks. (However, even a disk that isn't divided requires at least one partition.) In order to use the disk space allocated to the partition, the partition needs to be formatted for a file system. A *primary partition* contains a single volume and, in the simplest case in which a disk has only one partition, the volume occupies the entire disk. You can actually divide a disk drive into four primary partitions, resulting in four volumes, such as C:, D:, E:, and F:.

What if four drives aren't enough? The answer is to use an *extended partition* in addition to at least one primary partition (you're allowed one extended partition per disk). An extended partition contains one or more *logical drives*, enabling you to break up a single partition into many drives, each formatted separately. Any disk space not occupied by primary or extended partitions is called *unallocated space* (or free space).

To discuss a disk drive that contains operating system files, we need to use a few more terms. The primary partition that the computer accesses first when booting is called the *system partition*. On Intel-based computers, this is marked as the *active partition*. The partition that contains system files (which is often the same partition you boot to, but it doesn't have to be) is called the *boot partition*. As an example of the difference between these partition types, if you were to dual boot operating systems, one of the operating systems would be on a boot partition that is also the system partition and the other operating system would be on a boot partition that isn't a system partition.

Using the Disk Management Tool

Disk Management is an improved version of the Disk Administration tool in Microsoft Windows NT 4.0 and it replaces the FDISK command-line tool in Windows 95 with an easy-to-use graphical interface. When would you use the Disk Manager? Typically, not very often—most operations are fairly drastic in nature, and you'd only undertake them prior to installing a new operating system or when preparing new disk drives for use.

Disk Management works with basic volumes, the disk architecture used by all Microsoft operating systems, and with dynamic volumes, the new architecture provided by Windows 2000. While dynamic volumes are described here, the emphasis of this section is on working with basic volumes, which you'll likely be more familiar with from previous operating systems. Your system will use basic volumes unless you manually upgrade your disk to a dynamic disk using Disk Management.

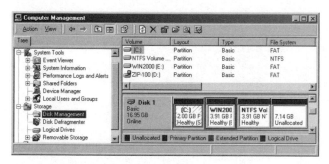

Figure 19-9

Use Disk Management to perform base-level tasks required on a disk drive.

As shown in Figure 19-9, when you select Disk Management in the console tree in the left pane, the lower half of the right pane displays each drive in your computer as a row in a table and each partition or unallocated space on the drive as a cell in that row. Cells are marked by color, so you can quickly see which are primary partitions, extended partitions, logical drives, free space, and so on.

By default, the cells are scaled according to capacity, with a logarithmic scale (meaning larger partitions, for example, will only look slightly bigger). You can change the color scheme and the scaling by clicking Settings on the View menu, so you could make partition cells reflect their actual (linear) proportional size or change the color of primary partitions to red, for instance.

Creating and Deleting Partitions and Logical Drives

You can use Disk Management to create a partition from unallocated disk space. Pre-configured computers are usually already partitioned for all available disk space, and Disk Management can't resize an existing partition. However, you might be adding a new disk drive that's not partitioned, or you might have created unallocated disk space on an existing drive, for example, by deleting an existing partition. Creating and deleting logical drives are handled in the same manner as creating and deleting a partition.

Caution

Creating or deleting a partition on the disk that you boot from might require you to edit your BOOT.INI file because the partition numbers will be changed and the file uses those partition numbers. The BOOT.INI file is a system file and editing this file can cause your system to fail to boot.

To create a partition in an unallocated drive space:

1. In the right pane, right-click the box representing the unallocated space and choose Create Partition.

2. In the Create Partition Wizard, click Next, and then click either Primary Partition or Extended Partition, and follow the wizard steps to finish creating the logical drive.

To create a logical drive in an extended partition:

1. In the right pane, right-click the box representing the extended partition and click Create Logical Drive.

2. In the Create Partition Wizard, click Next, click Logical Drive, and follow the wizard steps to finish creating the logical drive.

If your computer has a single disk drive with more than one partition, you can delete one of the partitions to create unallocated disk space. Or if you have a second disk drive, you can delete all partitions and start from scratch creating the partitions that you want (for instance, if you want to resize a partition). Disk Management will not allow you to delete any partition that you boot to or that contains operating system files. Note that this operation permanently removes all data, so be careful to back up first.

Caution

Before deleting any partitions, make sure you have backed up any data that you want to save in any volumes on that partition.

To delete a partition or logical drive:

1. Right-click the partition or logical drive and click Delete Partition.

2. Click Yes when asked if you want to delete the partition. (Note that you can't delete an extended partition until you delete all logical drives on it.)

Formatting Volumes and Changing their Properties

You can do a few more things with basic volumes and disks from within Disk Management. You can format a volume and change its properties, two tasks that you can also do from within any file browser.

- To format a volume, right-click the volume and click Format, enter the volume label, select a file format (FAT, FAT32, or NTFS), select the allocation unit size, and click OK.

- To open a volume's Properties dialog box, right-click the volume and click Properties. (*See "Other Disk Management Tasks," on page 372 to learn about what you can do in the Properties dialog box.*)

You can access volumes by using drive letters but you can also access them by mounting them on an empty NTFS folder, in which case they have a drive path instead of a drive letter. You might want to mount a volume so it has a drive path, for example, if you have a separate drive that you use for database files (say D:) and you want it to appear in Windows Explorer as a folder, perhaps called C:\Database. While you can change drive letters easily by selecting a new letter, you can change drive paths only by deleting the old path and adding a new one.

- To mount a volume on an empty NTFS folder, right-click the volume and click Change Drive Letter And Path, click Add, and then either type the drive path under Mount In This NTFS Folder, or click Browse to choose an empty folder on an NTFS volume. Click OK to finish.

- To change a drive letter, right-click the volume and click Change Drive Letter And Path, select the drive letter (if you have both a letter and drive path), click Edit, select a letter, click OK and then click Close. All data is preserved on the volume; only the drive letter changes. Be careful when changing drive letters because applications refer to volumes by drive letter and they might not be able to locate data or program components after you change a drive letter.

- To delete a drive path or letter, right-click the volume and click Change Drive Letter And Path, select the letter or drive path, click Remove, and click Yes when prompted.

If You're Coming From Windows NT 4.0

Windows NT has four advanced volume types that are only partially supported by Disk Management. These include the volume set, stripe set, mirror set, and stripe set with parity. If you need to use any of these advanced capabilities, your best bet is to use dynamic volumes, described next.

Also, if you're upgrading from Windows NT 4.0, you have the option of using a disk configuration saved by the Disk Administrator utility. To restore a configuration you've saved previously, click Restore Basic Disk Configuration on the Action menu and follow the steps. You can't store disk configurations using Disk Management.

Understanding Dynamic Disks and Volumes

Windows 2000 introduces a new scheme for allocating disk space called dynamic disks and volumes. A dynamic disk isn't limited to four partitions (in fact, partitions are eliminated) and it can have any number of dynamic volumes. So rather than having to figure out what kind of partitions you need and mounting volumes on those partitions, you can simply create dynamic volumes directly on a dynamic disk—as many as you need. You can upgrade a disk from basic to dynamic, and any existing partitions on that disk will become simple volumes. You can extend a simple volume across physical hard disks, in which case it becomes a spanned volume. You can't, however, extend a simple volume that contains the operating system.

Dynamic disks also support the advanced modes of the basic disk architecture, whose names are followed in parentheses here, including striped volumes (striped sets), mirrored volumes (mirrored sets), and

RAID-5 volumes (stripe sets with parity). Advanced modes are more typically used on servers rather than on workstations and are best left to experienced professionals to set up and configure.

Note

Dynamic volumes don't work with other operating systems, so you should avoid them if you are dual booting with another operating system. Also, they don't work on portable computers.

To upgrade a basic disk to a dynamic disk, right-click the disk drive box in the left column, choose Upgrade To Dynamic Disk, and then select the disks you want to upgrade and click OK.

Other Disk Management Tasks

You can perform some disk management tasks in a volume's Properties dialog box (see Figure 19-10). You can open the Properties dialog box from within Disk Management, or from any file browser, by right-clicking the volume or drive letter and clicking Properties. Here are some tasks you can perform using the volume's Properties dialog box:

- Perform disk cleanup for any FAT or NTFS drive, which identifies disk space you can free up.

- Set security options for NTFS drives. This includes setting a volume's permissions and also enabling auditing of users who access the volume.

- Set disk quotas on NTFS drives. Disk quotas let you manage the amount of storage used by users or groups on a volume.

Cleaning Up Your Disk

The General tab of the Properties dialog box for both FAT and NTFS volumes contains a Disk Cleanup option that helps you identify disk space you can free up. This feature spots items such as the Recycle Bin, Temporary Internet Files, and so on that you can empty or eliminate. To free up the amount of disk space that is listed next to the items, select the items you want and click OK. For some volumes, you'll see a couple of additional check boxes you can select: Compress Old Files, which compresses files you haven't used in a while, and Catalog Files For The Content Indexer,

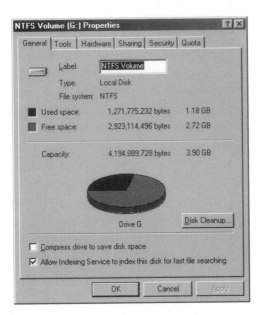

Figure 19-10

You can perform some disk management tasks in a volume's Properties dialog box.

which removes extraneous files left over by the Indexing Service. By clicking the More Options tab, you can gain further space by removing Windows components and installed programs; this has the same functionality as in Windows 98, although the tools you'll encounter during the removal process are slightly different.

An NTFS volume contains two more tabs in the Properties dialog box that provide most of the real power of NTFS: Security and Quota. These tabs encompass a great deal of functionality, and here's an overview of their features.

Setting Permissions and Auditing on NTFS Volumes

The Security tab lets you determine who can access the disk. By default, the Everyone group has full access to the disk but you can add or remove users or groups and set permissions for each user and group. By clicking the Advanced button in the Security tab, you can fine-tune permissions, set the owner of the volume, or enable and configure disk auditing. Setting security permissions on a volume is similar to setting permissions on a file or folder (*see "Setting Security Permissions on Files and Folders," on page 170 in Chapter 9*). The only difference is that volumes are at the top of the permissions inheritance chain, so you don't have to break the inheritance propagation from a parent to set permissions (there is no parent).

Disk auditing enables you to monitor who accesses or makes changes in an NTFS volume. You could use this feature, for example, if you want to log who's deleting (or trying to delete) files on a volume. Once auditing is established for a user or group, you'll receive audit events, which you can see by opening the Event Viewer and looking at the security log. (*See "Viewing Events," on page 358, for more information on viewing the event logs.*)

To enable auditing, you add a user to the audit list, edit the user, and specify the types of activities you want to monitor (for example, you can select both the Successful and Failed check boxes next to the Delete Subfolders And Files item). Figure 19-11 shows an example of auditing a user named Joanna Fuller. This also works for groups, by the way—setting an audit on a group logs events whenever a user belonging to that group performs the activity that you audit.

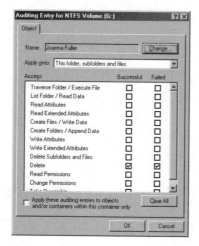

Figure 19-11

Auditing a user's attempted access to the disk provides audit events in the security log.

Before auditing will work, you'll also need to turn on object auditing in your local security policies. To do this, visit the Local Security Policy console in the Administrative Tools folder, open Audit Policy under Local Policies in the console tree, and enable audit object access (for example, double-click Audit Object Access, select both the Success and Failure check boxes, and click OK). Log off and log back on to make this the effective setting. (If you're on a domain network, the group policy set by your network administrator overrides your local setting.)

Setting Disk Quotas

You enable the other NTFS disk management tool, quota management, on the Quota tab, shown in Figure 19-12. Disk quotas let you manage how much disk space you allow any user or group on an NTFS volume. By default, quota management is disabled, but you can enable it by selecting Enable Quota Management and then clicking Quota Entries to add users or groups and allocate the amount of storage available to each quota entry. When a user with a quota entry exceeds the designated quota, you can choose to deny access to that person and/or to log an event. You can also log a warning event at a specified disk usage level, which is separately selectable for every user or group.

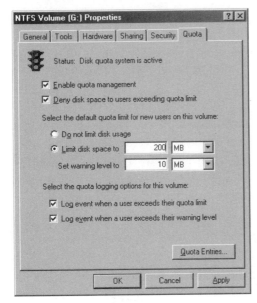

Figure 19-12

Use the Quota tab in a volume's Properties dialog box to manage disk usage.

Using the Disk Defragmenter

The Disk Defragmenter snap-in provides a convenient means of speeding up access to your hard drive. Files on your disk drive are actually composed of small units called clusters that are accessed fastest when they are located next to each other (that is, when they are contiguous). Over time, the clusters that make up a file end up being scattered about the disk, and when this occurs, the file is fragmented. The Disk Defragmenter does the job of making all clusters of each file contiguous.

Unlike the Disk Defragmenter in Windows 95, the Windows 2000 version enables you to analyze the volume first and it makes a recommendation about whether to defragment the volume. This is a useful service and saves time, because defragmenting a hard drive can take quite a while and you want to do it only when necessary.

To perform the analysis, select Disk Defragmenter in the console tree and you'll see a list of your system's volumes at the top of the right panel. Select a volume to analyze and click the Analyze button. While the analysis proceeds, you'll see the Analysis Display area graphically display fragmented and contiguous clusters, along with system files and free space. After the volume is analyzed, a dialog box will appear with a recommendation. If it recommends that you defragment the volume, you can click Defragment to immediately proceed, or click Close to defragment the volume later. You can also click View Report to see statistics such as the percentage of fragmentation and which files are most fragmented.

When you perform a defragmentation, the Defragmentation Display area shows a graphical view of the clusters as they are moved about on the volume. You can click Stop or Pause at any time if you need to. Figure 19-13 shows the Disk Defragmenter after a defragmentation operation is completed (notice that the Analysis Display area shows the state before the defragmentation and the Defragmentation Display area shows it after).

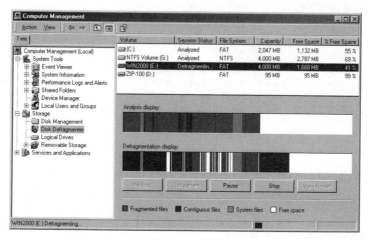

Figure 19-13

Use the Disk Defragmenter to increase your file access speed.

Managing Logical Drives

The purpose of the Logical Drives snap-in (as shown in Figure 19-14) is to enable you to configure NTFS permissions and set volume labels. While you can also set volume labels and permissions on any local drive in its Properties dialog box, this is the only control that lets you perform those operations on a remote computer. As with other remote capabilities, this can be useful when you don't want to visit the remote computer to set permissions.

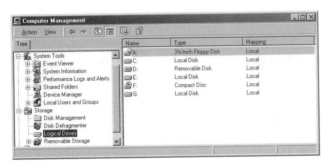

Figure 19-14

Use Logical Drives to manage NTFS volumes, especially on remote computers.

Services And Applications Snap-Ins

The Services And Applications node gives access to the Services snap-in and the WMI Control (discussed next) and the Indexing Service. It also provides access to the Internet Information Services if you've installed them.

About the WMI Control Service

Microsoft Windows Management Instrumentation (WMI) represents the core of an infrastructure aimed at reducing the maintenance and cost of managing components in a Windows NT or Windows 2000 enterprise network by enabling remote or automated administration. WMI is compliant with Web-Based Enterprise Management (WBEM), an industry initiative to develop a nonproprietary specification for accessing and sharing management information in an enterprise network. A WMI service running on any Microsoft platform (including Windows 95, Windows NT 4.0, and Windows 2000) encapsulates its resources as objects based on a specification provided by the Component Information Model (CIM). The

CIM Object Manager, part of the WMI, handles collecting this information and storing it in a repository. Another part of this infrastructure, MMC, enables the display of this information, while still other parts allow the use of scripts for automation and more. As you can no doubt surmise, this service is designed for networks that include administrators and, like the label on the appliance says, contains no user-serviceable parts.

Working with Services

A service is an operating system component that runs in the background and performs tasks invisible to users but important to some aspect of the computer's operation. If you click the Services And Applications node, you'll see a long list of services (see Figure 19-15), and those listed as Started in the Status column are currently running on your computer (or on the remote computer you're managing). The services listed as Automatic are started when the system starts. These are mostly services required by the system (click Startup Type to sort these to the top if you like).

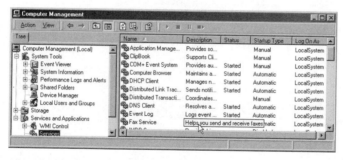

Figure 19-15

Click the Services node to see the list of services that can run on your system.

To disable a service, you can right-click the service and click Stop. To restart the service later, just right-click it again and click Restart. Some services also allow you to pause and then resume them, in which case those options appear on the menu when you right-click the service.

This concludes the Advanced Administration Tools section of this book. If you've read this far, you've covered a lot of ground and should have a fairly good appreciation of the capabilities of Windows 2000 Professional and how to make the most of them for your small business. Hats off to you for taking the time to explore and learn Windows 2000 Professional—your efforts will be well rewarded as you spend less time on your operating system and more time on your business!

Index

Q

R

Don Gilbert has been writing about computers and operating systems for more than fifteen years. He worked as a programmer before discovering he also enjoyed writing about technical subjects involving computers, eventually writing programming guides and Software Development Kits (SDKs) for Microsoft that described the inner workings of operating systems. His writing has appeared in several books published by Microsoft Press. Don has also contributed to Microsoft Internet Developer (MIND) magazine and has managed content for a Web site targeting Internet developers.

The manuscript for this book was prepared and submitted to Microsoft Press in electronic form by Studioserv (www.studioserv.com). Text files were prepared using Microsoft Word 2000. Pages were composed by Studioserv using Adobe PageMaker 6.52 for Windows, with text in Berkeley and display type in Frutiger. Composed pages were delivered to the printer as electronic prepress files.

Cover Graphic Designer
Patrick Lanfear

Cover Illustrator
Tom Draper Design

Interior Designer
James D. Kramer

Copy Editor
Gail Taylor

Illustrator
Steve Hussey

Principal Compositor
Steve Sagman

Principal Proofreader
Tom Speeches

Indexer
Audrey Marr

Proof of Purchase

0-7356-0856-3

Do not send this card with your registration.
Use this card as proof of purchase if participating in a promotion or
rebate offer on *Small Business Solutions for Microsoft® Windows® 2000 Professional*.
Card must be used in conjunction with other proof(s) of payment such as your dated
sales receipt—see offer details.

Small Business Solutions for Microsoft® Windows® 2000 Professional

WHERE DID YOU PURCHASE THIS PRODUCT?

CUSTOMER NAME

mspress.microsoft.com

Microsoft Press, PO Box 97017, Redmond, WA 98073-9830

OWNER REGISTRATION CARD   *Register Today!*   0-7356-0856-3

Return the bottom portion of this card to register today.

Small Business Solutions for Microsoft® Windows® 2000 Professional

FIRST NAME   MIDDLE INITIAL   LAST NAME

INSTITUTION OR COMPANY NAME

ADDRESS

CITY   STATE   ZIP

( )

E-MAIL ADDRESS   PHONE NUMBER

U.S. and Canada addresses only. Fill in information above and mail postage-free.
Please mail only the bottom half of this page.

For information about Microsoft Press®

products, visit our Web site at

mspress.microsoft.com